Collins | English for Exams

VOCABULARY AND GRAMMAR FOR THE TOEFL iBT® TEST

Ingrid Wisniewska, PhD

T0312395

Published by Collins
An imprint of HarperCollins Publishers
Westerhill Road
Bishopbriggs
Glasgow
G64 2QT

HarperCollins Publishers
Macken House
39/40 Mayor Street Upper
Dublin 1
D01 C9W8
Ireland

Third Edition 2024

10 9 8 7 6 5 4 3 2 1

© HarperCollins Publishers 2012, 2023, 2024

ISBN 978-0-00-869522-4

Collins® is a registered trademark of HarperCollins Publishers Limited

Academic Word List © Coxhead, Averil 2000

ETS, MYBEST, TOEFL and TOEFL iBT are registered trademarks of ETS. This publication is not affiliated with or endorsed by ETS.

www.collins.co.uk/elt

A catalogue record for this book is available from the British Library

Series Editor: Celia Wigley
Author: Ingrid Wisniewska
Author of additional content for third edition: Louis Harrison
Audio: New York Audio Productions
Typesetting: Sharon McTeir Creative Publishing Services and Jouve, India
For the Publisher: Gillian Bowman, Kerry Ferguson, Lisa Todd

Printed and bound in the UK by Ashford Colour Press Ltd.

A catalogue record for this book is available from the British Library.

If you would like to comment on any aspect of this book, please contact us at the given address or online.
E-mail: collins.elt@harpercollins.co.uk

Acknowledgements
We would like to thank those authors and publishers who kindly gave permission for copyright material to be used in the Collins Corpus. We would also like to thank Times Newspapers Ltd for providing valuable data.

This book contains FSC™ certified paper and other controlled sources to ensure responsible forest management.

For more information visit: www.harpercollins.co.uk/green

Contents

Grammar

Key grammar for the independent writing and speaking tasks

Key grammar for the integrated tasks (speaking and writing sections)

Key grammar for the reading and listening sections

Key grammar for all sections

Index of question types

Question type	Vocabulary Unit	Grammar Unit
Reading section		
Detail	11, 14, 19	12, 14, 17
Negative fact	14, 19	11, 14
Inference	1, 3, 7	11
Function	6, 7, 14, 19	17
Vocabulary	11	12, 14
Referent	2, 3, 7, 9, 11, 14, 19	11, 14, 17
Sentence summary/simplification	7, 11, 19	12, 14
Insert a sentence	3, 19	11, 12
Passage/Prose summary	14, 19	14, 17
Listening section		
Main idea	1, 4, 5, 10, 15	18
Purpose	1, 4, 5, 10, 15	13, 18
Detail	13	15
Function	4, 5, 10, 13	15, 18
Attitude	1, 5, 10	13, 18
Organization	1	15
Connecting content	5, 6	13, 18
Inference	15	13
Speaking section		
Paired choice	2, 10, 17	3, 4, 5
Campus matters	13, 17	1, 6
Academic reading and lecture	7, 20	2, 7, 9, 18
Academic summary	4, 5, 9, 10, 16	13
Writing section		
Integrated task	18	8, 10, 16, 19
Independent task (Personal Experience Essay)*	3, 6, 8, 12	1, 2, 3, 4, 5, 16, 20
Academic discussion task**	See pages 168–179.	See pages 168–179.

*Please note: Only on the <u>Paper Edition</u> of the TOEFL iBT® test.

**Please note: Only on the <u>Computer-based version</u> and the <u>Home Edition</u> of the TOEFL iBT® test.

See the Overview of the TOEFL iBT® test on page 180 for more information.

About this book

Who is this book for?

This book is intended as a preparatory tool for any student intending to take the TOEFL iBT® test. It provides an introduction to the vocabulary and grammar that are needed in all sections of the test.

The TOEFL iBT® test is offered in three ways:

- Test at a test center
- Test at home
- Test on paper

This book prepares you for all three options:

- the TOEFL iBT test on computer at a test center
- the Home Edition, and
- the TOEFL iBT Paper Edition.

This book has been fully updated to match the changes to the TOEFL iBT test that took effect on July 26 2023.

For more information on the differences between the versions of the test, please see the Overview of the TOEFL iBT® Test on page 180.

Updated information about test content can be found on ETS's website: https://www.ets.org/toefl/test-takers/ibt/about/content.html.

Why are vocabulary and grammar important to the test?

Vocabulary: A good knowledge of general academic vocabulary is essential for all four sections of the test. The reading and listening sections both have specific vocabulary questions that check understanding of vocabulary in context. Rubrics for the speaking section include "effective use of vocabulary" and rubrics for the writing section include "appropriate word choice and idiomaticity." The speaking and writing sections of the test also require you to read academic texts and listen to parts of lectures, and paraphrase or summarize them in your own words. As well as knowledge of academic vocabulary, you will need to be able to figure out the meaning of unfamiliar words by using context and applying knowledge of word roots, suffixes, and prefixes.

Grammar: Although the TOEFL iBT test doesn't have specific grammar questions, knowledge of English sentence structure and ability to understand and use a range of grammatical structures is necessary for all sections of the test. For the speaking section, you should be able to speak confidently, without obvious grammatical errors that could distort meaning. According to the speaking section rubrics, the candidate should "demonstrate effective use of grammar" and exhibit "a fairly high degree of automaticity with good control of basic and complex structures." For the writing section, students should display "facility in the use of language, demonstrating syntactic variety, appropriate word choice and idiomaticity." A good understanding of grammatical structures is also required to understand the passages and answer the questions in the reading and listening sections.

What kind of vocabulary is included in this book?

The vocabulary has been selected according to two criteria:

1. Main academic subject areas: arts, life science, social science, and physical science. Although you are not expected to have specialized content knowledge, you are expected to have a good understanding of the content-specific words that are commonly used in all of these academic areas. These are not all the words you will need, but will give you a starting point for expanding your vocabulary in each area.

2. The Academic Word List. This is a list of 570 words that are most commonly used in academic contexts. The selection is based on samples of academic texts from a wide range of subject areas and includes general academic words that are commonly used in all subject areas; it does not include subject-specific words. The Academic Word List can be found by searching "AWL headwords Victoria University of Wellington" or at: www.victoria.ac.nz/lals/resources/academicwordlist/awl-headwords.

This book also helps you develop word attack skills. Dictionary Skills and Word Building boxes throughout help you to notice roots, prefixes, and suffixes so that you can expand your vocabulary. Study Tip and Test Tip boxes give you strategies for maximizing your study efforts and how to approach specific test question types.

What kind of grammar is included?

The grammar points have been selected according to which grammar will be most useful for you in the test. You will need to have a general level of grammatical accuracy in order to achieve a high score. You will also need specific aspects of grammar for specific questions in the test.

What other skills do I need?

Good levels of vocabulary and grammar are essential in order to achieve a high score. However, you will also need to practice listening, speaking, reading, and writing, as well as academic skills, such as note taking, paraphrasing, and summarizing. You can develop these skills by reading and listening to authentic academic materials in English, as well as by using practice books such as *Collins Skills for the TOEFL iBT® Test: Reading and Writing* and *Collins Skills for the TOEFL iBT® Test: Listening and Speaking*.

How does this book help me prepare for the test?

In addition to helping you to learn and practice the vocabulary and grammar you will need for the test, this book will also help you to become familiar with the question types that you will meet in the test. Every unit in the book contains questions similar to those in the test, using texts that are shorter and easier than actual TOEFL iBT test questions. All the question types found in the test are practiced in a variety of different academic contexts. If you know what question types to expect, and what types of answers are required, this will increase your chance of achieving a high score.

The audio included with this book provides you with all of the listening passages for the Test Practice and Extra Practice questions. You can download the audio at www.collins.co.uk/eltresources.

This edition also includes a new unit with practice questions for the new Writing question 2: Academic discussion. This is Unit 21 and can be found on page 168. Sample answers to the practice questions can be found on page 195.

If you would like a set of complete practice tests, you might be interested in *Collins Practice Tests for the TOEFL iBT test*.

I hope you will enjoy using this book and good luck with the TOEFL iBT test!

Ingrid Wisniewska, PhD

Visual art and architecture

Read the words, definitions, and examples. Use your dictionary to find additional word forms for each word.

OVERVIEW

Word	Definition	Example
unique (adj)	original, different from anything else	A **unique aspect** of Turner's paintings is his **innovative** use of color.
aspect (n)	element, feature	
innovative (adj)	new, different, better than before	
vision (n)	concept, idea	Gaudi's **vision** of architecture **utilized** organic shapes to create highly decorative structures.
utilize (v)	use	
considerable (adj)	great, significant	The development of steel construction had **considerable impact** on **contemporary** architecture.
impact (n)	influence, effect	
contemporary (adj)	present day	
illustrate (v)	to add pictures to a book, to give an example	Leonardo da Vinci **illustrated** his notebooks with drawings and sketches which provide valuable **insights** into his **creative** processes.
insight (n)	a clear understanding	
creative (adj)	able to make new ideas	
signal (n or v)	indicate	The Impressionist art movement **signaled** a **shift** away from naturalism toward a more **abstract** representation of human experience.
shift (n or v)	move	
abstract (adj)	not realistic	
design (n or v)	outline, plan	The Bauhaus **design** movement attempted to **analyze** form in terms of basic universal principles.
analyze (v)	examine, think about something in detail	
seek (v)	attempt, try	The Impressionists **sought** to **depict** the **subjective** experience of light and color.
depict (v)	show, describe	
subjective (adj)	from an individual's point of view	
image (n)	picture	**Images** used in surreal art often attempt to **convey** aspects of the unconscious.
convey (v)	communicate, express	

Practice Exercises

A Choose the words from the chart opposite that best replace the words in italics.

1. The modernist movement has had a *significant*[a] *influence*[b] on *present day*[c] architecture and design.

   a _____ b _____ c _____

2. Surrealist art *attempts*[a] to *express*[b] *a picture*[c] of unconscious psychological processes.

   a _____ b _____ c _____

3. Nowadays architects use computer technology to *design*[a] 3D images of their *plans*[b].

   a _____ b _____

4. *An original*[a] *element*[b] of cubist art was the attempt to *show*[c] multiple viewpoints simultaneously.

   a _____ b _____ c _____

STUDY TIP

After reading an article, choose five key words from the text and note them in your vocabulary notebook. Then try to combine them into sentences about the theme of the article.

B Circle the best word to complete each sentence.

DICTIONARY SKILLS

€ POWERED BY COBUILD

When you look up a word in your dictionary, you will see an abbreviation after it that tells you what word class it belongs to. For example, *innovative* (adj = adjective), *innovate* (v = verb), *innovation* (n = noun).

To extend your vocabulary, take notes of other word forms of the words in the chart.

1. One of the most _____ aspects of modernism was the principle that form follows function.

   a innovative

   b subjective

   c considerable

2. Post-modernism in architecture represents a(n) _____ from a functional to a more decorative style.

   a signal

   b shift

   c insight

3. Many of Monet's paintings _____ water lilies from his garden.

   a utilize

   b depict

   c signal

4. Images in _____ art do not represent forms of real objects.

   a creative

   b subjective

   c abstract

C Complete the sentences with the correct form of words from the box.

analyze	creative	depict	illustrate	innovative

1. *The Old Guitarist* by Picasso is a _____ of human misery.
2. William Blake was a British Romantic painter, poet, engraver, and _____.
3. _____ is the ability to transform existing ideas and make something new.
4. Technological _____ have had a huge impact on modern art.
5. Scientific _____ of materials used in old paintings can help us to restore and conserve them.

Test Practice

A Read the sentences and answer the questions about each one.

1. Cubism signaled a shift away from representational art, that is, art that attempted to portray realistic scenes of people and places.

    According to the text, all of the following are true EXCEPT

    ○ Cubist art portrayed real people.

    ○ Cubist art was more abstract.

    ○ Representational art was more realistic.

    ○ Representational art preceded cubist art.

2. Modern art gave artists the freedom to express their inner vision in their art.

    According to the text, all of the following are true EXCEPT

    ○ Before modern art, artists were restricted.

    ○ Modern art allowed artists to innovate.

    ○ Modern art is abstract.

    ○ Modern artists have more choices.

3. The key aspect of modern architecture is that new materials are now available that have had significant impact on what types of designs are technically possible.

    According to the text, all of the following are true EXCEPT

    ○ New materials have influenced modern architectural designs.

    ○ Today's designs were not possible previously.

    ○ Modern architecture utilizes new materials.

    ○ Modern architecture is not influenced by old architecture.

TEST TIP: Reading section (negative fact questions)

In the reading section of the test, you will be asked to identify a fact that is NOT included in a longer reading passage. When answering negative fact questions, read all the options carefully. The incorrect options will usually paraphrase information in the text. The correct answer will often contain extra information not mentioned in the text, or contradict information in the text.

🎧 **B** Listen to part of a lecture in an art class and take notes. Then answer the questions.
Track 2

> Notes

1. Why does the professor mention the portrait of *The Two Fridas*?
   - ○ To show how Kahlo's art expressed her emotions.
   - ○ To explain aspects of Kahlo's inner life.
   - ○ To compare Kahlo and other artists.
   - ○ To explain the process of creating a painting.

2. What aspects of Kahlo's art does the professor mainly discuss in the lecture?
   - ○ Her use of color
   - ○ Her choice of subject
   - ○ Her influence on surrealism
   - ○ The influence of her life on her art

3. According to the professor, what is true about Kahlo's art?
   - ○ It is abstract.
   - ○ It is realistic.
   - ○ It challenges the viewer.
   - ○ It represents a cultural view.

4. According to the professor, how was Kahlo's art influenced by surrealism?
   - ○ It was abstract.
   - ○ It was subjective.
   - ○ It conveyed emotions.
   - ○ It expressed the unconscious.

5. What is the professor's attitude concerning whether Kahlo's art depicts social attitudes to women?
   - ○ He disagrees with this view.
   - ○ He thinks this view is doubtful.
   - ○ He thinks this theory is correct.
   - ○ He does not think this view is possible.

Literature

Read the words, definitions, and examples. Use your dictionary to find additional word forms for each word.

OVERVIEW

Word	Definition	Example
classic (n)	a book that represents the best of a particular genre	*On the Road* by Jack Kerouac is a **classic novel** of the 1950s. Although it is a work of **fiction**, it is based mainly on the **autobiographical** description of a road trip Kerouac took across the United States and into Mexico.
novel (n)	a book about imaginary people and events	
fiction (n)	stories about imaginary events	
autobiographical (adj)	describing true events in the author's own life	
set (adj)	placed, located	*The Great Gatsby* by F. Scott Fitzgerald is **set** during the 1920s in the United States. The story is **narrated** by a minor **character**, Nick Carraway, who describes the other people in the story with **contradictory** emotions of admiration, jealousy, and envy.
narrate (v)	tell a story	
character (n)	a person in a story	
contradictory (adj)	opposing	
inspired (adj)	describing the source of an idea	Charles Dickens' novel *David Copperfield* was partly **inspired** by his **experience** of working in a factory as a child.
experience (n)	past events that have happened to you	
realistic (adj)	giving an accurate picture of reality	John Steinbeck's novel *The Grapes of Wrath* is a **realistic** description of the economic depression of the 1930s that mainly affected industrialized countries seen from the **perspective** of one family of migrant workers in the United States.
perspective (n)	point of view	
prose (n)	ordinary written language, not poetry	The novel *Mrs Dalloway* by Virginia Woolf is written in an experimental form of **prose** using a narrative **technique** known as stream-of-consciousness, which **portrays** a continuous flow of thoughts while shifting perspective from one character to another.
technique (n)	method	
portray (v)	describe	
pseudonym (n)	an invented name that someone uses instead of a real name	Emily Brontë's novel *Wuthering Heights* was at first published under the **pseudonym** Ellis Bell in order to keep the author's real name **anonymous**. The book was praised for the **originality** of its subject matter and narrative **style**.
anonymous (adj)	unidentified, unnamed	
originality (n)	the condition of being completely new and different	
style (n)	way of doing something	

Practice Exercises

A Choose the best words to complete the sentences.

1. *The Age of Innocence* by Edith Wharton is a _____ novel of late-19th-century American literature.

    a narrative

    b classic

    c fictional

2. The *Sherlock Holmes* detective stories are _____ by Sherlock's friend Dr. Watson.

    a inspired

    b set

    c narrated

3. George Eliot was the _____ of the English author Mary Ann Evans.

    a pseudonym

    b character

    c perspective

4. Sylvia Plath's novel *The Bell Jar* is a semi- _____ novel based on her own experience.

    a anonymous

    b autobiographical

    c contradictory

5. Many of Jack London's stories were _____ by his life as a sailor and gold prospector.

    a written

    b set

    c inspired

WORD BUILDING

The prefix *auto-* has the meaning of *self*. Look up the meaning of other words that start with *auto-*, for example: *automatic, autonomy.*

B Complete the text with the correct form of words from the chart. Use your dictionary to help you.

Mark Twain was the [1]_____ of the 19th-century American writer Samuel Clemens. One of his most famous [2]_____ was *The Adventures of Huckleberry Finn*, which was first published in 1887. The work is a realistic [3]_____ of life in rural Mississippi in the late 1800s. The novel is written in a colloquial prose [4]_____ that was [5]_____ for the time. The story is [6]_____ by an uneducated 13-year-old boy who has a unique but limited [7]_____ on the main events. According to the author, the [8]_____ for the main character came from one of his childhood friends.

STUDY TIP

When trying to figure out the meaning of new words, read the surrounding text carefully. It can sometimes give a definition or some example of the meaning of the word.

STUDY TIP

The **Academic Word List** is a list of words that are most commonly used in academic contexts. The list is based on samples of academic texts from a wide range of subject areas. The 570 most commonly used words are arranged in sub-lists according to frequency. Each word in the list represents all the different forms of the word. For example, *analyze* also represents the words *analyst, analytic, analytical, and analytically*. The Academic Word List can be found at: www.victoria.ac.nz/lals/resources/academicwordlist/awl-headwords.

Note that the list includes *general* academic words that are commonly used in *all* subject areas.

Test Practice

A **Read the questions and choose the best answer.**

1. Narrated from the point of view of the character Sal Paradise, *On the Road* is a classic example of an autobiographical novel. It is written in a spontaneous style of prose that sounds like someone speaking directly to the reader without pausing to think or reflect.

The word spontaneous is closest in meaning to

○ original.

○ realistic.

○ fictional.

○ unplanned.

2. The novel *Frankenstein* by Mary Shelley was first published anonymously in 1818. Although known mainly as a science-fiction horror novel, it deals with many profound themes, such as the conflict between good and evil.

The word profound is closest in meaning to

○ interesting.

○ contradictory.

○ intense.

○ thought-provoking.

3. Jean Rhys's novel *Wide Sargasso Sea* was inspired by Charlotte Brontë's novel *Jane Eyre* and uses a stylistic device of shifting narrative voices to explore themes of power, dependence, and madness.

The word device is closest in meaning to

○ language.

○ version.

○ perspective.

○ technique.

B Read the transcript of a student response to question 1 in the speaking section (choice). Underline phrases you could use to talk about your own opinion.

Some people prefer to watch the film version of a book. Others prefer to read the original book. Which do you prefer and why?

In my opinion, reading a book and watching the film version of a book are two very different experiences. While both help to stimulate your imagination and engage the reader or viewer in a dramatic story, there are some important differences. Obviously, watching a movie is much faster than reading a book. Not only that, but you can also watch a film with friends and compare your opinions. Reading a book, on the other hand, makes you think about the characters more deeply. For example, when I read *Pride and Prejudice* by Jane Austen, I tried really hard to understand the characters and their motivation, but when I watched the movie, I just sat back and enjoyed the story. For this reason, I always try to read a book before watching the film version..

TEST TIP: Speaking section question 1 (paired choice)

To prepare for the speaking section of the test, practice speaking on a topic for 45 seconds (about 125–150 words).

If possible, record your voice and write a transcript of your response. Read the transcript carefully and try to improve the range of vocabulary. Then record your voice again.

When recording your voice, remember to pause often and try to sound natural, as if you were speaking to a person.

C Practice your reply to the question in exercise B. Write your spoken response here (or record your response and write the transcript here).

_____

_____

_____

_____

_____

_____

_____

_____

_____

_____

_____

_____

_____

_____

_____

_____

Music and dance

Read the words, definitions, and examples. Use your dictionary to find additional word forms for each word.

OVERVIEW

Word	Definition	Example
emerge (v)	become known	Modern dance **emerged** as an art form in the early 20th century. It represented a **rejection** of the conventional principles of classical ballet.
reject (v)	turn against, refuse to accept	
develop (v)	grow or change	Martha Graham **developed** modern dance techniques that were based on **concepts** of **contraction** and **release**.
concept (n)	idea	
contraction (n)	becoming smaller or tighter	
release (n or v)	let go	
performance (n)	show, display, concert	Modern dance **performances** utilize a range of **choreographic** techniques to create a unique form of self-expression.
choreographic (adj)	relating to dance movement	
combine (v)	mix, join together	Jazz music **combined** elements of African and European music traditions and **transformed** popular music in the 1920s.
transform (v)	change completely	
genre (n)	type, category, especially of music or literature	Blues is a musical **genre** that **evolved** from the songs of Black enslaved laborers in the American South.
evolve (v)	gradually develop over a period of time	
incorporate (v)	include	Tango is a form of music that **incorporates** classical and jazz music **rhythms**.
rhythm (n)	regular pattern (of sounds)	
consist of (v)	be formed of, comprise	Traditional Native American music typically **consists** of singing **accompanied** by percussion **instruments**, such as drums and rattles.
accompany (v)	happen at the same time	
instrument (n)	tool	

Practice Exercises

A Complete the sentences with words from the box.

choreographic	combine	concept	evolves	genre	instrumental	reject
release	rhythm	transformed				

1. If a place looks completely different, it is _____.

2. If you help something to happen, you are _____ in making it happen.

3. If something changes gradually, it _____.

4. If you mix two things together, you _____ them.

5. If you invent a new idea, it is an original _____.

6. If you say you don't want something, you _____ it.

7. Rock 'n' roll is one _____ of popular music.

8. If you _____ a new album, you offer it for sale to the public.

9. If a piece of music has a regular pattern of sound, it has _____.

10. Self expression in a modern dance performance usually involves a range of _____ techniques.

> **WORD BUILDING**
>
> The prefix *trans-* means to move from one place to another. *Transform* means to change from one form to another. Find the meanings of these other words with the prefix *trans-*: *transport, transmit, translate, transfer, transcribe, transfusion.*

B Complete the sentences with the correct form of words from the chart opposite. Use your dictionary to help you.

Milestones in Modern Dance

In the early years of the 20th century, Isadora Duncan was the first to ¹_____
a concept of dance that ²_____ of moving naturally in response to music.
She ³_____ dances in bare feet, wearing a simple flowing tunic, and
⁴_____ elaborate scenery and costumes in order to focus more attention on the
dancer. She ⁵_____ elements of folk dance, as well as Greek classical art into her art.
Her ideas caused a ⁶_____ in popular attitudes and contributed to the
⁷_____ of modern dance as an art form. In the 1930s, Martha Graham created
dance techniques that were ⁸_____ basic human movements such as breathing and
walking. In the 1970s, Twyla Tharp was the first ⁹_____ to create a type of dance that
¹⁰_____ both modern and classical ballet techniques.

Test Practice

A Read the passage and choose the best answer.

Development of the Blues

Blues music has influenced many other genres of music, from jazz to rock and country music. Blues originally evolved in the early 20th century in the rural Mississippi region, based on the unaccompanied rhythmic vocal narratives sung by Black enslaved laborers while working on plantations or farms in the 18th and 19th centuries. Enslaved people were often prohibited from owning musical instruments as they could be used to transmit messages, so the enslaved laborers created chants, hollers, spirituals, and work songs (known as *arhoolies*).

By the 1920s, blues had developed a very particular style based around three-line rhymed stanzas. These consisted of one line that was repeated and a final line of rhyming verse with typically between four and eight stanzas in one song. The style also included a repeating blues chord progression, which was the basis of the harmony, utilizing the three major chords of the musical scale.

After the abolition of enslavement, African Americans started to move to the towns and cities and the blues moved with them. The music was no longer only related to work, but was now a form of entertainment and self-expression. Traveling musicians started to become more widespread and they incorporated instruments such as guitar, harmonica, and banjo into their musical style. The lyrics of the blues often focus on themes of hardship, injustice, and suffering, as well as themes of love, jealousy, and sadness. A significant feature of blues singers is their ability to express suffering through personal experience.

---

1. According to the passage, *arhoolies* do NOT

- ○ tell a story.
- ○ use musical instruments.
- ○ have a strong rhythm.
- ○ accompany work.

2. The word transmit in the passage is closest in meaning to

- ○ send.
- ○ repeat.
- ○ travel.
- ○ provide.

3. The word stanza in the passage refers to

- ○ a song.
- ○ a type of instrument.
- ○ a set of lines.
- ○ a set of songs.

4. The word widespread in the passage is closest in meaning to

- ○ musical.
- ○ popular.
- ○ restricted.
- ○ skilled.

5. An introductory sentence for a summary of the passage is provided on the next page. Complete the summary by selecting the THREE answer options that express the most important ideas in the passage. Some sentences do not belong in the summary because they express ideas that are not presented in the passage or are minor ideas in the passage.

This passage describes the evolution of blues music.

○ _____

○ _____

○ _____

Choose 3 answers.

1. Blues music is associated with everyday life in the countryside of Mississippi.

2. Blues music often expresses sadness and suffering.

3. People in towns and cities used blues music to accompany their work.

4. Blues developed from songs that were sung by enslaved people on plantations.

5. The music developed a unique pattern and rhythm.

6. Blues musicians do not use musical instruments to accompany their songs.

TEST TIP: Reading section

When tackling the vocabulary questions in the reading section, try replacing the highlighted word with each of the answer options. Then, try reading the sentence. When you insert the correct answer option, the sentence should be logical and should support the main ideas of the passage.

B The following question is similar to question 2 in the writing section (independent task) of the Paper Edition of the TOEFL iBT test. Write notes for an essay of about 300 words.

Why do you think some genres of music are more popular than others? Which types of musical genres do you listen to and why? Use specific reasons and examples to support your answer.

Music I listen to:

Reasons:

Examples:

Music I don't listen to:

Reasons:

Examples:

Comparing and contrasting

Read the words and examples. Make additional examples using each word or phrase.

OVERVIEW

	Word or phrase	Example
To express similarity	similarity (between)	There are many **similarities between** painting and photography.
	both … and … have in common	**Both** painting **and** photography share several similarities. One feature that they **have in common** is that they can **both** express emotion.
	in the same way, similarly, likewise	Painting is sometimes used to record historic events. **In the same way**, photography is also often used to document history.
	like	**Like** painting, photography can express the subjective viewpoint of the artist. Photography, **like** painting, can express the subjective viewpoint of the artist.
	be similar to / resemble	Eighteenth century portraits **were similar to** photography because they aimed to present an accurate picture of reality.
	neither … nor	**Neither** painting **nor** photography is completely objective.
To express difference	difference (between)	One major **difference between** photography and painting is that we generally think of photography as being more realistic.
	whereas / while	**Whereas / While** a photograph is taken in a single moment, a painting usually takes much longer to create.
	on the other hand / however / by contrast*	A photograph captures an image of actual material things. A painting, **on the other hand**, can depict images from the artist's imagination.
	unlike / in contrast to / compared to	**In contrast to** painting, it is easy to produce multiple copies of a photograph.
	be different from (than) / differ (from)	Painting **is different from / differs from** photography because it draws attention to the technique used by the artist.

*These expressions can also be used at the beginning of a sentence. For example, *A photograph captures an image of actual material things.* **On the other hand**, *a painting can depict images from the artist's imagination.*

Practice Exercises

A Choose the correct word to complete each sentence.

1. _____ Van Gogh and Cezanne tried to create paintings that expressed the effect of light and color.

   a Like　　　　**b** Both　　　　**c** Compared to

2. In _____ to other artists, Jackson Pollock applied paint directly onto the canvas.

   a unlike　　　　**b** contrast　　　　**c** different

3. Warhol often used images of famous people in his art. _____, Basquiat incorporated elements of well-known images in his paintings.

   a Likewise　　　　**b** However　　　　**c** Similarity

4. _____ traditional art considered advertising to be a purely commercial activity, pop art of the 1960s used advertisements and dissociated them from their original context.

   a Unlike　　　　**b** Whereas　　　　**c** Compared to

5. _____ Picasso nor Matisse restricted themselves to just one style of art or one medium.

   a Both　　　　**b** Like　　　　**c** Neither

B Choose an appropriate word or phrase from the chart to complete the paragraph.

The Prose Style of Hemingway and Faulkner

Faulkner and Hemingway were two American authors who were ¹_____ writing in the same period of time in the 1920s–1950s. Faulkner, ²_____ Hemingway, wrote a large number of novels that are classics of modern American fiction. There are, ³_____, many ways in which their prose styles ⁴_____. One major ⁵_____ is sentence length. ⁶_____ Faulkner uses lengthy complex sentences with frequent repetition and long archaic words, Hemingway's prose is simpler, with shorter sentences that often ⁷_____ a newspaper report. Hemingway's dialog is simple and direct. Faulkner, ⁸_____, incorporates dialog into long, dream-like sequences that are almost poetic. Something that both writers have ⁹_____ is their ability to express strong emotions through their writing. Hemingway conveys strong emotions with just a few lines, ¹⁰_____ Faulkner who sometimes writes several pages about one scene. Rather than writing detailed descriptions of moods and feelings, Hemingway prefers to convey them through descriptions of actions and events.

STUDY TIP

One way to improve your speaking skills is to keep an audio journal. Make a recording each day about things you have seen, read about, or experienced. Try to use the new words that you studied recently. Listen to your recordings and identify ways in which they could be improved.

Test Practice

🎧 Listen to part of a lecture in an art class and take notes. Then answer the questions.
Track 3

1. What is the main topic of the lecture?

○ Whether art or graphic design is more complex

○ Different types of art and graphic design

○ How to compare art and graphic design

○ Problems with defining art and graphic design

2. According to the professor, what is NOT true about artists?

○ They create paintings.

○ They use their imagination.

○ They present their inner vision.

○ They start with a fixed purpose in mind.

3. What does the professor imply about graphic design?

○ It does not create a response in the viewer.

○ It is more commercial.

○ It is less skilled.

○ It has many interpretations.

Extra Practice

🎧 **A** Listen to the lecture again. Complete the notes opposite using the abbreviated forms of words from
Track 3 the box.

TEST TIP: Speaking section question 4 (academic summary)

In question 4 of the speaking section, you will listen to a lecture and take notes. The lecture will explain a term or concept and give concrete examples to illustrate that term or concept. Then you will be asked to give a spoken summary of the information and demonstrate an understanding of the relationship between the examples and the overall topic. In the test, you will have 20 seconds to prepare your response and 60 seconds to record it (approximately 125–150 words).

It is helpful to develop ways to organize your notes clearly using numbers, letters, symbols, and abbreviations when you listen. This will help you to record information from the lecture to use in your written response. One way to write quickly is to use short forms of words, without vowels. Look at the words in the examples below.

---

a feeling or point of view (POV) fixed purpose (fxd purp)

has several meanings (>1 mng) imagination (imag.)

materials and tools (mats + tools) product or service (prdct or serv)

take action (→ take actn) visible (vsble)

visual compositions (vis. comps)

Art + Graphic design: Similarities

1. Create

2. Have a range of

3. Use

Differences: Art

1. Expresses

2. Can have

3. Artist's presence is

Differences: Graphic design

1. Has a

2. Persuades

3. Sells

B Using points and examples from the lecture, explain how art and graphic design are similar and different. Write your spoken response here (or record your response and write the transcript here).

_____

_____

_____

_____

_____

_____

_____

_____

_____

_____

_____

_____

_____

_____

Biology

Read the words, definitions, and examples. Use your dictionary to find additional word forms for each word.

OVERVIEW

Word	Definition	Example
distinguish (v)	tell the difference	Modern humans can be **distinguished** from early humans by their more highly **evolved** brains.
evolved (adj)	developed over time	
estimate (n or v)	guess, judge, predict	**Estimates** of the actual number of **cells** in the human body **vary** widely.
cell (n)	smallest part of an animal or plant that can function independently	
vary (v)	differ	
genetic (adj)	related to genes (pattern of chemicals in cells)	**Genetic** mutations can be caused by environmental **factors**.
factor (n)	something that helps to produce a result	
identify (v)	recognize, name	The Human Genome Project **identified** 20,000–25,000 genes in human **DNA**.
DNA (deoxyribonucleic acid) (n)	sequence of genes carrying genetic instructions	
process (n)	series of actions or events	Photosynthesis is a **process** by which a plant produces food using sunlight, carbon dioxide, water, and **nutrients** from the soil.
nutrient (n)	substance that help organisms to grow and stay healthy	
adapt (v)	change in order to fit new conditions	Desert plants have **adapted** to dry conditions by growing long root **systems** that go deep underground to find water.
system (n)	network of parts that work together	
survive (v)	manage to live in difficult conditions	Some arctic animals **survive** in sub-zero conditions by developing an extra **layer** of fat to keep their bodies warm.
layer (n)	material that covers a surface	
classify (v)	categorize	**Organisms** are **classified** into groups according to shared **characteristics**.
characteristic (n or adj)	feature, trait, quality	
organism (n)	living thing	
microscopic (adj)	tiny	Plankton are **microscopic** organisms that float in the ocean and form a key **link** in the marine food chain.
link (n or v)	connection	

Practice Exercises

A Circle the best word to complete each sentence.

1. Reptiles can be _____ from other mammals by the fact that they are cold-blooded and have scales.

   a distinguished   **b** classified   **c** identified

2. An important _____ of amphibians is that they can live on both land and water.

   a gene   **b** system   **c** characteristic

3. Ocean fish cannot _____ in fresh water.

   a survive   **b** identify   **c** adapt

4. Skin is the outermost _____ of the human body.

   a cell   **b** layer   **c** link

5. Scientists _____ there are over 8 million species on Earth.

   a classify   **b** identify   **c** estimate

6. Minerals and vitamins are essential _____ for the human body.

   a nutrients   **b** links   **c** characteristics

7. One _____ in the development of biotechnology was the discovery of DNA.

   a system   **b** process   **c** factor

8. The number of red blood cells may _____ according to oxygen content.

   a estimate   **b** vary   **c** distinguish

DICTIONARY SKILLS

⊑ POWERED BY COBUILD

A good dictionary can tell you words that frequently occur together in a specific context. For example, words related to the *cardiovascular system* of the human body are: *cells, nutrients, oxygen, heart, lungs, blood, veins, arteries*. Drawing a diagram can also help you remember vocabulary.

WORD BUILDING

The suffix *-ic* is used to form adjectives: *microscopic, genetic, economic, electronic*. Some names of academic subjects add *-s* to form a noun: *economics, genetics, electronics*.

STUDY TIP: Vocabulary

Breaking a word into component parts can sometimes help you figure out its meaning. It can also help you expand your vocabulary. For example, *micro-* means small, and *scope*, means to see, so a *microscope* is something that helps you to see small objects. Other words with *micro-* are: *microbiology, microorganism, microchip, microeconomics*. Other words with *-scope* are: *telescope, stethoscope, periscope*.

B Complete the sentence with the correct form of the words in the box. Use your dictionary to help you.

cell	characteristic	identify	microscopic	survive

1. Microbiology is the study of organisms at a _____ (adj) level.

2. A _____ (n) magnifies objects that are too small to be seen by the human eye.

3. New DNA-based methods have been developed for the _____ (n) of species.

4. Climate change is threatening the _____ (n) of many living species.

5. Polar bears are _____ (v) by their long necks and powerful shoulders that make them excellent swimmers.

TEST TIP: Listening section

Take note of expressions that signal a digression from the main topic. Such expressions include: *By the way … As a side note … Incidentally … To change the topic …*

Expressions for returning to the main topic are: *To return to the main topic …To get back to the subject … To resume … To get back to the point … Anyway … Anyhow … At any rate …*

Test Practice

A Listen to part of a lecture in a biology class and answer the questions.

Track 4

1. What is the main idea of the lecture?

   ○ Genome sequencing

   ○ Use of technology to alter DNA

   ○ How to identify genetic characteristics

   ○ How to make food resistant to disease

2. Why does the professor mention biotechnology?

   ○ To distinguish it from genetic modification

   ○ As an example of genetic modification

   ○ To show how food can be modified

   ○ To explain how cheese is made

3. According to the professor, what is the definition of genetic modification?

   ○ Improving the genetic make-up of food

   ○ Changing the DNA of plants

   ○ Altering the genetic structure of organisms

   ○ Using technology to create new organisms

Track 5

4. Listen again to part of the lecture. Why does the professor say this?

   ○ To ask for help in creating a definition

   ○ To give an example of genetic modification

   ○ To emphasize the importance of a definition

   ○ To find out what students already know

5. According to the professor, what is true about GM foods?

   ○ They taste the same as other foods.

   ○ It is difficult to estimate its effects.

   ○ It has more nutrients than other foods.

   ○ It has a huge number of potential uses.

6. What does the professor imply is the most important reason for GM food products?

○ To prevent disease

○ To increase the food supply

○ To create new technology

○ To develop new medicines

Extra Practice

Track 4

A In question 4 in the speaking section (academic summary), you will listen to a lecture and take notes. Then you will be asked to give a spoken summary of the information. Listen again and make notes on the main ideas of the lecture.

Notes

Topic:

Definition:

Reasons for:

Why needed?

New technology:

B Using points and examples from the lecture, explain what genetic modification is and what its benefits are. Write your spoken response here (or record your response and write the transcript here). Use the phrases in the box.

The lecture is about …   The professor states that …   She claims that …
She suggests that …

Medicine and healthcare

Read the words, definitions, and examples. Use your dictionary to find additional word forms for each word.

OVERVIEW

Word	Definition	Example
procedure (n)	medical treatment in hospital or doctor's office	An ECG (electrocardiogram) is a medical **procedure** that is used to **monitor** the heart's electrical activity. The results of the test are **interpreted** by a doctor.
monitor (n or v)	check	
interpret (v)	decide what something means	
surgery (n)	process of cutting open a patient's body to provide treatment	Some types of dental **surgery**, such as tooth extraction, require only local **anesthesia**.
anesthesia (n)	use of drugs to prevent any experience of pain during surgery	
side-effect (n)	negative effect of a drug in addition to its main effect of treating an illness	One possibly dangerous **side-effect** of taking aspirin is stomach bleeding.
neurology (n)	study of the nervous system	**Neurology** is a branch of medicine dealing with **disorders** of the nervous system.
disorder (n)	illness, problem	
virus (n)	kind of germ that can cause disease	Influenza is a **virus** that is spread by coughing and sneezing. The **symptoms** are fever, sore throat, and a runny nose.
symptom (n)	sign	
hygiene (n)	cleanliness, sanitation	Maintaining hospital **hygiene** by sterilizing surgical instruments and washing hands frequently is vital to **preventing** the spread of **infection**.
prevent (v)	stop	
infection (n)	disease caused by germs or bacteria	
diagnose (v)	identify an illness or problem	New technologies such as MRI (magnetic resonance imaging) have made it easier for doctors to **diagnose** health conditions and **prescribe** the best **treatment**.
prescribe (v)	tell you what medicine is necessary	
treatment (n)	medical attention given to a sick person	
perception (n)	opinion, attitude	Negative **perceptions** of some mental illnesses still **persist** despite **advances** in public education and information.
persist (v)	continue	
advances (n)	progress, developments	
antibiotics (n)	drugs used to kill bacteria and infections	**Antibiotics**, such as penicillin, are drugs that are commonly used to treat **bacterial** infections.
bacterial (adj)	relating to small organisms that can cause disease	
modification (n)	alteration, change	Minor **modifications** to diet and lifestyle have been found to be **beneficial** in reducing hypertension (high blood pressure).
beneficial (adj)	having a positive effect	

Practice Exercises

A Match the terms with the correct examples.

1. a diagnostic procedure _____
2. a symptom _____
3. a prescription _____
4. a perception _____
5. a type of surgery _____
6. a virus _____
7. bacteria _____

a heart transplant
b chickenpox
c headache
d MRI scan
e dislike
f E. coli
g antibiotics

> **WORD BUILDING**
>
> The root *-scribe* can form several words related to the act of writing: *describe, transcribe, prescribe, inscribe, subscribe.*

B Circle the correct word to complete each sentence.

1. The interaction of two drugs may increase the risk of _____.

   a symptoms   **b** side-effects   **c** infection

2. _____ medicines cannot be bought over the counter.

   a prescription   **b** diagnosis   **c** treatment

3. Most cases of mental illness have a _____ cause.

   a bacterial   **b** neurological   **c** perceptive

4. New medical _____ can help to diagnose illnesses earlier.

   a surgery   **b** anesthesia   **c** procedures

5. The _____ of heart disease are chest pain, shortness of breath, and dizziness.

   a symptoms   **b** treatment   **c** diagnosis

6. Patients with diabetes usually have to _____ their blood sugar level.

   a prescribe   **b** persist   **c** monitor

7. A surgeon has to _____ the patient's symptoms in order to make a diagnosis.

   a monitor   **b** interpret   **c** prescribe

C Replace the words in italics with the correct form of one of the words from the chart opposite.

1. A *constant*[a] problem in medicine is the evolution of *infectious cells*[b] that are resistant to *medicine*[c].

   a _____   **b** _____   **c** _____

2. A radiologist will usually *evaluate*[a] the results of the X-ray and send a report to your doctor, who will *make a decision about*[b] your condition and *give*[c] treatment, if necessary.

   a _____   **b** _____   **c** _____

3. *Developments*[a] in modern technology have facilitated the use of minimally invasive surgical *techniques*[b], thus reducing the risk of *illness*[c] from bacteria.

   a _____   **b** _____   **c** _____

4. It is important to *check for*[a] possible *negative symptoms*[b] when taking these drugs and *alter*[c] the dose accordingly.

   a _____   **b** _____   **c** _____

Test Practice

A Read the passage and choose the best answer.

Modern Surgery Techniques

Surgery has traditionally been a medical practice that required invasive procedures to treat various illnesses and health conditions. The benefits of removing diseased organs far outweighed the possibly harmful and traumatic effects of cutting into the human body. Modern technology, however, has enabled the development of non-invasive and minimally invasive surgical techniques that allow surgeons to operate while making minor or no incisions .

Non-invasive procedures refer to techniques that do not require any incision into the skin. Examples of non-invasive techniques include ultrasound, X-rays, and magnetic resonance imaging (MRI), all of which are used for diagnostic purposes. MRI scans, for example, can help diagnose multiple sclerosis, brain tumors, cancer, and strokes, to name just a few conditions.

Minimally-invasive surgery refers to surgical techniques that require only the smallest possible incision into the skin. With keyhole surgery, for example, specially designed surgical scopes and instruments are inserted through the incision, enabling surgeons to gain access to the organs requiring treatment. Recent advances in robotic surgery have also allowed a greater flexibility and range of procedures to be addressed.

The benefits of this approach for the patient are numerous. Specifically, these procedures result in fewer complications for the patient in terms of recovery. There is also less likelihood of infection and less need for antibiotics or other drugs. Recovery time is faster and therefore time spent in hospital is shorter and considerably cheaper.

---

1. In paragraph 1, the author mentions invasive procedures in order to
   - ○ make the point that there are many different types of procedures.
   - ○ clarify the meaning of minimally invasive techniques.
   - ○ highlight the difference between traditional and modern surgery.
   - ○ give an example of surgical progress.

2. How does paragraph 2 relate to paragraph 3?
   - ○ They each present a different type of medical procedure.
   - ○ They contrast modern with traditional surgical techniques.
   - ○ Paragraph 3 gives a further example of the procedure in paragraph 2.
   - ○ Paragraph 3 describes advantages of the technique described in paragraph 2.

3. According to the passage, what is the main benefit of non-invasive techniques?
   - ○ To treat illnesses
   - ○ To identify illnesses
   - ○ To reduce recovery time
   - ○ To save money

4. According to the passage, what is one advantage of minimally invasive medical procedures?

○ They minimize recovery time.

○ They help diagnose major health conditions.

○ They are less complicated.

○ They require special instruments.

5. The word incisions is closest in meaning to

○ cuts.

○ illnesses.

○ techniques.

○ instruments.

B The following question is similar to question 2 in the writing section (independent task) of the Paper Edition of the TOEFL iBT test. Make notes for an essay of 300–400 words in response to the question.

Do you agree or disagree with the following statement? Advances in technology are helping us to live healthier and longer lives. Use specific reasons and examples to support your opinion.

> *Advances in Technology*
>
> *Benefits*   *Drawbacks*

C Write an introductory paragraph for your essay.

_____

_____

_____

_____

_____

_____

_____

_____

_____

_____

TEST TIP: Writing section question 2 of the Paper Edition of the TOEFL iBT test (independent writing task)

Remember that for question 2 in the writing section of the Paper Edition of the TOEFL iBT test, you do NOT need specialized knowledge of the subject. You may use examples based on your own experience. The criteria for a high-scoring response are: ability to respond to the question and express a clear opinion in a well-organized essay with good use of examples, correct grammar, and appropriate vocabulary.

PAPER EDITION ONLY

Animal behavior

Read the words, definitions, and examples. Use your dictionary to find additional word forms for each word.

OVERVIEW

Word	Definition	Example
migration (n)	movement of animals or humans from one place to another	The term **migration** is used to describe the movement of **populations** of butterflies, birds, or other animals.
population (n)	the people who live in a country, or the total number of animals in a region	
decline (v or n)	decrease	The number of bird species has **declined** because of changes in their natural **habitat**.
habitat (n)	natural home of a plant or animal	
climate (n)	general weather conditions	Rising temperatures due to **climate** change have **triggered** changes in migratory **patterns**.
trigger (v or n)	cause	
pattern (n)	repeated or regular way in which something is done	
endangered (adj)	that may soon disappear	Whales and polar bears are two examples of **endangered** species that are at risk of becoming **extinct**.
extinct (adj)	that does not exist any more	
species (n)	related group of plants or animals	Some **species** of insects, such as ants and honey bees, live together in groups known as **colonies**, where group members have highly specialized **functions**.
colony (n)	group	
function (n or v)	purpose, role	
mechanism (n)	device, method	Small fish have developed defence **mechanisms** to avoid **predatory** fish such as sharks.
predatory (adj)	killing and eating other animals	
herbivore (n)	organism that eats only plants	Giraffes are **herbivores** that live on a diet of leaves and eat an **average** of 75 pounds of food a day.
average (n or adj)	typical	
theory (n)	idea or set of ideas that tries to explain something	Darwin's **theory** of natural selection explains why some genetic **traits** tend to survive while others do not.
trait (n)	characteristic	
research (n or v)	study	Scientific **research** on animal behavior has **contributed** to the development of medicines for many human disorders.
contribute (to) (v)	help	

Practice Exercises

A Choose the words from the chart that best replace the words in italics.

1. Changes in animal *numbers*[a] can be *caused*[b] by lower temperatures.

   a _____ b _____

2. Different *types*[a] of birds follow different *traveling*[b] patterns.

   a _____ b _____

3. Some animals have a genetic *characteristic*[a] that enables them to change color as a *protection*[b] against *hunters*[c].

   a _____ b _____ c _____

4. Honey bees live in *groups*[a] called hives, where worker bees perform the *role*[b] of collecting food.

   a _____ b _____

5. Many species of fish are *at risk*[a] due to overfishing and may become *lost*[b] if fishing is not restricted.

   a _____ b _____

6. One *idea*[a] for the decline in the penguin population is the disappearance of ice fields, which are their natural *environment*[b].

   a _____ b _____

7. Although pandas eat *a typical amount*[a] of 80 pounds of bamboo shoots a day, they are not *vegetarians*[b], as they can also digest meat.

   a _____ b _____

8. The study of color production *methods*[a] in animals can *give*[b] useful insights to modern science.

   a _____ b _____

B Complete the paragraph with the correct form of words from the chart. Use your dictionary to help you.

Changes in Bird Migration
Rising temperatures are causing a shift in the migratory [1]_____ of birds in North America, pushing them to [2]_____ earlier in the year. This could [3]_____ species that are not able to adapt successfully to [4]_____ change. Recent [5]_____ shows that birds accelerated their schedule by an [6]_____ of 0.8 days per degree Celsius of temperature increase. Some studies suggest that changes in [7]_____ could [8]_____ to population [9]_____, putting many species at risk of [10]_____.

STUDY TIP

Read and listen to science- and medicine-related articles in the newspaper or online to keep up-to-date with the latest topics and to expand your vocabulary. For example, www.dsc.discovery.com has short videos on academic topics and www.npr.org has short stories on health, science, and other topics. As lectures are sometimes spoken in British or Australian English, it is also helpful to listen to news articles on the BBC (www.bbc.co.uk) or lectures on TED (www.ted.com).

Test Practice

Read the passage and answer the questions.

Social Organization of Ant Colonies

Ant colonies are divided into queens, males, and workers. The job of the queen is to lay eggs. The males generally do not work, but receive food from the workers until it is time for them to mate. They die almost immediately after mating. Workers are sterile females. Instead of reproducing, they perform a variety of roles that benefit the colony. They forage for food, defend the colony from attack, construct the nest, and take care of the queen. Only a small percentage of worker ants are foragers. They face greater risks as they are constantly exposed to external dangers from predators while hunting for food.

---

1. The author mentions the queen, males, and workers in the passage in order to illustrate
   - ○ functions of ant colonies.
   - ○ types of ant colonies.
   - ○ functions of ants.
   - ○ types of reproduction.

2. According to the paragraph, which of the following is NOT true about ant colonies?
   - ○ Each type of ant has a different function.
   - ○ Workers do not hunt for food.
   - ○ Males do not reproduce.
   - ○ Workers and queen ants are all female.

3. The word forage in the passage is closest in meaning to
   - ○ search.
   - ○ eat.
   - ○ carry.
   - ○ store.

4. The word sterile in the passage is closest in meaning to
   - ○ inactive.
   - ○ uncooperative.
   - ○ defensive.
   - ○ infertile.

5. Which of the sentences below best expresses the essential information in the highlighted sentence in the passage?
   - ○ Forager ants do not put their lives at risk when they hunt for food.
   - ○ The function of forager ants is to defend the colony from danger.
   - ○ Forager ants do not hunt for food unless they are safe from danger.
   - ○ Forager ants hunt for food despite facing constant danger outside the colony.

TEST TIP: Reading section

Look for words around the highlighted word to help you identify the meaning. Sometimes a word with a similar meaning can be found later in the same sentence or paragraph. For example, *They forage for food ... while hunting for food.*

B This question is similar to question 3 in the speaking section (academic reading and lecture). Read the paragraph and take notes of the main ideas.

> Lack of water and the extreme heat of the desert habitat create a survival problem for all desert organisms. Many desert animals have adapted physically and behaviorally to survive in these conditions. An example of a physical adaptation is the ability to store water; the gila monster is a species of lizard that can store water in the fatty cells in its tail. An example of behavioral adaptation is the kangaroo rat, which sleeps under the ground during the day and comes out at night to hunt for food when the temperatures are

C Now listen to part of a lecture on the same subject and add to your notes.

Track 6

D Complete the sample spoken response below, summarizing the information from both sources (or record your response and write the transcript here). Practice reading the response aloud. You have 60 seconds to provide your response (125–150 words).

Sample spoken response

Both the reading passage and the lecture are about _____.

The reading passage and the lecture describe two ways that _____ _____.

The first type of adaptation from the reading passage is that animals _____ _____.

One example from the reading passage is _____ _____.

One example from the lecture is _____ _____.

The second type of desert adaptation is that animals _____ _____.

One example from the reading passage is _____ _____.

One example from the lecture is _____ _____.

Opinions

Read the words and examples. Make additional examples using each word or phrase.

OVERVIEW

Function	Word or phrase	Example
Giving opinions	In my opinion, In my experience, From my point of view, It is my opinion that … I agree with the idea that … I personally believe that …	**In my opinion,** genetically modified food is a good way to increase world food production. **I agree with the idea that** genetically modified crops should be used to help to solve world food shortages.
Making generalizations	In general, Generally speaking, On the whole, For the most part, As a rule,	**In general,** genetically modified food has improved agriculture in many countries. **As a rule,** these crops are scientifically tested before being used.
Giving examples	For example, For instance, …, for example, … …, for instance, … As an example, As an illustration, … such as …	**For example,** genetically modified wheat is more resistant to pests and requires fewer pesticides. Some varieties of apple, **for instance,** have been modified to reduce browning after being cut. Some types of grain, **such as** rice, have been developed to increase their annual yield.
	especially (introduces an outstanding example)	Many crops, **especially** those grown in countries that are prone to drought, would not survive if they were not modified.
Elaborating (Giving further reasons)	In addition / Moreover / Additionally / Besides / Furthermore / Similarly	**In addition,** crops can be enhanced with multivitamins that benefit human health.
	In fact, (gives further information about an example that has already been mentioned)	**In fact,** some human diseases may be prevented if crops are fortified with nutrients.

Note: Notice the use of a comma when a transition phrase begins a sentence.

Practice Exercises

A Choose the correct word or phrase to complete each sentence.

1. *In / On* the whole, I think it is a good idea for people to have pets.

2. *In / On* general, I feel that pets are helpful to humans.

3. *In / As* a rule, most pets are good companions.

4. *On / For* the most part, cats are sociable animals.

5. Cats, *for / as* example, seem to enjoy living with people.

6. *On / In* addition, pets can be beneficial to our health by keeping us active.

7. *In / On* fact, domesticated cats would not be able to survive outdoors.

8. *Especially / Additionally,* having a pet is very comforting for older people.

9. *On / In* my opinion, cats are the best pets as they are so independent.

10. *Furthermore, / Similarly,* cats have distinct personalities so they make wonderful companions.

<table>
<tr><td>DICTIONARY SKILLS</td></tr>
<tr><td>☞ POWERED BY COBUILD</td></tr>
<tr><td>Domesticated in this context describes animals that are used to living with people. Use your dictionary to find other forms and meanings of this word. What does the root dom- mean?</td></tr>
</table>

B Complete the paragraph with words or phrases from the box.

especially	for instance	in addition	in fact	in general	in my opinion
on the whole	such as				

[1]_____, I disagree with the use of animals for medical science. [2]_____, it is not always helpful to use animals for testing. [3]_____, rats and mice are often used to test the safety of new drugs, but drugs used on mice are not always effective on humans. [4]_____, some drugs, [5]_____ aspirin, are helpful to humans, but harmful to animals. [6]_____, improved technology these days makes animal testing less necessary. Many drugs, [7]_____ those that are used for cosmetics or beauty products, do not need to be tested on animals. Although some animal testing may be essential, I feel that, [8]_____, animal testing causes unnecessary cruelty to animals.

C Complete the sentences using your own ideas.

What is your opinion about genetic modification of animals? Is it useful? Why or why not?

In my opinion, _____.

Generally speaking _____.

For the most part, _____.

For example, _____.

In fact, _____.

In conclusion, I believe that _____.

STUDY TIP

Transition words show logical connections between sentences and ideas. They help your reader to follow the logic of your ideas and make your essay clearer. Check that you have used transition words when you proofread your essay.

Test Practice

A The following question is similar to question 2 in the writing section (independent task) of the Paper Edition of the TOEFL iBT test. Read the question, then complete the essay below using the concept map provided.

In general, people are living longer these days. Discuss the reasons for this development and give specific examples.

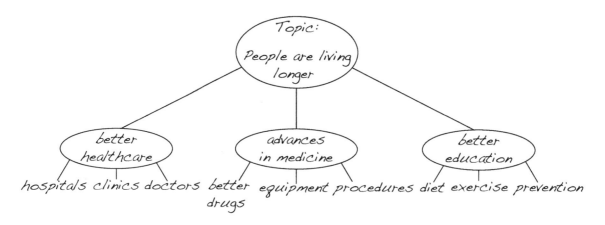

People are living longer these days for a number of reasons. The main reasons are _____,
_____,
and _____.
In general, _____. For example, _____.
In addition, people are living longer because _____. In the past,
_____ but now _____.
A further reason for the increase in longevity is _____.
In conclusion, _____, _____, and
_____ are enabling people to live longer. That is
why some countries have an increasing number of older people.

B Read the following questions. They are similar to questions that may come up in the independent task in the writing section. In this question, you may be asked to agree or disagree with a statement and explain why. Choose one question and use the concept map to plan a 300-word response.

Do you agree or disagree with the following statement? Medical advances are the most important development of the 21st century. Use specific reasons and examples to support your response.

Do you agree or disagree with the following statement? It is more important to be healthy than to be rich. Use specific reasons and examples to support your response.

TEST TIP: Writing section

Before you start writing, make a quick plan. You could use a concept map to organize your ideas. As you write, think about how to incorporate transition words to connect your ideas.

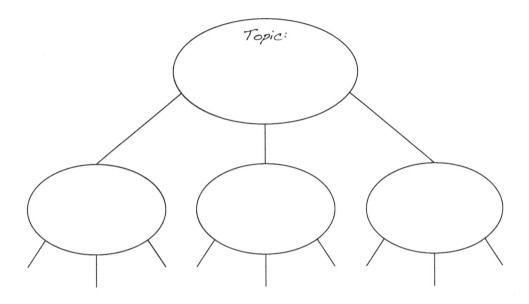

C Now write the essay (300 words).

_____

_____

_____

_____

_____

_____

_____

_____

_____

_____

_____

_____

_____

_____

_____

_____

History

Read the words, definitions, and examples. Use your dictionary to find additional word forms for each word.

OVERVIEW

Word	Definition	Example
period (n)	length of time, era	The Stone Age is the **period** of human history before the **invention** of metal tools.
invention (n)	something that has been devised by someone	
construct (v)	build	The earliest known pyramids were **constructed** in 2600 BCE (Before the Common Era) when pharaohs **ruled** over the **kingdom** of Egypt.
rule (v)	have control over	
kingdom (n)	country that is ruled by a king or monarch	
society (n)	community, large organized group of people	The **society** of **ancient** Rome was divided into a **hierarchy** of two main classes: the patricians, who were wealthy and powerful, and the plebeians, who were workers.
ancient (adj)	very old	
hierarchy (n)	social structure where upper levels have control over lower levels	
document (n)	piece of text that is stored so it can be accessed later	The Magna Carta of 1215 was an important historical **document** that **restricted** the power of the king in England.
restrict (v)	limit	
civilization (n)	society with its own organization and culture	One reason for the success of ancient Egyptian **civilization** was the development of irrigation systems.
settler (n)	immigrant, person who goes to live in a new country	English **settlers** arrived in Plymouth, Massachusetts, in 1621 and **founded** the first permanent European colony in New England.
found (v)	start, set up, establish	
overthrow (v)	remove a government or leader by force	In 1789, the people of France **overthrew** the **monarchy** and eventually **established** a republic.
monarchy (n)	system of government where a king or queen has control of power	
establish (v)	start, create, set up, found	
revolutionary (adj)	that changes the existing system	The American **Revolutionary** War was **declared** in 1775 when the thirteen colonies in North America decided to become independent from the British Empire.
declare (v)	assert, pronounce	

Practice Exercises

A Choose the correct word to complete each sentence.

1. Historians obtain information from primary sources such as _____ of eyewitness accounts.

    a documents   **b** inventions   **c** constructions

2. The _____ in Ancient Egypt placed the Pharaoh and his family at the top, merchants and craftspeople in the middle, and farmers at the bottom.

    a hierarchy   **b** monarchy   **c** revolution

3. In 17th-century England, the right to vote was _____ to men who owned property.

    a declared   **b** restricted   **c** ruled

4. Historians are usually very interested in old _____ about the lives of ordinary people.

    a settlers   **b** documents   **c** societies

5. The right of everyone to vote was _____ in the United States with The Voting Rights Act of 1965.

    a constructed   **b** overthrown   **c** established

6. An absolute _____ is a political system where one person has complete power over a country.

    a revolution   **b** hierarchy   **c** monarchy

7. The ancient African _____ of Axum was located in present day Ethiopia and reached its height under King Ezana in the 4th century.

    a republic   **b** kingdom   **c** society

8. The _____ of the steam engine revolutionized transportation by making possible the steam train and the steamboat.

    a establishment   **b** invention   **c** declaration

B Complete the paragraph with the correct form of words from the chart.

The Aztec Empire

By the 13th century, groups of Aztecs had migrated southward into Mexico. They [1]_____ in the valley of Mexico and [2]_____ the twin capitals of Tenochtitlán and Tlatelolco some time after 1325. After destroying the opposition, the Aztec Emperor Tlacecl ordered all historical [3]_____ to be burned so that they could create their own version of the country's history. The Aztecs were aggressive and militaristic and quickly expanded their territory beyond the valley to the borders of Guatemala. Aztec [4]_____ was divided into an elaborate [5]_____ of social status, with a small group of [6]_____ and nobility at the top who controlled land and resources.

STUDY TIP

When you finish reading an article in a journal, magazine, or online, ask yourself what the main points of the article were. Write them down. Then look back through the article and check if you have included all the main points. Doing this regularly will increase your confidence in being able to distinguish main ideas from details.

Test Practice

Read the passage and answer the questions.

The French Revolution

The French Revolution was a crucial moment in the modern history, of not only Europe, but the world. [1] ■ During this period, French citizens overthrew a centuries-old system of government that placed power in the hands of a few and abolished institutions such as absolute monarchy and the feudal system. Like the American Revolution before it, the French Revolution was influenced by the concept of popular sovereignty. [2] ■ This was a belief that the source of a nation's governmental power lies with its citizens and should benefit its citizens. [3] ■ Although at times it descended into unnecessary chaos, the Revolution played a critical role by showing how modern nations can be shaped by the will of the people. [4] ■

---

1. The word crucial in the passage is closest in meaning to
   ○ important.
   ○ necessary.
   ○ successful.
   ○ dangerous.

2. The word abolished in the passage is closest in meaning to
   ○ established.
   ○ challenged.
   ○ introduced.
   ○ eliminated.

3. Look at the four squares [■] that indicate where the following sentence can be added to the passage. Where would the sentence best fit?

   The French Revolution began in 1789 and ended in the late 1790s with the ascent of Napoleon Bonaparte.

   Answer _____

TEST TIP: Reading section (insert a sentence questions)

Review the given sentence and see if there are any words that refer to it in the paragraph. In this case, the phrase *during this period* refers back to a description of the time. Therefore, the correct answer is [1].

Extra Practice

🎧 Track 7

A This question is similar to question 4 in the speaking section (academic summary). Listen to part of a lecture from a history class. Complete these notes as you listen.

Main topic

Impact 1
Before

After

Result

Impact 2
Before

After

Result

Conclusion

B Using the points and examples from the lecture, explain how the steam engine impacted England and the United States. Complete the sample spoken response. Practice reading the response aloud. You have 60 seconds to provide your response (125–150 words).

Sample spoken response

In the lecture, the professor talks about the _____.

The professor mentions two ways that _____

_____.

According to the professor, the steam engine increased _____.

Before the steam engine, people _____.

Afterward, goods could _____

_____.

The second major impact the professor mentions _____.

The steam engine led to the construction _____.

Before the steam engine, _____

_____.

Afterward, people _____

_____.

It was the beginning of _____.

43

Business and economics

Read the words, definitions, and examples. Use your dictionary to find additional word forms for each word.

OVERVIEW

Word	Definition	Example
economy (n)	way of managing resources in a country	A market **economy** is one that is based on the interaction of **supply** and **demand**.
supply (n or v)	the quantity of something that people are willing to sell	
demand (n or v)	the quantity of something that people are willing to buy	
inflation (n)	increase in prices	The 1970s was a period of high **inflation** in the United States, when the **overall** level of prices more than doubled.
overall (adj)	general	
firm (n)	company	A **firm** can raise **capital** from **investors** by becoming a public company and selling its **shares** on the stock market.
capital (n)	large amount of money needed to start a business	
investor (n)	someone who gives money to a company hoping that it will increase in value	
shares (n)	units of a company's value that people can buy and trade	
budget (n or v)	financial plan	The annual **budget** of a country is a way for the government to **allocate** funds to different **sectors** of the economy.
allocate (v)	give, assign, distribute	
sector (n)	part	
generate (v)	create, make	The main goal of a company is to **generate** the maximum amount of **profit** for its shareholders.
profit (n or v)	money gained when something is sold	
measure (v)	find out the size, amount, or speed of something	The size of a country's economy is **measured** by the annual total **output**, which is known as the GDP (Gross Domestic Product).
output (n)	something that is produced	
promote (v)	encourage people to buy something	Advertising is an important way for companies to **promote** their products and increase their **market** share.
market (n)	customers, or area where something is sold	
collapse (n or v)	sudden and complete fall	High-risk lending by financial institutions led to a **collapse** in the housing market and the financial **crisis** of 2008.
crisis (n)	emergency	
compete (v)	take part in a race or a contest	In a free market, companies **compete** with each other on price so that many **consumers** will buy their products.
consumer (n)	buyer, user, customer	

Practice Exercises

A Choose the correct form of words from the chart opposite that best replace the words in italics.

WORD BUILDING

The word *crisis* can co-occur with a number of adjectives: *financial crisis, economic crisis, political crisis, severe/ major crisis, reach a crisis point.*

1. Companies *contest*[a] with each other by trying to persuade the *customer*[b] that their product is better than the others.

   a _____ b _____

2. The government's *financial plan*[a] is one way of influencing the country's *financial system*[b].

   a _____ b _____

3. To start a company, it is necessary to find *people with money*[a] who are willing to provide *finance*[b].

   a _____ b _____

4. The wealth of a country can be *estimated*[a] according to the average *productivity*[b] of each person.

   a _____ b _____

5. *An overall increase in prices*[a] can sometimes lead to an economic *emergency*[b].

   a _____ b _____

6. In many countries, construction is one *part*[a] of the economy that *creates*[b] a lot of employment.

   a _____ b _____

7. Many *businesses*[a] use TV and social media to *advertise*[b] their products.

   a _____ b _____

8. The price of oil rises when the *amount people want to buy*[a] is high and the *amount available*[b] is low.

   a _____ b _____

B Complete the paragraph with the correct form of words from the chart.

Marketing
Marketing is more than just advertising or [1]_____ your product. First of all, a [2]_____ has to develop a product that [3]_____ will want to buy. This involves doing careful research to find out where there is a gap in the [4]_____. Second, the price has to be [5]_____, that is, sold at a price that customers will be prepared to pay. If it is priced too high, [6]_____ will be low. If it is priced too low, there will not be enough [7]_____. A large part of the marketing [8]_____ will be [9]_____ to advertising so that customers can get to hear about the product. Finally, there has to be a sufficient [10]_____ of the product available in places where people will be likely to buy it.

STUDY TIP

Use online resources to improve your vocabulary. Many websites have interactive activities designed to help you prepare for the TOEFL iBT test. Examples of some key search terms are: *TOEFL speaking practice, TOEFL writing topics, TOEFL practice tests.*

Test Practice

🎧 **Listen to the lecture and take notes. Then answer the questions.**

Track 8

1. What is the main topic of the lecture?
   - ⭘ Different ways of managing the economy
   - ⭘ Advantages of a mixed economy
   - ⭘ Problems with a planned economy
   - ⭘ Difference between public and private companies

2. According to the professor, what is one problem with a free market economy?
   - ⭘ Goods are too expensive.
   - ⭘ Products are not of the best quality.
   - ⭘ Only profitable goods are produced.
   - ⭘ There is more supply than demand.

3. According to the professor, which of the following is a problem with a planned economy?
   - ⭘ There is insufficient supply.
   - ⭘ Goods are of poor quality.
   - ⭘ Government controls production.
   - ⭘ There is no profit.

4. What does the professor imply about changing from a planned to a market economy?
   - ⭘ It can have a range of economic effects.
   - ⭘ It has a beneficial effect.
   - ⭘ It can lead to unemployment.
   - ⭘ It takes a long time.

🎧 5. Listen again to part of the lecture. Then, answer the question. Why does the professor say this?

Track 9
   - ⭘ To introduce a digression
   - ⭘ To ask for students' opinions
   - ⭘ To review what students know
   - ⭘ To outline today's lecture

TEST TIP: Listening section (inference questions)

Inference questions ask you to make a judgment based on information that is strongly implied, but not directly stated, in the lecture. Inference questions may be worded as follows: *What does the professor imply about ...? What can be inferred about ...? What is probably true about ...?* Watch out for incorrect answer options that are true but not supported by information in the lecture, or information that contradicts information in the lecture.

Extra Practice

Track 8

A In question 4 in the speaking section (academic summary), you will listen to a lecture and take notes. Then you will be asked to give a spoken summary of the information and demonstrate an understanding of the relationship between the examples and the overall topic. Listen again and make notes on the main ideas of the lecture.

> *Main topic*
>
> *Type 1*
>
> *Benefits*
>
> *Problems*
>
> *Type 2*
>
> *Benefits*
>
> *Problems*
>
> *Conclusion*

B Using points and examples from the lecture, explain the two types of economic system and what their advantages and drawbacks are. Write your spoken response here (or record your response and write the transcript here). You have 60 seconds to provide your response (125–150 words). Use the phrases in the box.

> The lecture is about …   The professor states that …   She claims that …
> She implies that …

_____

_____

_____

_____

_____

_____

_____

_____

_____

_____

_____

Sociology and archeology

Read the words, definitions, and examples. Use your dictionary to find additional word forms for each word.

OVERVIEW

Word	Definition	Example
investigate (v)	examine, explore, study, analyze	Sociologists **investigate** social groups and their **structure**.
structure (n)	organization	
issue (n)	topic	Sociological **issues** that relate to the internet include **identity** and the **nature** of social interaction.
identity (n)	who you are	
nature (n)	the basic quality or character of something	
data (n, pl)	statistics	Social researchers can collect **data** by using **surveys**, questionnaires, or interviews.
survey (n)	a series of questions asked in order to find out information about a large number of people	
examine (v)	study carefully, inspect	Archeology is the study of past people and cultures by **examining** material evidence **ranging** from **artifacts**, such as pottery and stone tools, to architecture and landscape.
range from ... to ... (v)	vary	
artifact (n)	object	
excavate (v)	uncover, find	Archeologists have **excavated** a **site** in France that may provide new **evidence** of society in the Stone Age.
site (n)	place	
evidence (n)	proof	
diversity (n)	variety	Anthropology is the study of human **diversity** around the world and studies cultural differences in social **institutions**, cultural beliefs and values, and communication styles.
institution (n)	a large important organization Ex. university, church, bank	

Practice Exercises

A Choose the best words to complete the sentences.

1. Recent sociological studies are ᵃ_____ social networks and their
   ᵇ_____.

   a investigating   conducting   involving

   b identity   institution   structure

2. One ᵃ_____ that sociologists study is the interaction between individuals and
   social ᵇ_____, such as schools.

   a survey   data   issue

   b participants   institutions   artifacts

3. Anthropologists sometimes ᵃ_____ research that
   ᵇ_____ traveling to remote parts of the world.

   a observe   conduct   excavate

   b conducts   investigates   involves

DICTIONARY SKILLS

POWERED BY COBUILD

The prefix *ex-* means *out of*: *excavate* means to take out of the ground. Use your dictionary to find the meanings of these words: *exhale, extract, expel, expand, exclude.*

4. Archeologists in France and southern Spain have ᵃ_____ stone pots and other
   ᵇ_____ that provide ᶜ_____ of prehistoric civilization.

   a observed   excavated   involved

   b artifacts   issues   sites

   c identity   evidence   diversity

5. A ᵃ_____ that was ᵇ_____ by researchers in Sweden found that
   there was a link between depression and diet.

   a survey   site   data

   b involved   conducted   investigated

B Complete the text with the correct forms of words from the chart.

Anthropological Research Methods

Cultural immersion describes the process by which an anthropologist lives among a certain group of people for a period of time in order to get a better understanding of the ¹_____ of their social ²_____. This can ³_____ living with the group for many months or years.

In studies of this kind, researchers can sometimes take part in the social group they are ⁴_____ by taking a job or another social role. This is known as ⁵_____ observation. Researchers can explain their research role to the people in the group, although this can sometimes have an adverse effect on the ⁶_____. Another approach is to conceal their ⁷_____ and pretend to be a member of the group.

A famous example of this second type of research was ⁸_____ by Erving Goffman in his ⁹_____ into life in psychiatric hospitals. Goffman worked as a member of staff in the hospital which enabled him to gather a more accurate picture of life in a psychiatric ¹⁰_____.

Test Practice

A Read the paragraph and answer the questions.

Cultural Anthropology

Cultural anthropology of the 20th century was greatly influenced by the so-called culture history school, founded by Franz Boas, a German-born American. He supported the idea that researchers should collect evidence of the diversity of human social structures and behavior by observing people in their natural environs. In his view, the task of the anthropologist was to go out into the field to observe and gather facts and artifacts, record social and cultural processes, and use this data as the basis of a theoretical description. This emphasis on fieldwork and firsthand observation influenced a whole generation of sociologists and cultural anthropologists.

---

1. The word field in the passage is closest in meaning to
   ○ team.
   ○ subject.
   ○ environment.
   ○ research.

2. The word firsthand in the passage is closest in meaning to
   ○ direct.
   ○ careful.
   ○ social.
   ○ expert.

3. Which of the following is implied about anthropologists before Boas?
   ○ They did not study other cultures.
   ○ They did not base their theories on observation.
   ○ They did not gather enough evidence for their theories.
   ○ They did not agree on theoretical research methods.

B Read the paragraph and answer the questions.

Ancient Peoples of the American Southwest

Nowhere in North America has the study of the past been so fascinating as in the study of the Anasazi, also known as the "ancient ones," the native peoples of the Southwest who lived in this region between 850 CE and around 1200. [1] ■ Excavations at Chaco Canyon in New Mexico provide evidence of a sophisticated social structure. [2] ■ Artifacts ranging from exquisite pottery and jewelry to stone tools for making flour offer unique insights into the nature of life in this arid climate where water was scarce and soil conditions extremely poor. Without a written history, however, we can only speculate about the details of their daily lives. [3] ■ Archeologists disagree about the type of social organization that governed these communities, with some theorizing a hierarchical organization, and others a more egalitarian one. [4] ■ One thing that all agree on, however, is that the reason these settlements were completely abandoned by the end of the 13th century was most probably due to climatic change.

---

1. The word arid in the passage is closest in meaning to

    ○ dry.

    ○ extreme.

    ○ variable.

    ○ unusual.

2. The word egalitarian in the passage is closest in meaning to

    ○ powerful.

    ○ equal.

    ○ sophisticated.

    ○ complex.

3. According to the text, artifacts of the Anasazi provide evidence of

    ○ social structure.

    ○ written history.

    ○ daily lives.

    ○ climate conditions.

4. Look at the four squares [■] that indicate where the following sentence can be added to the passage. Where would the sentence best fit?

    Data collected from this and other sites reveal that the Anasazi were expert farmers and skilled craftsmen.

    Answer _____

5. Which of the sentences below best expresses the essential information in the highlighted sentence in the passage? Incorrect choices change the meaning in important ways or leave out essential information.

    ○ We cannot guess anything about the details of their lives.

    ○ We can guess details of their lives even without written records.

    ○ We can develop theories based on written records.

    ○ A written history would not help us to imagine their daily lives.

TEST TIP: Reading section (insert a sentence questions)

Review the given sentence and see if there are any words that refer to it later in the paragraph. In question 4 above, the words *this and other sites* refer back to *excavations*. Therefore, the correct answer is [2].

Cause and effect

Read the words and phrases. Study the examples. Make your own examples using each word or phrase.

OVERVIEW

Function	Word or phrase	Example
Expressing causes (Reasons)	One reason for … was … . There were several reasons for … . One reason was … .	**One reason** for the financial crisis in 2008 was lack of regulation in the banking sector. **There were several reasons for** the economic downturn in 2008. **One reason was** the collapse of the housing market.
	One reason why (clause) was … . There were several reasons why (clause). One reason was … .	**One reason why** people were unable to repay their mortgage was the increase in the interest rate. **There were several reasons why** people were unable to repay their mortgage. **One reason** was the increase in the interest rate.
	Due to … Owing to … Because of … (These are prepositions and are followed by a noun or noun phrase. Use *the fact that* to introduce a clause.)	**Due to** the decrease in demand, many companies were forced to downsize their workforce. **Owing to** *the fact that* there was a decrease in demand, many companies were forced to downsize their workforce.
Expressing effects (Results)	Consequently, As a result, Therefore, For this reason, As a consequence,	Many companies went bankrupt. **Consequently,** there was a rise in unemployment.
	This means that … . This can / may / might mean that … . This results in … . This can / may / might result in … . One of the main results / effects is … . An important result / effect is … .	There are stricter regulations on lending money. **This means that** it is more difficult to borrow. More people are renting houses than buying. **This may result in** an increase in rent prices. The number of house sales has fallen dramatically. **One of the effects** has been a decline in the construction of new homes.

Note: Information about using conjunctions *because, since,* and *so* to express cause and effect can be found in Grammar Unit 13.

STUDY TIP

Notice that the expressions listed in the chart are for formal written English. In spoken English, we usually use *because*, *since*, and *so* to express cause and effect.

Practice Exercises

A Underline the cause and draw a wavy line under the effect in each of the following pairs of sentences. Then rewrite them using one of the transition phrases in the chart.

1. There has been a decline in the number of bookstores. Many people are buying books online.

   _____

2. More people are working from home. Communication by computer is faster and more efficient.

   _____

3. People watch movies at home on the internet. Fewer people are going to movie theaters.

   _____

4. Too many people try to text and drive at the same time. There are many car accidents.

   _____

B Complete the paragraph with words or phrases from the box. Some words can be used more than once.

as a result	because of	cause	consequently	due to	effect	reason
result	result in	resulted	therefore	meant that		

The Industrial Revolution [1]_____ in enormous changes to the way society was organized in Europe, the US and some other countries. The most popular view is that the main [2]_____ was the invention of new technology, most notably, the steam engine. [3]_____ improved machinery, craft industries that were traditionally carried out in the home were replaced by factories. This [4]_____ people started to move to the towns and cities for work. [5]_____, towns and cities became larger and more crowded. Another [6]_____ was that goods could be produced cheaply and in greater quantities. [7]_____, more people could afford to buy them and their quality of life improved.

Another view, however, is that an important [8]_____ for placing workers in large factories was that employers could have greater control over their workers. [9]_____, they had to work longer hours and produce more. Technology was [10]_____ developed in order to speed up their productivity.

In the 20th century, the Information Revolution is also having an [11]_____ on the organization of our society. [12]_____ the invention of the internet, people can communicate more quickly and efficiently than ever before. One [13]_____ of this may be that in the future more people will work from home. It is possible that this may [14]_____ a change of attitude concerning how much control employers need to have over their workers.

STUDY TIP

Transition words show logical connections between sentences and ideas. They help your reader to follow the logic of your ideas and make your essay clearer. Remember to use **a variety** of transition words and avoid repeating the same ones over again.

Test Practice

A Read the following questions. They are similar to question 2 in the writing section (independent task) of the Paper Edition of the TOEFL iBT test. Choose one question and use the concept map to plan a 300-word response. (Note: In the test you <u>won't</u> be given any choice about which question you do.)

1. How does social networking influence people's behavior? Use reasons and specific examples to support your answer.

2. What effect has the internet had on the economy and business? Use reasons and specific examples to support your answer.

3. What impact have cell phones had on our society? Use reasons and specific examples to support your answer.

TEST TIP: Writing section

Before you start writing, make a plan using a concept map to organize your ideas. Think of two reasons to support your argument and one or two examples or details for each reason.

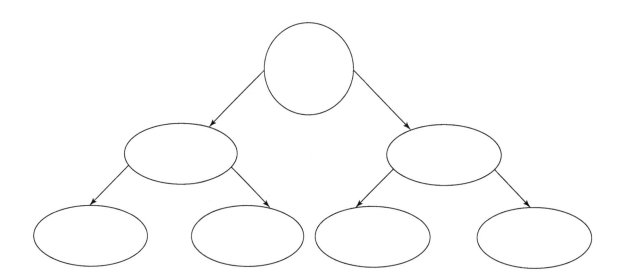

B Now write your essay. Remember to use a variety of transitions.

Introduction

_____

_____

_____

_____

_____

_____

_____

Effect 1

_____

_____

_____

_____

_____

_____

_____

Effect 2

_____

_____

_____

_____

_____

_____

_____

Conclusion

_____

_____

_____

_____

_____

_____

_____

Technology and computers

Read the words, definitions, and examples. Use your dictionary to find additional word forms for each word.

OVERVIEW

Word	Definition	Example
app (application) (n)	software that can run on a computer or cell phone, usually with a specific function such as paying bills online	**Installing** this **app** on your cell phone can help you keep track of your assignments.
install (v)	download a computer program onto your computer or cell phone	
access (n or v)	permission to use something	All students have free **access** to online resources within the library **network**.
network (n or v)	large number of computers that have a connection with each other and that work together	
laptop (n)	small computer that you can carry with you	**Laptops** may be borrowed for in-library use and are **configured** to connect to the campus **wireless** network.
configure (v)	install a technical specification on a computer	
wireless (or Wi-Fi) (adj)	that can connect to the internet without needing an internet access point	
data (n)	information, especially facts and numbers	All personal **data** will be **deleted** from the **hard drive** at the end of the day.
delete (v)	remove	
hard drive (n)	data storage device inside your computer	
password (n)	secret word or phrase that allows you to use a computer system	Students will need a **password** to **log on** to their internet account.
log on (v)	access a computer system by typing a password	
spreadsheet (n)	type of program that stores data in tables or charts	When using computers for word, data, and **spreadsheet** processing, it is recommended that you save your work frequently to your **removable media**.
removable media (n)	storage device that can be removed. Ex. flash drive / USB	
shortcut (n)	icon that links to a program or file on your computer	You can install **shortcuts** to college websites or to your internet **browser** on your desktop.
browser (n)	software that allows you to search for information on the internet	

Practice Exercises

A Choose the correct words to complete the sentences.

1. Please report any _____ connection problems to the library staff.

   a data   **b** shortcut   **c** network

2. All documents will be _____ when you return your laptop.

   a configured   **b** deleted   **c** installed

3. You can search for information by typing keywords into your internet _____.

   a password   **b** browser   **c** network

4. New software has already been _____ on all the library computers.

   a deleted   **b** connected   **c** installed

   > **WORD BUILDING**
   >
   > *-able* is a suffix you can add to verbs to make them adjectives: *downloadable*, means it can be downloaded. What do these mean: *acceptable, available, usable, readable?*

5. Saving data onto your flash drive will free up space on your _____.

   a browser   **b** hard drive   **c** network

6. You can _____ your email account with your password.

   a install   **b** configure   **c** access

7. The network in the library is wireless, and all our laptops are _____ to connect to it.

   a posted   **b** configured   **c** deleted

8. Downloading this _____ onto your laptop will give you access to coursework for online classes.

   a data   **b** spreadsheet   **c** app

B Match the sentences with the correct word to complete them.

1. You can store personal _____ on a flash drive.   **a** data
2. You can click uninstall to _____ this program..   **b** icon
3. I downloaded a new _____ for an online dictionary.   **c** chatroom
4. A good way to view numerical data is on a _____.   **d** log on
5. Visit our web store to purchase and _____ our new app.   **e** network
6. People can meet each other online in a virtual _____.   **f** delete
7. You can reconfigure your software by accessing the _____.   **g** spreadsheet
8. You can _____ to the internet using your password.   **h** install
9. People can share data if they are connected to the same _____.   **i** hard drive
10. This _____ on my screen is a shortcut to my email account.   **j** app

Test Practice

A Listen to part of a conversation between a student and a librarian and take notes. Then answer the questions. You may use your notes.

Track 10

1. Why does the student speak with the librarian?

○ To borrow a laptop

○ To find some materials

○ To find out how to access the internet

○ To ask about the availability of internet

2. What is implied about the student?

○ He does not know much about laptops.

○ He has not accessed the library network before.

○ He is not good at using the internet.

○ He has never used a laptop before.

3. What will the student probably do next?

○ Check his email

○ Go to the cafeteria

○ Listen to a lecture online

○ Borrow a book

TEST TIP: Listening section (purpose questions)

A purpose question asks you the reason that a speaker visits a professor or specific office on campus. In order to answer correctly, you must be able to understand why the conversation is taking place and draw a conclusion about the main reason for the conversation. Usually the correct answer will include reworded information from the conversation. Watch out for false clues that are not the real purpose of the conversation!

B This question is similar to question 2 in the speaking section (campus situation). Read the announcement. You have 45 seconds.

Important Changes to Library Laptop Policy

Policies regarding overdue fines for laptops will change as of September 10. The policy changes are as follows: Fines for overdue laptops will be $20 per day for every day or portion of a day that the laptop is overdue. Once a fine is applied, students will not be able to check out a laptop until that fine is paid. Fines must be paid online with a credit or debit card. The purpose of these changes is twofold: (1) to increase the availability of laptops across campus by reducing the number of overdue laptops; and (2) to pay for costs of repairing or reconfiguring damaged laptops.

🎧
Track 11

Now listen to two students as they discuss the announcement. Take notes as you listen.

Notes

Main change

Student's opinion

Reason 1

Detail

Reason 2

Detail

C The man expresses his opinion of the new policy. State his opinion and explain the reason he gives for holding that opinion. Write a transcript of your spoken response here (or record your response and write a transcript of it here). You have 60 seconds (125–150 words).

_____

_____

_____

_____

_____

_____

_____

_____

_____

_____

_____

_____

_____

_____

_____

_____

_____

Climate and environment

Read the words, definitions, and examples. Use your dictionary to find additional word forms for each word.

OVERVIEW

Word	Definition	Example
temperature (n)	how hot or cold something is	Climate is often described in terms of average **temperature** and **precipitation** over time.
precipitation (n)	rainfall	
fundamental (adj)	important	Climate patterns play a **fundamental role** in the formation of **ecosystems**.
role (n)	function, influence	
ecosystem (n)	relationship between all the living things in a particular area	
atmosphere (n)	layer of gases around the Earth	Warmer global temperatures in the **atmosphere** can **lead to** climate changes that affect rainfall patterns, storms and **droughts**, and sea level.
lead to (v)	cause	
drought (n)	period of time without rain	
fossil fuel (n)	oil, gas, coal	When **fossil fuels** are burned, carbon **emissions** known as greenhouse gases are **released** into the atmosphere.
emission (n)	something that is discharged into the atmosphere	
release (v)	allow to escape, discharge	
absorb (v)	take in	Solar energy is **absorbed** by the atmosphere and some of it is **reflected** into space by ice and snow.
reflect (v)	send back	
ecologist (n)	someone who studies relationships between plants, animals, people, and the environment	**Ecologists** are studying **sustainable** farming methods that will not **deplete** the Earth's resources.
sustainable (adj)	that can be maintained or continued	
deplete (v)	reduce, diminish	
deforestation (n)	cutting down trees over a large area	There has been a high rate of **deforestation** in the **tropical** rainforests of Australia.
tropical (adj)	referring to a climate zone that is hot and wet, near the equator	

Practice Exercises

A Match the words with the correct examples.

1. precipitation _____
2. fossil fuel _____
3. emission _____
4. temperature _____
5. ecosystem _____
6. ecologist _____

a carbon dioxide
b 20 degrees Celsius
c tropical rainforest
d scientist
e 16 inches per year
f natural gas

DICTIONARY SKILLS

⊂ POWERED BY COBUILD

The prefix *de-* indicates something is *removed* or *taken away*. Use your dictionary to find out what these words mean: *decline, deconstruct, defoliate, desalinate, depopulate.*

B Choose the best words to complete the sentences.

1. Climate change affects _____, such as the polar regions.

   a temperatures   b emissions   c ecosystems

2. The overuse of _____ is increasing carbon dioxide in the atmosphere.

   a fossil fuels   b emissions   c precipitation

3. Warmer temperatures can _____ changes in migration, breeding, and food availability.

   a deplete   b lead to   c release

4. Because of their light color, ice and snow _____ solar energy into space.

   a release   b absorb   c reflect

5. Climate scientists study long-term trends in the _____ of the Earth's atmosphere.

   a drought   b precipitation   c temperature

6. Forests _____ carbon dioxide from the atmosphere.

   a absorb   b release   c melt

C Complete the passage using words from the chart.

Environmental indicators play a fundamental [1]_____ in our understanding of climate change and its causes. Examples of climate change indicators include [2]_____, precipitation, sea level, and greenhouse gases in the [3]_____. Climate change affects local [4]_____ in a variety of ways. [5]_____ are studying both the causes of climate change and its impact. For example, in the polar regions, melting ice has reduced the amount of solar heat that is [6]_____ into space and also [7]_____ the natural habitat of polar bears. In tropical rainforest zones, deforestation has reduced the amount of carbon dioxide that the forests can [8]_____. Scientists and producers need to work together to develop methods of [9]_____ production that will reduce the consumption of [10]_____ and help slow down global warming.

Test Practice

Read the passage about a topic in environmental science.

Deforestation

The tropical rainforests play a crucial role in sustaining life on our planet. They are vitally important to the environment. However, the rainforests around the world from Australia to Brazil are being depleted at a dramatic rate. Recent estimates are that deforestation has reduced the amount of tree cover on our planet by more than 50 percent. Forests are cut down for many reasons, but most of them are related to the increase in human population.

A major contributing factor is the clearing of land for agriculture. [1] ■ Farmers cut down forests to cultivate crops or to provide grazing land for their livestock. [2] ■ When trees are cut down for agriculture, they are not replaced with new trees. [3] ■ Not only animal species, but also plants with as yet undiscovered potential medicinal uses are destroyed with a resulting decrease in biodiversity. [4] ■ The preservation of animal and plant species is essential for maintaining the future sustainability of life on our planet.

A second cause of deforestation is the use of wood for construction and manufacturing, as well as for paper production. Legal and illegal logging in many countries has destroyed large areas of forest and this has led to a degradation of soil conditions. Trees not only provide shade and protection that keep soil moist, their roots also hold the soil together, preventing erosion. Land that has been cleared for cultivation easily becomes barren and more susceptible to damage from floods and droughts.

Trees play an important role in absorbing greenhouse gases. Without trees, larger amounts of greenhouse gases enter the atmosphere and contribute to air pollution and global warming. Trees are also very important in the process of precipitation. The leaves of the trees contribute humidity to the atmosphere through the process of transpiration. Fewer trees mean that there is a reduction in humidity in the air, which affects not only the local ecosystem, but weather patterns globally, potentially harming agricultural production around the world.

---

1. In paragraph 1, the author mentions the increase in human population in order to

   ○ show that trees are important to the planet.

   ○ make the point that deforestation is harmful.

   ○ argue that deforestation is unnecessary.

   ○ explain why trees are being cut down.

2. The word this in paragraph 3 refers to

   ○ paper production.

   ○ the destruction of large areas of forest.

   ○ logging activity.

   ○ degradation of soil conditions.

3. The word susceptible in the passage is closest in meaning to

   ○ predictable.

   ○ vulnerable.

   ○ resistant.

   ○ sufficient.

4. Which of the following statements is supported by paragraph 4?

    ○ Less rain means less pollution.

    ○ More pollution means less rain.

    ○ Less humidity means higher temperatures.

    ○ Fewer trees mean less rain.

5. Look at the four squares [■] that indicate where the following sentence can be added to the passage. Where would the sentence best fit?

    As a result, the natural habitats for many unique wildlife species are permanently lost.

    Answer _____

6. An introductory sentence for a brief summary of the passage is provided below. Complete the summary by selecting the THREE answer options that express the most important ideas in the passage. Some sentences do not belong in the summary because they express ideas that are not presented in the passage or are minor ideas in the passage.

Tropical rainforests are vital to sustaining life on earth.

    ○ _____

    ○ _____

    ○ _____

Choose 3 answers.

1. Many new medicines have been discovered from rainforest plants.

2. Forests are being destroyed to produce food and building materials.

3. When trees are cut down, it reduces biodiversity in plant and animal species.

4. Flooding mainly occurs in places where forests have been cut down.

5. Forests play an important role in preventing climate change.

6. Trees keep the soil moist, preventing erosion.

TEST TIP: Reading section (Passage/Prose summary questions)

In order to answer a passage/prose summary question, you must be able to recognize the main ideas of the passage. The correct answers will usually contain reworded information from the passage and are major ideas from the passage. Out of the six answer options, you need to choose three that summarize the passage. Watch out for answer options that do not summarize the main ideas, include information not mentioned in the passage, contradict the facts from the passage, or include minor details.

Chemistry, physics, astronomy

Read the words, definitions, and examples. Use your dictionary to find additional word forms for each word.

OVERVIEW

Word	Definition	Example
gravity (n)	force that causes objects to be attracted toward each other because they have mass	The Earth's **gravity** is a natural **phenomenon** that causes objects to fall to the ground.
phenomenon (n)	something that is observed to happen or exist	
velocity (n)	speed and direction of travel	A speedometer measures the **velocity** of a moving train or car and its rate of **acceleration**.
acceleration (n)	change in velocity	
altitude (n)	height above sea level	At high **altitudes** there is less **oxygen** in the Earth's atmosphere and it becomes more difficult to breathe.
oxygen (n)	gas that forms part of the Earth's atmosphere and is essential for life	
hydrogen (n)	colorless, highly flammable gas	**Hydrogen** is the lightest **element** in the Periodic Table.
element (n)	one of the simplest chemical substances which cannot be broken down	
dense (adj)	having a lot of mass when compared to its volume	Wood is less **dense** than water, which is why it floats. That means it has less **mass** per cubic inch.
mass (n)	the amount of material in something	
satellite (n)	object in space that circles around another object	Most planets have natural **satellites** or moons that **orbit** around them.
orbit (v or n)	move around another object in a curved path	
nucleus (n) (pl. nuclei)	central part of an atom	When two or more **nuclei fuse** they **generate** energy.
fuse (v)	join together	
generate (v)	create	
atom (n)	smallest unit of matter	A typical **atom** consists of a nucleus of **protons** and **neutrons** with a system of **electrons** orbiting the nucleus.
proton, neutron, electron (n)	subatomic particles	

Practice Exercises

A Choose the best words to complete each sentence.

1. ᵃ_____ is the lightest ᵇ_____ and has been used in the past to lift airships.

    a velocity   hydrogen   oxygen   **b** element   atom   nucleus

2. The International Space Station is an artificial ᵃ_____ that ᵇ_____ the Earth.

    a orbit   electron   satellite   **b** generates   orbits   accelerates

3. Gold and copper have a high ᵃ_____ and therefore do not float in water.

    a density   altitude   gravity

4. The ᵃ_____ of an object determines its ᵇ_____ force.

    a mass   orbit   nucleus   **b** atomic   gravitational   dense

5. At high ᵃ_____ climbers sometimes use ᵇ_____ cylinders to help them breathe.

    a velocity   altitude   gravity   **b** hydrogen   satellite   oxygen

6. ᵃ_____ can involve an increase or a decrease in ᵇ_____.

    a gravity   density   acceleration   **b** velocity   atoms   elements

7. A(n) ᵃ_____ is the central part of a(n) ᵇ_____.

    a satellite   atom   nucleus   **b** atom   proton   electron

8. ᵃ_____ are positively charged, whereas ᵇ_____ are negatively charged.

    a protons   neutrons   electrons   **b** neutrons   electrons   protons

B Complete each paragraph below with words from the box. Then summarize the main ideas of each paragraph.

1.

atom	electron	nucleus	orbit	satellites

The ᵃ_____, which is a negatively charged subatomic particle, was discovered in 1897 by the scientist J. J. Thomson. He proposed a "plum pudding" model of atomic structure, where positive and negative charges are equally distributed throughout the ᵇ_____. This theory was later disproved by Rutherford in his famous gold-foil experiment, which led him to propose that the atom had a large ᶜ_____ containing all of its positive charge. His model showed how electrons could ᵈ_____ a positively charged nucleus, like ᵉ_____ around a star.

Summary:

_____

_____

_____

_____

_____

2.

hydrogen	mass	neutrons	oxygen	phenomenon	protons

Scientists later discovered that the nucleus of an atom consists of two types of particles: ^a_____ that are positively charged and ^b_____ that have no charge. The position of an element in the Periodic Table depends partly on its ^c_____, or the number of protons in the nucleus of its atoms. ^d_____ has an atomic number of 1, whereas ^e_____ has an atomic number of 8. Both are gases and can combine with each other to form water, a ^f_____ that is known as bonding.

Summary:

_____

_____

_____

_____

3.

acceleration	altitude	generate	gravity	velocity

The exploration of space required the development of rockets that would be able to attain sufficient ^a_____ to achieve extreme altitudes. In order to escape from Earth's ^b_____, a rocket has to achieve a speed of 40,000 kph (25,000 mph), which requires a very powerful engine and a great deal of fuel. Even with the most powerful engine available, it would not be possible to ^c_____ sufficient ^d_____ to lift a rocket and all its fuel to the required ^e_____. To solve this, scientists developed the multi-stage rocket.

Summary:

_____

_____

_____

_____

Test Practice

Listen to part of a seminar in an astronomy class. Then answer the questions.

Track 12

1. What is the professor mainly discussing?
- ○ Differences between planets and stars
- ○ Difficulty of identifying stars and planets
- ○ A theory about how stars and planets developed
- ○ The number of planets and stars

Track 13

2. Listen again to part of the lecture. Why does the professor say this?
- ○ To interrupt
- ○ To explain
- ○ To contradict
- ○ To correct

3. Why does the professor mention nuclear fission?
- ○ To give an example of a way to generate energy
- ○ To avoid confusion with nuclear fusion
- ○ To describe the radioactive activity of a star
- ○ To compare two types of energy

4. What does the professor say about atomic matter?

○ It is a mixture of helium and hydrogen   ○ It is known as plasma

○ It cannot exist in space   ○ It cannot exist in stars

5. For each point below, place a checkmark in the correct column.

	Planets	Stars
Generate light		
Have a hot center		
Have hydrogen and helium		
Reflect light		
Generate energy		
Have low density		

TEST TIP: Listening section (connecting content questions)

This type of question tests your understanding of the relationships between different ideas in text. They may ask you to organize information in a different way. It is sometimes presented in the form of a table where you have to check boxes. Take clear notes while you listen, clearly identifying main ideas and details.

Extra Practice

Track 12

A In question 4 in the speaking section (academic summary), you will listen to a lecture and take notes. Then you will be asked to give a spoken summary of the information and demonstrate an understanding of the relationship between the examples and the overall topic. Listen again and make notes on the main ideas of the seminar. Remember to organize your notes clearly and use abbreviations.

> Notes

B Using points and examples from the lecture, explain the differences and similarities between planets and stars. Write your spoken response here (or record your response and write the transcript here). You have 60 seconds to provide your response (125–150 words). Use the phrases in the box.

> The lecture is about …   The professor compares …   The professor explains that …

Reporting verbs

Read the words, definitions, and examples. Use your dictionary to find additional word forms for each word.

OVERVIEW

Verb	Meaning	Example
Reporting verbs followed by a *that* clause		
argue, propose*	give reasons why something is true	The professor **argues** that biodiesel is an important fuel for cars.
hold the view, believe, consider	have an opinion	She **holds the view** that adding fluoride to water is beneficial to our health.
claim, assert	say something that may or may not be true	He **claims** that nuclear power is better for the environment than fossil fuels.
suggest, imply, indicate*	make you think something is true by stating it in an indirect way	The research **suggests** that the Earth's ozone layer is being depleted.
mention*	say something without giving much information	The passage **mentions** that ultra-violet radiation is damaging to humans.
demonstrate*, illustrate*	show, make something clear	The experiment **demonstrates** that rust is formed when iron reacts with oxygen and water.
make the point, emphasize*	highlight a specific piece of information	The professor **makes the point** that chlorine has many important industrial uses.
Reporting verbs followed by a noun		
support	agree with something	The author **supports** the view that GM foods can help to solve food shortages.
challenge, query	question whether something is true	He **challenges** the argument that GM food can damage the Earth's ecology.
contradict, refute	say the opposite	The professor **contradicts** the reading passage by arguing that nanotechnology will change our view of chemistry.
define, give a definition	explain the meaning of something	She **defines** the meaning of an organic compound.
identify	describe	The professor **identifies** three types of materials: solids, liquids, and gases.
expand on	give further examples or explanation of a previously mentioned topic	She **expands** on the topic of chemical reactions by giving two further examples.

Notes: 1. These verbs* can also be followed by a noun. For example, *The study demonstrates the importance of restricting carbon emissions.* 2. For use of these verbs with the impersonal passive, see Grammar Unit 17.

Practice Exercises

A In each sentence, cross out one word choice that does *not* fit.

The ancient Greeks were the first to [1]*suggest / argue / define* that there might be one simple substance from which all other substances were made. Some Greek philosophers [2]*claimed / illustrated / proposed* that this substance might be water. Other philosophers [3]*held / took / said* a different view. They thought it was air. Others [4]*contradicted / disagreed with / emphasized* both of these views. They thought the simplest substance was fire or earth. Eventually, they [5]*supported / proposed / argued* that there were four elements: earth, air, fire, and water. They [6]*held / argued / had* a theory that these four elements could be combined to make gold. For hundreds of years, people [7]*claimed / demonstrated / asserted* that it was possible to make gold from other metals, but none of them were able to [8]*demonstrate / illustrate / emphasize* this. In 1677, Robert Boyle [9]*challenged / contradicted / illustrated* the Greek theory of elements. He [10]*proposed / argued / expanded* that elements must be simple substances that cannot be broken down into other substances. This definition is still in use today.

> **WORD BUILDING**
>
> *Have* and *hold* collocate with *opinion*. *Have*, *hold*, and *take* collocate with *view*. Ex. *I **have**/**hold** the **opinion** that … . I **have**/**hold**/**take** the **view** that … .* Notice the use of articles in these expressions: have/hold **the** same/opposite opinion, have/hold/take **the** same/opposite view, have/hold **a** similar/different opinion, have/hold/take **a** similar/different view.

B Complete the paragraph with words from the box.

believed	demonstrated	expanded	identify	proposed	supported

A Russian professor of chemistry, Dmitri Mendeleev, first [1]_____ that elements could be grouped in a tabular form according to their chemical properties. He [2]_____ that grouping elements according to their atomic mass made it possible to [3]_____ recurring patterns. Although there were gaps in the pattern, he [4]_____ that gaps would be filled by subsequent discoveries. Chemists subsequently [5]_____ on his work and discovered new elements that [6]_____ his theory and completed the missing gaps in the Periodic Table.

> **STUDY TIP**
>
> When recording reporting verbs in your notebook, you may want to group them according to their meaning. For example, those that express doubt, those that express certainty, and those that are neutral. You may also find it helpful to write example sentences that are memorable for you, perhaps related to your own experience, or to your own field of study. Use a good dictionary to check that both the meaning and the structure of your examples are correct.

C Complete the sentences using words from the chart.

1. A liquid in which a substance dissolves is called a solvent.

   The professor _____ the meaning of the term "solvent."

2. When you add instant coffee to a cup of hot water, it dissolves very quickly.

   But when you stir it into cold water, the coffee does not dissolve.

   The example _____ that hot water is a better solvent than cold water.

3. Oxygen is dissolved in water and heat can reduce the oxygen content of the water. By the way, this is why some species of fish die if the water is too warm.

   The professor _____ that some fish can die if the water is too warm.

4. Three main causes of water pollution are fertilizers, industrial chemicals, and sewage.

   The passage _____ three causes of water pollution.

5. Some people say that companies should be obliged to avoid pollution and remove waste, but in that case, extra costs will be passed on to the consumer.

   Some people say that pollution should be banned, but the professor _____ this view. He _____ that goods and products will become more expensive.

6. Everyone should do as much as possible to avoid pollution because we are all responsible for it.

   He _____ that everyone is responsible for preventing pollution.

D Read the lecture and complete the sentences.

Nanotechnology is the science of using changing matter on a very small scale – the nanoscale. The field is expanding rapidly and has the potential to improve our daily lives. Let me give you two examples. One is something that you probably use every day – sunscreen. Many types of sunscreen use nanoparticles. These are tiny chemical compounds that scientists create by working with molecules. The size of these particles makes them easier to rub onto your skin and that means you have better protection from the sun. Another example is clothing. Recently scientists have started putting layers of nanoparticles on cloth in order to provide protection from the harmful rays of the sun.

Another development in the field has been advances in the use of nanotechnology to create microchips. Microchips have been getting smaller and smaller. In the future, however, microchips may be created by applying chemical compounds to a tiny silicon chip. For example, a tiny camera that can be injected into your body, or a tool that can travel through your veins and arteries to cure diseases. Now some think it is possible that this technology may not always be used for positive purposes, but at the moment there is great excitement about the future possibilities of this technology.

1. The professor defines _____.

2. He claims that _____.

3. He identifies _____.

4. The two examples illustrate _____.

5. He expands on _____.

6. He makes the point that _____.

7. Some people query _____.

8. He asserts that _____.

Test Practice

A This question is similar to question 4 in the speaking section of the test (academic summary). Remember to use a variety of reporting verbs in your response.

Track 14

Listen to part of a lecture in a chemistry class. Take notes as you listen.

Notes

Topic

Point 1

Reason

Point 2

Reason

Using the points and examples in the lecture, explain how CFC gases affect the Earth's atmosphere. Write your spoken response (or record your response and write the transcript here).

_____

_____

_____

_____

_____

_____

_____

_____

_____

_____

College campus vocabulary

Read the words, definitions, and examples. Make additional examples using each word or phrase.

OVERVIEW

Word	Definition	Example
academic adviser (n)	someone who gives students advice about their study	Your **academic adviser** can help you decide which **electives** to choose.
elective (n)	optional class that is part of your degree	
scholarship (n)	sum of money that is given by a college to students for study	I was able to get a **scholarship** to study abroad, but I had to apply for **financial aid**, too.
financial aid (n)	way of obtaining money to pay tuition fees	
transcript (n)	document that shows a student's grades	I need two copies of my **transcript** for my application to **grad school**.
grad (graduate) school (n)	study that follows the completion of undergraduate study	
freshman (n or adj)	first-year college student	**Freshmen** often have to take required courses, while some advanced courses are only for **sophomores** and **juniors**.
sophomore (n)	second-year student	
junior (n)	third-year student	
major (n)	main area of specialization	My **major is** in urban studies but I'm also taking **credit** courses in biology.
credit (n)	unit of study	
assignment (n)	written work that forms part of the course requirements	All **assignments** must be handed in by the **due date**. Contact your instructor if you need to have an **extension**.
due date (n)	the date an assignment has to be handed in	
extension (n)	additional time beyond the original due date	
tuition (n)	fees for instruction	**Tuition** covers the cost of instruction, but does not cover **dorm** fees, food, or books.
dorm (dormitory) (n)	accommodation for students on campus	
make-up test (n)	test that you can take if you were unable to attend the original test date	Your instructor may allow a **make-up test** if you have a good reason for being **absent**.
absent (adj)	not present in class	

Practice Exercises

A Complete the sentences with words from the chart opposite.

1. If you are _____ due to an illness or emergency, you may be allowed to take a _____.

2. Students who wish to apply for _____ should speak with their _____.

3. Students can sometimes get _____ to cover the cost of _____.

4. You can graduate when you have completed the correct number of _____.

5. I stayed in a _____ for my _____ year and it was a great start to my college experience.

6. _____ that are not handed in by the _____ will not be accepted.

7. All of your grades are recorded on your college _____.

8. If you don't declare your _____ before the end of your _____ year at college, you may not be able to graduate.

B Complete the conversation with words from the chart.

Lisa: How's everything, Amy? How do you like living on campus?

Amy: The [1]_____ is really great, and my roommate is so nice. I've made a lot of friends already.

Lisa: How are you managing budget-wise?

Amy: Not too bad, I have a [2]_____ that covers all my [3]_____ and I got some [4]_____ to help pay for accommodation and books and stuff.

Lisa: That's good! How're your classes going?

Amy: Well, [5]_____ year is pretty tough. We have to study at least three hours a day on top of classes. But hopefully [6]_____ year will be easier. So far I haven't missed any [7]_____ on my [8]_____ so I'm not behind on anything. If I have a problem, I can always speak with my [9]_____.

Lisa: Are you still planning to go to [10]_____ once you finish your degree?

Amy: Yes, that's the plan anyway!

C Read the passage and study the words in bold. Then write the correct words (1–10) without looking back at the passage.

Undergraduate Degrees in the United States

Degree courses at U.S. colleges and universities consist of classes in a variety of subject areas. Each class has a certain number of credits. You usually need a total of 120+ credits to graduate, with 30+ in your **major**, as well as a sufficient grade-point average (**GPA**), which is the average grade (translated into "points") for all classes. Your major is your chosen area of specialization and you usually have to **declare** your major by the end of your sophomore year (sometimes earlier). Depending on which major you choose, some classes are **mandatory**, and some are electives. Freshmen often have to take classes that are **prerequisites** for more advanced classes. In some cases, credits can be **transferred** from one college or university to another if a student decides to switch schools. An **associate's degree** is a two-

---

Continued over page →

year degree that can also be gained at a **community college**. A **bachelor's degree** is a four-year degree. The academic year at most U.S. schools is divided into two 15-week **semesters** starting in September and ending in June. Graduation, also known as **commencement**, is a ceremony when undergraduate students receive their degrees, and is attended by the **faculty**, students (in their academic caps and gowns), and parents.

1. make an official decision: _____

2. average grade: _____

3. period of time: _____

4. university professors: _____

5. two-year degree: _____

6. graduation: _____

7. two-year college: _____

8. required: _____

9. has to be done first: _____

10. move: _____

STUDY TIP: Speaking section question 2 (campus matters)

To familiarize yourself with relevant vocabulary for this task, visit websites of universities in the United States. You may find useful vocabulary and information in the sections for Student Affairs, the Office of Residential Life, Student Financial Services, or online student newspapers.

Test Practice

A Read the announcement. You have 45 seconds.

Announcement from the Office of Residential Life

Effective from the fall semester, dorm rooms will be available only to freshmen. All sophomores, juniors, and seniors currently living in dorms will be required to find off-campus accommodation. The reason for this is due to the fact that there are insufficient dorm rooms to accommodate all students who wish to live on campus. Priority will be given to freshmen in order to help them successfully adjust to college life and their new surroundings and afford every student with an opportunity to experience dorm life for one year.

Track 15

Now listen to two students as they discuss the announcement. Take notes as you listen.

Notes

Student's opinion

Reason 1

Detail

Reason 2

Detail

Practice Exercises

A Choose the correct word or phrase.

1. *Thanks to / In terms of* low interest rates, more people bought houses.

2. Construction companies built more homes *as a result of / as well as* the increased demand.

3. *Rather than / Due to* repaying their loans, homeowners borrowed more money.

4. *Given / Except for* the oversupply of housing, it was inevitable that prices would start to fall.

5. *In the case of / Instead of* making a profit by selling their home, they made a loss.

6. House prices fell by almost forty percent *compared to / as well as* the previous year.

7. *In the case of / In terms of* people who were unable to repay their loans, properties were repossessed by the banks.

8. *In terms of / Due to* the economic impact, the results were unemployment and a downturn in growth and productivity.

> **DICTIONARY SKILLS**
>
> ⊆ POWERED BY COBUILD
>
> *In case* is a conjunction and *in case of* is a preposition. They are used to express something that you think might happen. Examples: *They took a credit card in case they ran out of cash. They took raincoats in case of bad weather.* Use your dictionary to check other uses of the word *case*.

B Rewrite each sentence using one the prepositions provided. You will have to change some verbs into nouns or gerunds.

1. During the dot com bubble in the late 1990s, many new internet companies received capital investment, but they did not make any profits. (despite)

    _____

2. Internet companies aimed to develop new technologies and increase their market share. (in addition to)

    _____

3. Shares in internet companies continued to rise but then fell sharply. (instead of)

    _____

4. There was a crash and many people lost their investments. (thanks to)

    _____

5. Most internet companies collapsed, but two companies eventually exceeded market expectations. (except for)

    _____

6. Share values in technology stocks fell dramatically, but other share prices did not fall as much. (compared with)

    _____

7. There were some social benefits because the dot com bubble enabled many developments in technology that are used today. (in terms of)

    _____

STUDY TIP

When reading academic articles, look for examples of how prepositions are used. Underline them and identify exactly how they show the relationship between different parts of a sentence or paragraph. Try to paraphrase the sentences. Try to integrate these prepositions into your writing when you practice test questions or when you write in your journal.

Test Practice

This question is similar to question 1 in the writing section of the test (integrated task).

A Read the passage and identify the main points.

A market-driven economy is characterized by periods of economic expansion and contraction, also known as boom and bust. This pattern is repeated regularly, although not for fixed time periods. It is not possible to predict the length of a cycle, which can be measured in terms of months or years. The cycle is influenced by many factors, including inflation, politics, and natural events and it affects all aspects of economic life.

During the expansion phase of the cycle, there is an increase in wealth and productivity. Thanks to high consumer confidence, there is a demand for new products, which generates jobs. Banks are more likely to lend money to new enterprises and companies are willing to invest in development of new products and technologies. Benefits of this phase of the cycle include increased salaries and a generally higher standard of living.

The contraction phase of the cycle occurs when the economy starts to slow down. Because of reduced demand for goods, there is a decrease in employment and a decline in salaries. In spite of these negative effects of the cycle, there are also social benefits. Due to increased competition, weaker companies are forced to go under and only those that produce quality products in an efficient manner are able to survive. This results in more efficient production and use of resources.

 **B** Now listen to part of a lecture in a business class and take notes.

Track 16

Notes

TEST TIP: Writing section question 1 (integrated writing task)

Remember to include the main points from both the reading passage and lecture. Do not copy sentences from the reading passage, try to paraphrase them. Do not give your opinion. Make a brief outline of your response before starting to write. For example, in this question, you could summarize the points from the reading passage and follow this with a summary of the points in the lecture. Alternatively, you could take each point separately and show how the lecture challenges each point in the reading passage.

C Summarize the main points made in the lecture, being sure to explain how they challenge specific points in the reading passage. Write 3–4 paragraphs.

_____

_____

_____

_____

_____

_____

_____

_____

_____

_____

_____

_____

_____

_____

_____

_____

_____

_____

_____

Extra Practice

Read the paragraph and circle the mistakes. Rewrite the incorrect sentences below.

The reading passage asserts that economic bubbles are a natural correction to unrealistic prices. It suggests that instead to focus on their negative impact, we should look at the positive effects. The passage explains that thanks for the dot com bubble in the late 1990s, society benefited from many new technologies that were developed, in spite from the financial losses that were incurred by investors. The professor disputes this view. He argues that, with the possible exception to the dot com bubble, economic bubbles rarely have any positive impact. On the case of the housing bubble, for example, risky lending practices by banks caused many people to lose their homes.

_____

_____

_____

_____

_____

_____

Paraphrasing

Read the examples. Make your own examples using each strategy.

OVERVIEW

Paraphrasing means restating something in your own words. In order to paraphrase successfully, it is helpful to use synonyms, antonyms, and general words or phrases that simplify, explain, define, or categorize the expressions you want to paraphrase.

	Example	Paraphrase
Use synonyms	The **global** population has **increased significantly**.	The **world** population has **risen considerably**.
	Scientists predict that the population will **exceed** 10 billion.	**Experts estimate** that the population will **be more than** 10 billion.
Simplify	There is **insufficient** housing to meet the demand.	There is **not enough** housing to meet the demand.
	People are **migrating** from **rural to urban areas**.	People are **moving** from **the country to the city**.
Use phrases that explain or define	There has been **a fall** in the **rural population**.	**Fewer people** live in the **country**.
	Urban populations are growing.	**More people** live in **towns and cities**.
Use categories or examples	Overcrowding puts a strain on **social infrastructure**.	Overcrowding puts a strain on **schools and hospitals**.
	Consumption of **fossil fuels** is increasing.	Consumption of **oil, gas and coal** is increasing.
Use other word forms	Towns and cities have **expanded** rapidly.	There has been a rapid **expansion** of towns and cities.
	Experts are unsure whether the economy will remain **stable**.	Experts are unsure about the **stability** of the economy.
Use antonyms	It is **difficult** to find work in rural areas.	It is **not easy** to find work in rural areas.
	Living in a city is **more expensive** than in the country.	Living in the country is **cheaper** than in a city.

Note: To paraphrase successfully, you may need to change the grammatical structure of the original sentence as well as some of the vocabulary. For further practice with paraphrasing, see Grammar Unit 8.

Practice Exercises

A Use your dictionary to complete the chart.

Adjective	Noun	Synonym	Antonym
1. wealthy	_____	_____	_____
2. rapid	_____	_____	_____
3. similar	_____	_____	_____
4. strong	_____	_____	_____
5. certain	_____	_____	_____
6. rise	_____	_____	_____
7. create	_____	_____	_____
8. remove	_____	_____	_____
9. depart	_____	_____	_____
10. transmit	_____	_____	_____

B Complete each sentence with different words so that it has the same meaning.

1. Many people are migrating from the country to the cities.

   Many people are _____ _____ areas and _____ to _____ areas.

2. Young people are doubtful about employment.

   Young people are _____ about _____.

3. People in the cities generally have a higher standard of living.

   People in the cities are _____ _____.

4. There are many advantages to life in the city.

   Life in the city has many _____.

5. People have better access to hospitals, schools, and shops.

   They have better access to _____.

6. Some people think that life in the cities is more stressful.

   Some people _____ that life in the country is more _____.

C Choose the correct word or phrase to complete the paraphrase (in italics) of each sentence.

are dying	are living longer	available resources	decrease	in the last hundred years
are living longer	is increasing rapidly	not rising	poor people	richer	used up

1. In the last century, the world's population has increased many times over.

   The number of people living on Earth has grown significantly _____.

2. Human population growth is constrained by the availability of food, water, and land.

   The amount of _____ *limits population growth.*

DICTIONARY SKILLS

€ POWERED BY COBUILD

con-, co-, and col- are prefixes that mean *combine or join. Conurbation means urban areas that have combined together.* Use your dictionary to find the meanings of these words: *converge, concordant, conflate, confluence, concentric, consensus.*

3. Once those resources are depleted, the world population will start to decline.

There will be a _____ in population growth when these resources are

_____.

4. Lower mortality rates and longer life expectancy have contributed to the rapid population growth.

Population is increasing because fewer people _____ and many

people _____.

5. The countries in which poverty levels are the highest are generally those that have the most rapid increases in population.

There are more _____ in countries where the population is

_____.

6. Population is stable or falling in countries where there is more wealth.

The population isn't _____ in countries that are

_____.

Test Practice

Read the passage and answer the questions.

Effects of Population Growth

The rapid increase in global urbanization constitutes one of the greatest issues facing the world in the coming decades. It is estimated that the global urban population will double over the next 30 years. Cities in some countries are rapidly transforming into mega cities – massive conurbations of more than 20 million people.

The rapid growth of these cities is a reflection of the considerable economic growth in these newly developing economies. [1] ■ The absence of infrastructure such as roads and water supply in many cities leads to a lower quality of life for their citizens. In many cities, it has resulted in the emergence of heavily populated urban areas with substandard housing. [2] ■ Furthermore, the impact of ever-increasing demand for energy, food, goods, and other resources by urban populations is causing degradation of the surrounding environment, which in turn exacerbates the migration of rural populations. [3] ■

On the other hand, urbanization can also have a positive impact. [4] ■ Countries with highly urbanized populations tend to have a generally higher standard of living and their economies are more stable. Cities can deliver education, health care, and other services more efficiently than rural areas because of their advantages of scale and proximity. In both the Global North and South, cities generate the most wealth and provide extensive opportunities for employment and investment. However, evidence suggests that the prosperity generated by cities does not automatically reduce poverty; on the contrary, in many cities, inequalities have increased.

---

1. The word massive in the passage is closest in meaning to

○ complex.   ○ wealthy.

○ huge.   ○ expensive.

2. The word it in the passage refers to

○ water supply.   ○ economic growth.

○ lower quality of life.   ○ absence of infrastructure.

3. Which of the sentences below best expresses the essential information in the highlighted sentence in the passage? Incorrect choices change the meaning in important ways or leave out essential information.

○ The urban population needs food, but people are not able to afford it.

○ People are moving to the cities because there are more resources there.

○ People are moving to the countryside because there are not enough resources in the cities.

○ More people are moving to the city because demand for resources is destroying rural areas.

4. The author identifies advantages of scale and proximity as two factors that

○ facilitate better facilities in cities.   ○ cause problems for people in cities.

○ make life in cities more expensive.   ○ make life in rural areas better.

5. An introductory sentence for a brief summary of the passage is provided below. Complete the summary by selecting the THREE choices that express the most important ideas in the passage. Some sentences do not belong in the summary because they express ideas that are not presented in the passage or are minor ideas in the passage. This question is worth two points.

The passage discusses the effects of population growth.

○ _____

○ _____

○ _____

Answer options

1.   Large cities have many wealthy as well as many poor people.

2.   Cities with over 20 million people are known as metacities.

3.   Social inequality in cities is decreasing.

4.   The high demand for resources is damaging to the environment.

5.   The increasing world population presents many problems.

6.   There is less economic stability in cities.

6. Look at the four squares [■] that indicate where the following sentence can be added to the passage. Where would the sentence best fit?

Yet these cities are also the location of increasing poverty, disease, and pollution.

Answer _____

TEST TIP: Reading section (passage summary and sentence summary questions)

Both passage summary and sentence summary questions paraphrase important ideas in the passage. For passage summary questions, read all the answer choices carefully, paraphrasing the answer choices in your own mind. Then decide which ones most accurately reflect the main ideas of the passage. For sentence summary questions, read the highlighted sentence and paraphrase it in your own words. Then read the answer options.

Prefixes and roots

Read the roots, prefixes, definitions, and examples. Use your dictionary to check the meanings of each word. Find other words with the same root or prefix.

OVERVIEW

A **root** is the base of a word to which **prefixes** and **suffixes** can be added to create new words. Prefixes go before the root and suffixes follow the root. Prefixes and roots of academic words often come from Latin or Greek.

Root or prefix	Meaning	Examples
Roots that describe number		
uni- / mon- / sol-	one	unify, uniform, monopoly, monarch, solitary
du- / bi-	two	dual, duplicate, bicycle, bilingual, biped
tri-	three	triple, triangle, tripod
quad-	four	quadruple, quadrangle, quarter
pent-	five	pentagon, pentathlon
dec-	ten	decade, decimal, decimeter
cent-	hundred	centenarian, centigrade, century
Roots that describe size or value		
multi-	many	multiply, multitude, multi-purpose
min- / micro-	small, tiny	miniature, minimum, microscopic
mega- / macro- / magni-	large, great	magnitude, magnify, macroeconomics
equi-	equal	equivalent, equity, equitable, equidistant
Roots that describe movement		
-vert- / -vers-	change or turn	reverse, versatile, convert, diversion
-pel-	push, force	compel, expel, repellent
-port-	carry	portable, transport, import
Prefixes that describe relationships and movement		
pre-	before	prehistoric, previous
re-	again or back	revisit, restructure, replace, refinance
pro-	move forward or up	propel, proceed, propose, protect
com-	together	compress, combine, commit, compel

Practice Exercises

A Match the words in the left with the most appropriate field of study on the right.

1.	megabyte _____	**a**	chemistry
2.	pentathlon _____	**b**	languages
3.	equidistant _____	**c**	history
4.	century _____	**d**	geometry
5.	bilingual _____	**e**	computer science
6.	centigrade _____	**f**	physical education

B Complete the sentences using words from the chart.

1. A three-sided shape is a _____.

2. A hundred-year-old person is a _____.

3. A great number of things is a _____.

4. A very small version of something is a _____.

5. If you force someone to do something, you _____ them to do it.

6. An exact copy of something is a _____.

C Choose the best word to complete each sentence.

1. A magnifying glass is used to make objects look *bigger* / *smaller*.

2. Macroeconomics is the study of economic factors on a *large* / *small* scale.

3. When a power plant converts coal or gas, it is *changed* / *pushed* into electricity.

4. A quadrangle is a courtyard surrounded by buildings on *three* / *four* sides.

5. A microchip is a *large* / *tiny* piece of silicon with an electronic circuit.

6. A portable computer is one that you can *carry* / *change*.

7. An equilateral triangle is a shape with *three* / *four* sides of the *same* / *different* lengths.

8. The Pentagon is a building that has *four* / *five* sides.

9. The United States has a bicameral legislature. That means it is has *two* / *three* chambers.

10. A monopoly is when power is controlled by *one* / *many* organization(s).

STUDY TIP

Learning prefixes and roots helps you to increase your vocabulary. Each prefix or root can help you to recognize multiple groups of words with related meanings. For each prefix or root, try to think of one key word that is very familiar to you. For example, *century* (= *a hundred years*). This may be a good word to help you remember the root *cent-*, which means a *hundred*. Use this word as the key word to help you identify other words with the same prefix or root.

D Read the passage and study the words in bold. Then paraphrase the meaning of each word or phrase in your own words.

Development of the Metric System

The metric system is an international **decimalized system** of measurement. It was first introduced in France **in the 18th century** and was intended to provide **a universal measurement system**. Prior to this, there were **widely divergent** measurement units used in different regions of the country, sometimes depending on what type of object was being measured. This resulted in many errors and fraudulent practices. It also held back **scientific progress** and caused difficulty with the **import and export** of goods to other countries.

To solve this problem, politicians in France set up a commission to come up with an **invariable** unit of measurement to **replace** all existing systems. The commission **proposed** a unit based on the distance from the North Pole to the equator, which is **equivalent** to ten million meters. In 1795, the metric system became **compulsory** in France. Most countries now use the metric system with two exceptions being the United Kingdom, which has only partly **converted**, and the United States.

---

1. decimalized system: _____
2. in the 18th century: _____
3. a universal measurement system: _____
4. widely divergent: _____
5. scientific progress: _____
6. import and export: _____
7. invariable: _____
8. replace: _____
9. proposed: _____
10. equivalent: _____
11. compulsory: _____
12. converted: _____

Test Practice

This question is similar to question 3 in the speaking section (academic reading and lecture). In this question, you will read a paragraph and then listen to part of a lecture on the same topic. The lecture usually extends or provides examples of the topic in the reading passage. You will have 45 seconds to read the passage. After the lecture you will have 30 seconds to prepare your answer and 60 seconds to respond.

Read the passage about the Magna Carta. Then listen to part of a lecture in a political science class. You may take notes.

The Magna Carta

The Magna Carta, or Great Charter, originally issued in 1215, is a document that challenged the sole authority of the monarch to rule England. It was originally proposed by a group of powerful English landowners or barons who wanted to limit the king's power and protect their privileges. It was the first time that an English king had been compelled to sign a document by his subjects. It was first passed into law in 1225. The Magna Carta established that the king had to consult Parliament on important issues, and also established the universal right to justice according to due process of law. It influenced the development of many constitutional documents, such as the United States Constitution and Bill of Rights, and is considered one of the most important legal documents in the history of democracy.

🎧
Track 17

The professor describes the influence of the Magna Carta. Explain how the Magna Carta influenced the U.S. Constitution.

Write a transcript of your spoken response (or record your response and write the transcript here).

_____
_____
_____
_____
_____
_____
_____
_____
_____
_____
_____
_____
_____
_____
_____
_____
_____
_____
_____

TEST TIP: Speaking section question 3 (academic reading and lecture)

Start your response by stating the connection between the reading passage and the lecture.

In the lecture, the professor describes how the Magna Carta influenced the U.S. Constitution.

The reading passage describes the reasons for the introduction of the Magna Carta in 1215 and the professor explains its influence in later centuries.

First, the reading passage states that the Magna Carta was proposed by … and was intended to … .

Then the professor explains how the Magna Carta influenced … .

Review of verb forms

Study the explanations and examples in the chart. Make your own examples based on each rule.

OVERVIEW

	Explanation	Example
Present	Use the **simple present** for habits, routines, and facts.	Some people **check** their email dozens of times each day.
	Use the **present continuous*** to describe things that are happening now, or are changing.	Online learning **is becoming** more popular.
Past	Use the **simple past** to describe things in the past and **used to** to emphasize that things were different in the past.	In the past, people **sent** postcards and **wrote** letters. They **used to buy** books in bookstores.
	Use the **past continuous*** to describe an activity that was in progress in the past, often to contrast it with a single event.	Scientists developed the internet when they **were looking** for a way to create a national computer communication network.
	One way to use the **present perfect** is to describe past events that have an effect on the present.	Cell phones **have expanded** our friendship networks.
	Another use of the **present perfect** is to describe completed events at an unspecified time in the past.	A recent survey found that the majority of people **have used** the internet at some time to buy or sell something.
	A third use of the **present perfect** is to describe a period of time up to and including the present.	Most countries **have had** internet service for a number of years.
	Use the **present perfect continuous*** to emphasize the temporary nature of the ongoing nature of the activity.	People **have been using** social media to organize political protests.
	Use the **past perfect** to talk about events that happened before a past event.	Cell phones were invented in the 1970s, but **had been** in development since the 1940s.
	Use the **past perfect continuous** to stress the ongoing nature of the activity.	They **had been trying** to find a way to reduce the size of the phones for several years.
Future	Use **will** to make predictions.	In the future, laptops **will be** even thinner and lighter.
	Use **going to** for plans.	Our company **is going to** upgrade its computer system.
	The **future perfect** describes something that will be in the past at a future time.	In 20 years' time, people **will have forgotten** how to read books.

* Some verbs (including *like*, *be*, *belong*, *believe*) rarely take the continuous form.

Note: For a full explanation of all verb forms and their uses, please consult a grammar reference book.

Practice Exercises

A Choose the correct verb form.

1. Nowadays cell phones *get* / *are getting* smaller and more powerful.

2. The internet *starts* / *is starting* to influence our social relationships.

3. Video conferencing *provides* / *is providing* us many opportunities to study and learn.

4. In the past, people *were communicating* / *communicated* by letter or phone.

5. Twenty years ago, people *didn't take* / *didn't use to take* pictures all the time.

6. Cell phones *enabled* / *have enabled* us to stay in constant contact with each other.

7. Because of the internet, people *have communicated* / *have been communicating* more than before.

8. Before the internet, no one *had* / *has* ever tried to create one-to-one marketing tools.

9. By the year 2050, virtual reality *will* / *is going to* revolutionize the entertainment industry.

10. In 20 years' time, students *will stop* / *will have stopped* using libraries.

> **DICTIONARY SKILLS**
>
> POWERED BY COBUILD
>
> Use your dictionary to review the correct simple past and past participle forms of irregular verbs.

B Complete the sentences with your own ideas.

1. Many people **use** the internet to _____.

2. Many children **are learning** how to _____ by using the internet.

3. The internet **is bringing** people closer together because _____.

4. In the past, people **used to** _____, but now they _____.

5. People in remote countries didn't _____ but now they _____.

6. The internet **has changed** the way we _____.

7. In the future, people **will use** the internet to _____.

8. By the time they are adults, children of today **will have forgotten** about _____.

C Each of these sentences contains errors in verb forms. Circle and correct the errors. More than one option may be possible.

1. In 20 years' time artificial intelligence is change the way we live.

2. When I started work 25 years ago, nobody having a computer on his or her desk.

3. I've noticed that people who commute by train to work often worked on the train.

4. Classrooms now having interactive whiteboards, so teachers can access the internet while they were teaching.

5. The government is implemented a new policy for the use of technology in education.

6. Due to the budget cuts, the university has had 10% less to spend on technology next year.

7. At the beginning of the last century, most people hadn't had the opportunity to go to university.

8. Many people are considering the internet as the most significant invention of all time.

Test Practice

A Read the introduction and first paragraph of a response to the independent writing task in the writing section. Complete the text with the correct verb forms.

Many people say that the internet is the most important invention ever. Do you agree or disagree with this and if not, what do you believe to be more important? Use specific reasons and examples to support your opinion.

> The invention of the internet [1]_____ (affect) our lives in many ways. It
> [2]_____ (transform) the way we communicate, the way we shop, and the way we get
> our news. Many people [3]_____ (say) that it is the most important invention ever. I
> [4]_____ (agree) with this opinion for several reasons.
>
> One way in which our lives [5]_____ (change) because of the internet is the way we
> communicate. In the past, people wrote letters and postcards. It sometimes [6]_____
> (take) several days for a letter to arrive by mail. Nowadays, people [7]_____ (send) each
> other emails and messages instantly. They often [8]_____ (hold) video conferences
> online. People [9]_____ (start) to communicate with a large network of people via
> the internet. In the future, we [10]_____ (develop) even faster and better ways of
> communicating with people all around the world. In 20 years' time, we [11]_____ (stop)
> using paper and pens and perhaps even paper books and magazines.

B Now continue with the second paragraph of the essay. Try to use a variety of tenses in your writing.

A second way that the internet _____

_____

_____

_____

_____

_____

_____

_____

_____

_____

_____

_____

C Read the announcement. You have 45 seconds.

Communication and Media Studies

The introductory course for Communication and Media Studies will now take place online in order to faciliate the participation of a larger number of students. Course evaluation will include attendance at online sessions, student participation in online discussions, as well as completion of all assignments. Students who wish to enroll in this course should do so before the end of Week 1. If you have any questions, please contact the department office.

🎧
Track 18

Now listen to two students as they discuss the announcement. Take notes as you listen.

> *Notes*
> *Main topic*
> *Reason*
> *Woman's opinion*
> *Reason 1*
> *Reason 2*

The woman expresses her opinion of the announcement. State her opinion and explain the reasons she gives for holding that opinion.

Write your spoken response (or record your response and write your transcript here).

According to the announcement _____

_____

_____

The woman is / isn't happy with this decision.

Her first reason is _____

Her second reason is _____

Extra Practice

Read the following paragraph from an integrated writing task and find the errors in the verb forms. Write the correct forms.

In the reading passage, the author states that ebooks **becomes** more popular in the United States. The professor **is supporting** this view and says that ebooks have had an effect on reading habits. It was **predicts** that by 2015, the number of ebooks **outnumbers** print books. However, this has still not happened. The use of ebooks **continuing** to lag behind the use of print books.

STUDY TIP

Keeping a journal is a good way to improve your writing. Try to write at least a paragraph every day. Here are some questions that will help you to practice a range of tenses. *What or who has influenced you most in your life? What new skills are you learning right now? What have you done in your life that you are most proud of? What are your plans for the future? What will the world be like in 50 years' time?*

Review of articles

Study the explanations and examples in the chart. Write your own examples based on each rule.

OVERVIEW

Explanation	Example
Use *a* or *an* with singular count nouns that are not specific. Use *the* with specific nouns (singular, plural, or non-count).	**A** town needs **a** good transportation system to grow.
	The transportation system in my town is very efficient.
Use *a* or *an* the first time you mention a singular count noun. Use *the* when you mention it again. Note: Do not use *a* or *an* with non-count nouns or with plural nouns.	There is **a** beautiful art gallery in my city. If you visit my city, you should definitely go and see **the** art gallery.
Do not use an article with plural nouns or non-count nouns when you mean things *in general*. Use *the* when you are being specific.	**Large cities** are usually quite stressful places to live.
Use *the* when there is only **one** of something, with superlatives, and with *first*, *last*, *next*, and *only*.	In my opinion, Paris is **the** most beautiful city in **the** world. It is **the** first place I will visit on my trip to Europe.
Do not use an article before a noun that is preceded by a possessive adjective (***my***), demonstrative adjective (***this***, ***that***), or quantifiers (***no***, ***some***, or ***any***).	When I was a student at **that** university, I traveled with **my** friend in Europe and we visited **some** amazing cities.
Use *the* after *some of, all of, none of.*	**Some** people were friendly to us.
	Some of **the** people were friendly to us.

Additional rules

Some common types of nouns do **not** use any articles. These include:

Names of academic subjects (*geography*), languages (*Spanish*), sports (*baseball*).

Many geographical place names use *the*. These include:

Names of oceans (*the Pacific Ocean*), mountain ranges (*the Rockies*), rivers (*the Mississippi*), deserts (*the Sahara*), and points on the globe (*the North Pole*).

Do not use *the* with names of continents (*Asia*), countries (*Canada*), states (*Arizona*), cities (*New York*), or streets (*Fifth Avenue*). Note: An exception is *the United States*.

Practice Exercises

A Circle the correct article.

1. I have never visited **the** / – Australia.

2. English is **the** / – only language that I speak well.

3. All of **the** / – students in my class plan to study overseas.

4. I once traveled to Italy with **the** / **a** friend.

5. I prefer to visit **the** / – cities that have a lot of museums.

6. I stayed with a host family in Mexico City. **A** / **The** family taught me Spanish.

7. I would like to climb – / **the** Himalayas one day.

8. – / **The** library in my school has a lot of computers.

9. I have never seen – / **the** Indian Ocean.

10. My favorite subject is **the** / – history.

> **DICTIONARY SKILLS**
>
> ⊑ POWERED BY COBUILD
>
> Use your dictionary to find out whether nouns are count or non-count. Count nouns are shown as n-count and non-count nouns as n-noncount. Some nouns can be used as both count and non-count with slightly different meanings. Use your dictionary to find out whether these nouns are count, non-count, or both: *experience, time, money, work*.

B Match the sentences in exercise A with the correct rule.

a   academic subject _____

b   name of country _____

c   mountain range _____

d   something in general _____

e   non-specific _____

f   second mention _____

g   used with *only* _____

h   after *all of* _____

i   name of ocean _____

j   something specific _____

C Each of these sentences contains errors in article use. Correct the errors.

1. Many people visit the Nepal to climb Himalayas.

2. Most important subjects to study at school are the history and geography.

3. I kept the journal about my trip while I was traveling in United States.

4. Some of people in the my family went on a trip down Amazon River in Brazil.

5. We traveled by train around the India and visited capital city of New Delhi.

6. Hotel where we stayed in New York was across from large art gallery.

7. I have a picture of Thailand on my wall. A picture reminds me of best holiday I have ever had.

8. The travel is an important way to learn about culture and people of other countries.

9. My trip across the Asia was most exciting adventure I've ever had.

10. Paris and London are the popular destinations for the tourists.

STUDY TIP

Ask your teacher or a native English speaker to read your practice essays and correct them. Notice which sentences have mistakes with articles. Rewrite the sentences in your notebook. Try to notice if there is a pattern to your errors. Which rule is most difficult to remember and why?

Test Practice

A The following question is similar to question 3 in the speaking section (academic reading and lecture). In this question, you will read a paragraph and then listen to part of a lecture on the same topic. The lecture usually extends or provides examples of the topic in the reading passage. You will have 45 seconds to read the passage. After the lecture you will have 30 seconds to prepare your answer and 60 seconds to respond.

Read the passage about volcanoes. Then listen to part of a lecture in a geology class.

You may take notes while you listen.

Volcanoes

A volcano is an opening on the surface of the Earth that allows gas, magma, and ash to escape from beneath the Earth's crust. Magma is made of molten rock, crystals, and dissolved gas. When this material escapes, it causes an eruption. Magma that emerges from the Earth's crust is known as lava. Sometimes the magma pours gradually out of the opening and slides down the sides of the volcano. Sometimes it explodes violently , sending pieces of rock and ash high into the sky. The lava eventually cools and forms layers of rock, ash, or other material. .

🎧
Track 19

Explain what volcanoes are and how they are classified using the examples given in the lecture.

Write a transcript of your spoken response (or record your response and write the transcript here).

_____

_____

_____

_____

_____

_____

_____

_____

_____

_____

_____

_____

_____

_____

TEST TIP: Speaking section question 3 (academic reading and lecture)

Start your response by summarizing the main idea of the reading passage.
According to the reading passage, … . The reading passage states that … .
Then describe the connection between the reading passage and the lecture.
The lecturer goes on to describe … . The lecturer then explains … .

B Read the following example of a response to question 2 in the writing section (independent task) of the Paper Edition of the TOEFL iBT test. In this question, you will be asked to write an essay about a familiar topic. Complete the sample response with *a*, *the*, or [-].

Some people like to travel with a friend. Other people prefer to travel alone. Which do you prefer? Use specific reasons and examples to support your choice.

In my opinion, it is far more interesting to travel with _____ companion than it is to travel alone. Although _____ some people prefer to travel alone, and don't like to take _____ companion with them, I think that if you travel with _____ friend it is better for two main reasons: it is safer and you are never lonely.

First of all, traveling alone in _____ strange country can be quite dangerous. If you don't know _____ customs or _____ language, you can easily find yourself in _____ difficult situation. It is better not to be alone. In addition, it sometimes helps to have _____ friend who can watch _____ your bags while you go to buy _____ tickets, or if you want to get _____ some food. A friend can help you out if you feel tired or sick. Once when I traveled to _____ Malaysia, I got a bad case of the flu, and my friend was able to go to _____ pharmacy for me and get _____ some medicine. If I had been alone, I don't think _____ stranger would have done that for me.

Another good reason to travel with a friend is that you always have someone to talk to. You can discuss _____ sights that you saw that day. You can exchange _____ opinions and experiences and compare _____ your impressions. Furthermore, it is fun to make _____ plans for _____ next day. You can discuss problems such as how to get from one place to another, and find _____ solution by working on it together. It is a good way to learn about _____ cooperation. When I traveled with a friend on _____ trip to _____ Europe, we became good friends and are still friends today.

In conclusion, it is my opinion that traveling with a friend is a much more enjoyable way to travel. I would advise anyone to go with a friend when they go on _____ trip.

C Now write your own response to this question, arguing the opposite side of the argument. Use the notes to help you. In the test, you will have 30 minutes to plan, write, and revise an essay of about 300 words.

_____

_____

_____

_____

_____

_____

_____

_____

_____

_____

_____

_____

_____

_____

_____

Subject-verb agreement

Study the explanations and examples in the chart. Make your own examples based on each rule.

OVERVIEW

A **singular subject** must have a **singular verb**. A **plural subject** must have a **plural verb**.

Explanation	Example
Singular count nouns, non-count nouns, and gerunds have a singular verb.	A part-time job **helps** you to be more independent.
Sometimes the subject and verb can be separated by a number of words or phrases.	Getting a job while you are a student **teaches** you how to manage your own time.
If the subject consists of more than one singular count noun, non-count noun, or gerund, then the verb is plural.	The increase in tuition costs **has** made it more difficult for some students financially.
(But note that two gerunds can also be considered as one activity. Ex. *Working and studying at the same time **is** very difficult*.)	Dealing with customers and managing accounts **are** two skills you can learn from doing a part-time job.
If the sentence starts with **here** or **there**, the verb depends on the noun that follows.	Here **is** an example of how a part-time job can help you learn new skills.
	There **are** two reasons why I hold this opinion.
Use a singular verb with **each, every, any, everyone, anyone, no one**, and **none**.	I think that everyone **needs** to have some work experience as part of his or her education.
Use a plural verb with **all, most**, or **some**.	Most people **like** to earn some extra money while they are students.
Use a singular verb with **neither** + (singular noun) **nor** + (singular noun).	Neither school nor university fully **prepares** you for the world of work.
But, if the second noun is plural, or if both nouns are plural, use a plural verb.	Neither the faculty nor the students **want** to see an increase in the tuition.
Use a plural verb with **both ... and ...** .	Both faculty and students **want** to see more work placement opportunities for students.
Some nouns look plural but are singular: *physics, economics, politics, statistics, news*.	Economics **is** one of my most difficult classes.
Some nouns have unusual plurals: *alumni, criteria, data, media, phenomena* (but note that *data* and *media* are often used with singular verbs).	The criteria for a successful job application often **include** work experience.
The verb agrees with the noun that follows *a lot of*. In formal academic writing, it is better to use *a large number of* (with count nouns) and *a great deal of / a large amount of* (with non-count nouns).	*A lot of / A large number of* students **have** part-time jobs.
	A lot of / A great deal of / A large amount of money **is** spent on advertising.
One of takes a singular verb because it refers to "one."	One of the best reasons to run your own company **is** to have complete independence.
Collective nouns (*family, government, team, staff, faculty, committee*) normally use singular verbs.	The management team **has** decided on a new financial strategy.

Note: In the chart, the subjects are highlighted and the verbs are in bold.

Practice Exercises

A Read the sentences and circle the correct verb form.

1. Economics and politics *is / are* important ways to learn about history.

2. Businesses *is / are* under pressure to make higher profits.

3. None of the managing directors *is / are* willing to reduce his or her salary.

4. Investing money in the financial markets *is / are* becoming more risky.

5. There *is / are* several important reasons for the rising cost of energy.

6. The government *is / are* introducing more regulation of the banking sector.

7. Everyone *is / are* concerned about rising inflation and unemployment.

8. Neither the economists nor the banks *is / are* able to predict the stock markets accurately.

9. The faculty *is / are* unable to agree on the department budget for next year.

10. A large number of candidates *is / are* applying for work placements this year.

11. Learning how to manage your budget *is / are* important in any work environment.

12. Each of our employees *is / are* encouraged to give feedback on company policy.

B Read the following example of a spoken response to question 1 in the speaking section (paired choice). Choose the correct verb forms.

Some people think it is a good idea for students to have a part-time job during college. Others think it is a bad idea. Which do you think is better and why?

I have a part-time job and a lot of my friends who are students ¹*has / have* part-time jobs, too. There ²*is / are* two main reasons why I think this is a good idea. First, I think that having a job ³*helps / help* you to manage your time. Here ⁴*is / are* an example. Before I got a part-time job, I was often late for class and late with my homework. But after getting a job, I realized that being punctual ⁵*is / are* so important. Neither employers nor other staff members ⁶*is / are* happy if someone ⁷*is / are* late, or ⁸*doesn't / don't* finish his or her work. Second, having a part-time job ⁹*is / are* a great way to be independent. No one ¹⁰*likes / like* to borrow money from parents or friends, and taking out huge loans ¹¹*isn't / aren't* a good idea either. Earning money and deciding how to spend it ¹²*is / are* important aspects of becoming an independent adult.

STUDY TIP

Edit your essays carefully for subject-verb agreement. As you write, keep in mind whether the subject of your sentence is singular or plural. Practice identifying the subject of your sentence. Identify errors that you make most frequently. Rewrite the correct sentences in your notebook.

Test Practice

A The following question is similar to question 1 in the speaking section (choice). Make notes on your answer.

Some people think it is better to work for a company. Others prefer to run their own business. Which do you think is best and why?

> Notes
>
> My opinion
>
> Reason 1
>
> Reason 2
>
> Reason 3

Now write a transcript of your spoken response (or record your response and write your transcript here). Check your work carefully for subject-verb agreement.

_____

_____

_____

_____

_____

_____

_____

_____

_____

_____

_____

TEST TIP: Speaking section question 1 (paired choice)

In question 1 you are usually asked to answer a question using examples from your own experience. Read the question and spend 15 seconds making a few notes. Your answer should take about 45 seconds.

Remember to restate the question and state your opinion clearly at the beginning. For example: *Although some people prefer to work for a company, I personally would prefer to run my own business. My reasons for this are: First … For example … Second … For example … Finally … For example … .*

B The following is an example of question 2 in the writing section (independent task) of the Paper Edition of the TOEFL iBT test. Make an essay plan, being sure to include at least three reasons to support your opinion.

Do you agree or disagree with the following statement? The amount of money you earn is the most important reason for choosing a job. Use specific reasons and examples to support your answer.

My plan

Agree or disagree?

Reason 1

 Detail

 Example

Reason 2

 Detail

 Example

Reason 3

 Detail

 Example

Now write the <u>introductory paragraph</u> of your essay. Check your work carefully for subject-verb agreement.

_____

_____

_____

_____

_____

_____

_____

_____

Comparative structures

Study the explanations and examples in the chart. Make your own examples based on each rule.

OVERVIEW

Comparative structures are used to say how two things or people are similar or different.	
-er adjective + *than* / *more* + adjective + *than* Use *more* with adjectives of more than two syllables and some two-syllable adjectives. *less* + adjective + *than* Note irregular forms: *better, worse, further*.	Cities are becoming **larger** and **more crowded**. Life in rural areas tends to be **less expensive** and **less stressful**.
more + noun *fewer / less* + noun Use *fewer* with count nouns and *less* with non-count nouns.	**More people** live in cities today than ever before. Large cities often have **fewer parks** and green areas than small towns. Small towns generally have **less crime** than large cities.
Add *much, far, considerably,* or *significantly* to make a comparison stronger.	Cities are **significantly larger** now than they were 20 years ago. High-rise buildings are **far more common** in large cities than in small towns.
Negative comparative structures	
not as + adjective + *as*	Rural areas are **not as crowded as** cities.
not as many / much + noun + *as* Use *many* with count nouns and *much* with non-count nouns.	There are **not as many** job opportunities in rural areas **as** there are in towns. There is **not as much** pollution in rural areas **as** there is in towns.
Equal comparative structures	
as + adjective + *as*	Living in a small town is **as healthy as** living in the country.
as many / much + noun + *as*	There are **as many** museums and other cultural opportunities in smaller towns **as** in cities.

Practice Exercises

A Complete the paragraph with words from the box.

as	considerably	content	fewer	friendlier
more	much	smaller		

My hometown is much ¹_____ than the other cities in my region. It has ²_____ schools and colleges, and there are not ³_____ many stores, museums, or libraries. Nevertheless, I love my hometown because I think the people there are ⁴_____ than in other places. Life is ⁵_____ less stressful and people have ⁶_____ free time. As a result, they are ⁷_____ happier and more ⁸_____ than those who live in larger cities.

B The paragraph below contains eight errors in comparative forms. Circle and correct the errors. More than one option may be possible.

Somebody wants to build a factory in your hometown. Do you support or oppose this plan?

If a factory is built in my hometown, there will be many advantages. First, there will be many more employment. Second, roads will be more good and transportation will be more faster. There will also be much more educational and recreational facilities. Unfortunately, there will also be some disadvantages. The town will not be peaceful as before and it will be very more polluted. Much more people will come to work here. The town will probably become more crowded and there will be less parks and trees. On the whole, however, I feel that there are more advantages than disadvantages and I would support this plan.

C These are examples of types of topics in question 2 of the speaking section (paired choice). Write two comparative sentences to compare each pair of topics.

1. texting / speaking face to face

   _____

   _____

2. traveling by train / by car

   _____

   _____

3. taking a long vacation / a short vacation

   _____

   _____

4. eat at home / go out to a restaurant

   _____

   _____

5. getting news on the internet / reading a newspaper

   _____

   _____

TEST TIP: Speaking section question 1 (paired choice)

In this question, it does not matter which choice you make. The important thing is to show that you can evaluate the two choices and say why one is better than the other. In your answer, you should mention the benefits of your choice and also the drawbacks of the alternative. This question tests your ability to:

1. Express and justify likes, dislikes, values, preferences.

2. Take a position and defend it.

3. Make a recommendation and justify it.

Test Practice

A The following question is similar to question 1 in the speaking section (choice). Make notes.

Some people prefer to live in a city. Others prefer to live in the country. Which do you think is better and why?

> Notes
>
> My opinion
>
>
> Reason 1
>
> Reason 2
>
> Reason 3

Now write a transcript of your spoken response (or record your response and write the transcript here). Check your work carefully for correct use of comparative structures.

_____

_____

_____

_____

_____

_____

_____

_____

_____

_____

_____

B Read the following example of a question that is similar to question 2 in the writing section (independent task) of the Paper Edition of the TOEFL iBT test. Plan, write, and revise your written response to the question.

It is better for children to grow up in the countryside than in a big city. Do you agree or disagree? Use specific reasons and examples to develop your essay.

Opinion

Reason 1:

• Detail

• Example

Reason 2:

• Detail

• Example

Reason 3:

• Detail

• Example

_____

_____

_____

_____

_____

_____

STUDY TIP: Writing section question 2 of the Paper Edition of the TOEFL iBT test (independent writing task)

There are five main types of essay questions in this section of the test. They are:

1. Compare and contrast
2. Agree or disagree
3. Preference
4. Description or explanation
5. Imaginary or hypothetical situations

Use a library or online resource to find more examples of TOEFL iBT essay questions. Practice identifying the types of questions and choose examples of each type to practice your essay planning and writing skills.

PAPER EDITION ONLY

Modals (present and future)

Study the examples in the chart. Make your own examples based on each verb.

OVERVIEW

Modal verbs are used before the infinitive of other verbs. They add meanings connected with certainty or obligation, expressing the speaker's attitude to an action or event.	
Obligation or necessity	
have to / need to	Everyone **has to** / **needs to** reduce their energy consumption.
No obligation or necessity	
don't have to / needn't	You **don't have to** / **needn't** make major lifestyle changes to cut back on energy consumption.
Advice or recommendation	
should / ought to	Governments **should** / **ought to** spend more money on protecting the environment.
shouldn't	Governments **shouldn't** allow factories to produce pollution.
Certainty or uncertainty	
will (sure)	A rise in the Earth's temperature **will** affect animals and marine life.
would (hypothetical)	Reducing energy consumptions **would** also reduce pollution caused by gas emissions.
may / might (less certain)	Governments **may** / **might** introduce stricter laws.
could (possible)	Companies **could** reduce pollution by creating more products with recyclable packaging.
Ability or permission	
can	We **can** develop alternative sources of energy.
Past and passive forms	
To form the **past** with *would*, *should*, *could*, *may*, and *might*, use the modal + *have* + past participle.	They **should have monitored** the effects of global warming more carefully.
	We **might have reduced** energy consumption sooner, if we had known about its effects on the environment.
To form the **passive**, use the modal + *be* + the past participle.	Energy consumption **has to** / **should be** reduced.
	Animals and marine life **will be** affected by a rise in the Earth's temperature.
To form the **past passive**, use the modal + *have* + *been* + the past participle.	More money **could have been spent** on protecting the environment.

Note the difference in meaning between the two past forms of *need*: *didn't need to do* (something you didn't do because it wasn't necessary) and *needn't have done* (something that you did that wasn't necessary).

Also, note there are more modals, but these are the ones most useful for the test.

Practice Exercises

A Complete the paragraph with modal verbs from the chart.

Global warming ¹_____ (possibly) be permanently changing the Earth's climate. Climate scientists agree that global warming ²_____ (definitely) impact on all wildlife and marine habitats. Some people believe that we ³_____ (not necessary) be too concerned as these changes are happening only very gradually. Others believe that governments ⁴_____ (urgent) take action immediately. They insist that all countries ⁵_____ (advise) restrict carbon dioxide emissions and that they ⁶_____ (not a good idea) wait until it is too late. Scientists have recently predicted that average global temperatures ⁷_____ (possible) increase between 1.4 and 5.8 degrees Celsius by the year 2100. Changes resulting from global warming ⁸_____ (less certain) include rising sea levels, as well as an increase in severe weather events. Everyone ⁹_____ (ability) take action now by taking measures to increase energy efficiency and reduce consumption. Even the smallest reduction ¹⁰_____ (possible) help to slow down the effects of global warming.

> **WORD BUILDING**
>
> The root *duc-* in the word *reduce* means *to lead*. *Reduce* means *lead back (cut down)*. *Duc-* or *duct-* is found in many words. Examples: *educate (lead into knowledge)*, *introduce (lead people to know each other)*. Use your dictionary to find the meaning of these words: *abduction, induction, deduce conduct, aqueduct.*

B Rewrite these sentences using the passive form.

1. Everyone should do more to protect the environment.

   _____

2. They should have detected the effects on the environment much sooner.

   _____

3. We shouldn't use gas and coal to produce energy.

   _____

4. Governments will have to pass stricter laws to protect the environment.

   _____

5. We could have prevented the harmful effects of global warming.

   _____

6. They shouldn't have built nuclear power plants in an earthquake zone.

   _____

C Read the following response to question 1 in the speaking section (choice). Choose the best modals in the response to complete it.

Some people say that every city should have a car-free day once a month. Other people say it would cause a lot of problems. Which side do you support and why?

I agree with the view that cities [1]**would** / **should** have a car-free day once a month. First, if people used their cars less, there would be less pollution. The air [2]**would** / **will** be cleaner, and there [3]**would** / **will** be less noise. Second, if people use alternative methods of transportation, they [4]**may** / **should** realize that they [5]**have to** / **needn't** use their car quite so often. In fact, they [6]**might** / **have to** start to enjoy walking or riding a bicycle to work or school on a regular basis and as a result they [7]**could** / **need to** become healthier. Of course this idea [8]**should** / **may** be a little inconvenient for people who have to travel a long way to work. Those people [9]**may** / **might** have to stay at home on car-free days, which [10]**wouldn't** / **needn't** be good for them or their employers. But on the whole, if there were a car-free day every month, I think people [11]**should** / **might** appreciate the parks and trees in the city and start to walk around the city more. People [12]**might** / **can** also become a little friendlier and happier. I think this would be a very good idea in my city.

STUDY TIP

The criteria for question 1 of the speaking section (choice) include pace, fluency, and intonation, as well as vocabulary and grammar usage. You will also be graded on your ability to support opinions with personal details and to organize your response so that it is clear and easy to understand. Practice by recording your response within the allocated time of 45 seconds. Make a brief plan of the main points before you start to speak. Listen to your recording. Did you speak naturally and clearly? Were your ideas well organized? Did you use appropriate grammar and vocabulary to express your ideas?

D These are examples of the types of topics that may come up in question 1 of the speaking section (choice). Write two sentences using modal verbs to answer each question.

1. Some people think that TV should only be for education, while others think it should be for entertainment. Which side do you support and why?

   _____

   _____

2. Students should not use cell phones during class. Do you agree or disagree?

   _____

   _____

E The following question is similar to task 2 in the writing section (independent essay) of the Paper Edition of the TOEFL iBT test. Think of three sentences that would use modals in your answer to this question.

Some people think governments should spend money exploring outer space (for example, traveling to Mars and to other planets). Other people disagree and think governments should spend this money to help solve problems here on Earth. Which of these two opinions do you agree with? Use specific reasons and details to support your answer.

   _____

   _____

   _____

   _____

Test Practice

Remember to use transition words and phrases to guide your listener through the organization of your ideas. *There are three main reasons for my opinion. The first reason is … The second reason is … In addition … Finally … .*

The following question is similar to question 1 in the speaking section (choice). Make notes for your answer.

Some people enjoy living in a climate where it is warm all year. Others prefer to live in a climate where there are four seasons. Which type of climate do you prefer and why?

> Notes
>
> My opinion
>
>
> Reason 1
>
> Reason 2
>
> Reason 3

Now write a transcript of your spoken response (or record your response and write the transcript here). Think about how you could use modals in your answer.

_____

_____

_____

_____

_____

_____

_____

_____

_____

_____

_____

_____

_____

_____

Conditional sentences

Study the explanations and examples in the chart. Write your own examples based on each type of conditional. Include some examples using negative verbs for one or both clauses.

OVERVIEW

Conditional sentences are used to talk about a result that depends on something else happening first.

Explanation and structure	Example
Zero conditional: a result that always or usually happens Condition: *If* + (present), Result: (present)	If you **stay** in a dorm on campus, you **make** more friends. You **make** more friends if you **stay** in a dorm on campus.
First conditional: a result that is possible and likely Condition: *If* + (present), Result: (*will* + verb)	If she **takes** a part-time job, she'll **have** less time to study. She'll **have** less time to study if she **takes** a part-time job.
Second conditional: a result that is possible but less likely Condition: *If* + (past), Result: (*would* + verb)	If I **had** more time, I **would join** an academic study group. I **would join** an academic study group if I **had** more time.
Third conditional: a result that is hypothetical, a different result of something that has already happened Condition: *If* + (past perfect), Result: (*would* + *have* + past participle)	If he **had worked** more on his assignment, he **would have passed** the class. He **would have passed** the class if he **had worked** more on his assignment. If I **were*** you, I'd talk to your academic advisor. I wouldn't take any extra classes if I **were*** you.

Note:
1. If the condition is first, there is a comma. There is no comma if the result is first.
2. *Was* and *were* are both correct as first and third person singular forms of the verb be in second conditional sentences. *Was* is more usual in spoken English; *were* is more usual in formal and written English.
3. Conditional sentences can also be a mixture of different types. For example, *If I had sent in my application earlier, I would have a job now*.

Practice Exercises

A Complete the sentences with the correct form of the verbs in parentheses.

1. If you are absent from class too often, you _____ graduate. (not able to)

2. He _____ get a part-time job if he doesn't have enough money. (have to)

3. If she fails this class, she _____ enough credits. (not get)

4. We _____ the test if we had studied harder. (not fail)

5. If they knew more about science, they _____ better grades in biology. (get)

6. He wouldn't have become a teacher if he _____ to grad school. (not go)

B Complete the sentences using the phrases in the box.

join an academic study group	not get a grade	not have enough money
get a discount on books	not have so many classes	not study harder
save your work onto a flash drive	spend more time traveling	

1. If you have a student ID, _____.

2. If I don't get a part-time job, _____.

3. If you moved off campus, _____.

4. If she doesn't hand in her assignment on time, _____.

5. He won't get a good grade _____.

6. She will find the class easier _____.

7. I would have more free time _____.

8. You wouldn't have lost your assignment _____.

C These are examples of types of topics in question 2 of the writing section (independent essay) of the Paper Edition of the TOEFL iBT test. Complete each sentence with your own ideas.

1. If I could change one thing about my hometown, _____.

2. If I could study a subject I had never studied before, _____.

3. If I could meet a famous person from history, _____.

4. If I could go back in time, _____.

5. If I could meet a famous singer or sportsperson, _____.

6. If I were asked to choose one thing to represent my country, _____.

7. If I could invent a new life-changing product, _____.

8. If I were to travel for one year, _____.

STUDY TIP

In the speaking section, you can speak from your notes. Practice making clear notes and speaking from them. Record your voice. This will help you to sound confident and calm during the test. Remember to finish with a strong concluding sentence by using signpost words, such as *Finally ... In conclusion ... To summarize ... To conclude ...* . Do NOT add any personal comments at the end of the recording. Please note: Taking notes is not a requirement of the TOEFL iBT test, i.e. if you prefer not to take notes, you don't have to.

Test Practice

Track 20

A The following question is similar to question 2 in the speaking section of the test (campus situation). Read the announcement. Then listen to a conversation on the same topic. Take notes.

Announcement

Starting in the fall semester, all freshmen will be required to take an academic composition class in their first year. This is so that all students become familiar with the standard of academic writing required in their courses. It will also help students to understand the importance of academic rules, such as being careful to avoid plagiarism.

Notes

Main change
Reason 1
Reason 2
Woman's opinion
Reason 1
Detail
Reason 2
Detail

The woman expresses her opinion of the announcement. State her opinion and explain the reasons she gives for holding that opinion.

According to the announcement _____

The reason for this is _____

_____

The woman agrees / disagrees with this decision.

Her first reason is _____

_____

Her second reason is _____

_____

In addition, she thinks that _____

_____

B The following question is similar to question 2 in the speaking section (campus situation). Read the announcement. Then listen to a conversation on the same topic. Take notes.

Track 21

Notice from the Office of Student Affairs

In an effort to reduce traffic on campus, students and staff will be required to register for on-campus parking and purchase a one-year parking permit. A valid parking permit will be required at all times in any of the university parking lots. Starting next semester, metered parking will no longer be available. Permits for visitors can also be purchased depending on availability.

Notes

The man expresses his opinion of the announcement. State his opinion and explain the reasons he gives for holding that opinion.

Write your spoken response (or record your response and write the transcript here). You have 60 seconds (125–150 words).

TEST TIP: Speaking section question 2 (campus matters)

In this question, you will read a short text about a college campus situation. It may be an announcement or an article. First, you will read the text. Then you will listen to two students talking about the situation. Take notes during the conversation as you will hear it only once. One of the students will either agree with or oppose the information in the reading passage. Begin your answer by briefly describing the campus situation. Then state the speaker's opinion including some supporting details.

Transition words and phrases

Study the explanations and examples in the chart. Make your own examples using each word or phrase.

OVERVIEW

Transition words and phrases help the reader or listener to make connections between different pieces of information in an essay or in a presentation.

Function	Word or phrase	Example
Sequence	To begin with, At first, First of all, First, Next, Then	**To begin with**, the lecturer describes several types of animal communication. **Then** she goes on to give some examples of each type.
Contrast	However, On the other hand, In contrast, Unlike …	Bees feed on nectar and pollen from plants. Wasps, **on the other hand**, also eat small insects. **Unlike** bees, wasps can sting multiple times.
Comparison	Both … Like … Compared with (…), Similarly,	**Both** leopards and cheetahs are wild cats that have spotted markings on their coats. **Compared with** leopards, cheetahs have a more streamlined body and can run much faster.
Result	Consequently, As a result, Therefore, For this reason,	Bats are mainly active at night. **Consequently**, they have developed echolocation as a way to find their prey in the dark. Bats transfer pollen from one plant to another. **As a result**, many plants depend on bats for survival.
Addition	Furthermore, In addition, Additionally, Moreover,	The blue whale is the largest mammal on earth. **Furthermore**, it can live to be 80–90 years old. Whales use clicks and whistles to communicate with each other. **In addition**, they use their tails to make slapping noises on the water.
	Not only … but also*	Fish **not only** communicate using gesture and motion, **but** they can **also** use electric impulses. **Not only** do bats use squeaks to navigate, **but** they **also** use them to identify each other. *

Note: *When *not only* is used at the start of sentence, an auxiliary verb is used (except with the verb *be*) which is followed by the subject.

Practice Exercises

A Choose the correct words to complete the paragraph.

Tortoises and Turtles

[1] **Both / Like** tortoises and turtles are reptiles that have a shell on their back. One difference between them, [2] **however / moreover**, is that tortoises spend most of their time on land, while turtles tend to stay in water. [3] **Compared with / In addition to** tortoises, turtles have webbed feet that are adapted for swimming. Tortoises are herbivores. [4] **Therefore / Moreover**, they feed on a diet of plants and fruit. [5] **Unlike / Furthermore** tortoises, turtles are omnivorous and can eat meat as well.

B Rewrite the sentences using the words in parentheses.

1. Moths belong to the category *Lepidoptera* and so do butterflies. (both)

   _____.

2. Cheetahs live in groups, but leopards are solitary. (on the other hand)

   _____.

3. Food is scarce in the winter so bears go into hibernation in order to conserve energy. (consequently)

   _____.

4. Crocodiles have large, pointed teeth and so do alligators. (like)

   _____.

5. Pandas are good swimmers. They are also good at climbing trees. (moreover)

   _____.

6. Elephants have very thick wrinkly skin. It can retain water to help them stay cool. (as a result)

   _____.

7. Iguanas eat leaves and plants, but chameleons are carnivores. (however)

   _____.

8. Bats help to pollinate plants. They eat insects and disperse seeds, too. (not only…but also)

   _____.

DICTIONARY SKILLS

POWERED BY COBUILD

The prefix *omni-* means *all* or *everything*. Use your dictionary to find the meaning of these words: *omniscient, omnipresent, omnipotent*.

C Complete the paragraph with the phrases from the box.

also	consequently	first	in addition	not only
	on the other hand		then	

DICTIONARY SKILLS

⋐ POWERED BY COBUILD

The root word *audi-* means *to hear* or *listen*. Use your dictionary to find the meaning of these words: *auditorium*, *audition*, *audible*.

According to the passage, honeybees work together in a colony to collect food from flowers and bring it back to the hive. [1]_____, they identify which flowers have the best source of nectar and pollen. [2]_____, they go back to the hive and tell the other bees where they are. The lecturer goes on to explain that bees communicate this information to each other using a type of dance. [3]_____ does the dance indicate the distance of food from the hive, but it [4]_____ communicates the direction. The dance involves waggling forward in a straight line at a certain angle. The length of the line indicates the distance. The angle of the line, [5]_____, indicates the direction. [6]_____, the quality of the food source is indicated by the degree of energy in the dance. The other bees watch the dance carefully. [7]_____, they learn where to find the best sources of food.

Test Practice

A The following question is similar to question 3 in the speaking section (academic reading and lecture). In this question, you will read a passage and then listen to a lecture on the same topic. The lecture usually extends or gives examples of the information in the passage.

Read the passage in 45 seconds and make notes below.

Animal Communication

Animal communication can be defined as when an animal sends a signal that is perceived by another animal and alters its behavior in some way. There are four main types of animal communication. These are: auditory, visual, tactile, and chemical. Auditory communication includes vocalizations and other non-vocal sounds such as clicking, scratching, or knocking. Visual communication includes the display of color and specific movements, gestures, or facial expressions. Tactile communication includes touching, grooming, or fighting. Chemical communication uses pheromones that can be perceived through chemoreceptors using the sense of taste or smell.

Notes

B Now listen to part of a lecture in an ecology class and take notes.

Track 22

Notes

Complete the spoken response below. (Note that in the test, you will rely only on your notes.) If possible, record your response and listen to it. You have 60 seconds to give your spoken response.

The professor describes two examples of animal communication. Use the information from the passage and the lecture to explain how these examples relate to animal communication in general.

According to the passage, _____.

There are _____.

The lecturer gives two examples of _____.

The first example _____.

In addition, _____.

The second example, on the other hand, _____.

Furthermore, _____.

Like whales, ants can also _____.

Not only _____.

Both examples show that _____.

TEST TIP: Speaking section question 3 (academic reading and lecture)

In this type of question, you need to summarize both the reading passage and the listening and show how they relate to each other. You do not need to express an opinion or add any other information.

Reported speech (1)

Study the explanations and examples in the chart. Make your own examples.

OVERVIEW

Reporting verbs are used to describe what a person or a reading passage says. They are used in academic writing to indicate information taken from sources and convey the writer's interpretation of the material cited.

Structures with reporting verbs	Example
Reporting verb + *that* clauses Examples: *state, argue, claim, maintain, assert, indicate, suggest, show, agree, disagree*	The passage **states** that TV benefits language development in children. Research **indicates** that language skills are improved by watching TV. The author of the passage and the professor (both) **agree** that TV is beneficial to language development.
Reporting verb + noun Examples: *reject, refute, contradict, question, challenge, identify, describe, present* *Agree / Disagree + with +* noun *Refer + to +* noun *Agree / Disagree* can also stand alone without an object or a clause following it.	The professor **contradicts** the ideas in the passage. The passage **presents** two types of language development. The professor **agrees with** this conclusion. The passage **refers to** a recent study. The author of the passage asserts that … but the professor **disagrees**.
That clauses are often used after these nouns to give more information about the noun: *argument, chance, danger, difficulty, effect, evidence, fact, possibility, problem, risk.*	The study provides **evidence** that … The author supports **the argument** that … Research suggests **the possibility** that …

Note: *Say* and *tell* are more often used in spoken language (and are therefore more suitable for questions 3 and 5 in the speaking section than the writing section). *Tell* must be followed by an object. For example: *He **tells** us that TV is an important educational tool.*

For more information about the meaning of different reporting verbs, see Vocabulary Unit 18.

Practice Exercises

A Choose the correct word or words to complete each sentence.

1. The passage _____ that children who watch TV have improved language development.

   a agrees   b claims   c gives

2. The passage _____ to a study of 200 pre-school children.

   a refers   b claims   c provides

3. The professor _____ with the view that TV programs can be educational.

   a agrees   b refutes   c suggests

4. The passage gives an example to _____ how TV programs helped speech development.

   a argue   b contradict   c show

5. The passage maintains that TV is beneficial but the professor _____ .

   a claims   b refutes   c disagrees

6. The research reveals _____ many TV programs are not educational.

   a the fact   b the fact that   c the fact of

> **WORD BUILDING**
>
> The prefix *dis-* can be used to make a verb or an adjective into its opposite. Example: *disagree = not agree*. Use your dictionary to find the meanings of these words: *disappear, distrust, disobey, dislocate, disqualified, dissatisfied*.

B Complete the text with words from the box.

argues	concludes	gives	refutes	shows	that	to	with

The passage [1]_____ that educational programs on TV have a positive effect on young children. However, the professor disagrees [2]_____ this conclusion and [3]_____ evidence that [4]_____ educational programs are not beneficial for pre-school children. The reading passage suggests [5]_____ children who watch TV have better language skills. The professor [6]_____ this point by referring [7]_____ studies showing that pre-school children who watched TV had slower speech development. She [8]_____ that children's TV should be monitored more carefully.

C Find and correct the mistake in each sentence.

The passage agrees the idea that TV has educational benefits for children. The author refers with a study that found improved language development in pre-school children. The professor contradicts to this idea. She claims that several studies to show the opposite. She refers to evidence of language skills were delayed in some children. She identifies that three ways in which educational TV can be improved.

STUDY TIP

Practice summarizing news stories or academic articles. Write the summaries in your journal using a wide variety of reporting verbs.

D Read the following summaries. Summarize the connections in the content between them using reporting verbs.

1. **Reading passage:** The language people speak controls how they think. Not only does language shape our thoughts, it limits our perceptions of the world.

   Lecture: Brain research has shown that thoughts are independent of language. Although language can cause differences in thought, it does not determine how we think.

   _____

   _____

   _____

   _____

   _____

2. **Reading passage:** It is much easier to learn a second language during childhood than as an adult. This is because there is a critical period in childhood up to the age of around fifteen, during which children can easily acquire any language they are exposed to.

   Lecture: Adults also have many advantages that children do not have, such as study skills and strategies that can speed up the learning process.

   _____

   _____

   _____

   _____

   _____

3. **Reading passage:** Most children begin to speak around the age of ten to eighteen months. However, they learn to understand words a long time before that. Several studies have shown that hearing language being used around them stimulates a child's brain to grow.

   Lecture: Young children need to be provided with many different kinds of linguistic stimuli so that they can develop their language skills. It is important not to criticize or correct mistakes because they are part of the learning process as it is possible that this may inhibit language development.

   _____

   _____

   _____

   _____

   _____

Test Practice

The following question is similar to question 1 in the writing section (integrated task). In this question, you will read a passage and then listen to part of a lecture on the same topic. The lecture may support or challenge the ideas in the passage.

Read the passage and take notes on the left below.

It is often supposed that when individuals have successfully learned several languages, it is because they have a natural aptitude for language learning. While this may be true in some cases, recent research shows that the experience of learning a second language itself makes learning a new language easier. After learning a second language successfully, individuals can transfer effective language learning strategies to other languages so that they become better language learners. This may explain why bilingual children, who grow up speaking two languages, are generally better language learners later on in life.

A second benefit of foreign language learning is that it increases critical thinking skills and creativity. Recent research has shown that students who are learning a foreign language regularly score higher grades in both verbal and math tests. This is because second language learning is not just a linguistic activity, it also involves problem-solving, which helps develop higher level cognitive abilities.

Track 23

Now listen to part of a lecture in an education class and complete the notes below.

Notes

Main idea of passage	*Main idea of lecture*
Benefit 1	*Benefit 1*
Reason	*Reason*
Benefit 2	*Benefit 2*
Reason	*Reason*

Now answer the question. You may use your notes. Summarize the main points in the lecture, being sure to explain how they support the ideas in the reading passage. Use reporting verbs.

_____

_____

_____

_____

_____

_____

_____

_____

Reported speech (2)

Study the explanations and examples in the chart. Make your own examples.

OVERVIEW

Reporting verbs are often followed by nouns or noun clauses.

Structure	Example
(*describe*, *explain*, *discuss*, *illustrate*, *show*) + noun	The passage **describes** the causes of earthquakes.
(*explain*, *illustrate*, *show*) + *that* clause Note that *describe* and *discuss* cannot be followed by a *that* clause.	The professor **explains** that earthquakes are caused by a number of different factors.
(*describe*, *explain*, *illustrate*, *show*) + *wh*-clause (*what*, *why*, *how*, *when*, *where*, or *who*) The word order in these clauses is the same as in a simple sentence (*wh*-word + subject + verb + object). The noun clause represents a question about the object or complement of the verb. (*What are the causes of earthquakes?*)	The passage **describes** what the causes of earthquakes are. The passage **explains** why it is difficult to predict earthquakes. The examples **show** how earthquakes and tidal waves are connected. The diagram **illustrates** where earthquakes occur.
When the noun clause is about the subject, the word *what* replaces the subject, and the verb follows *what*. (*What causes earthquakes? What happens in an earthquake?*)	The passage **explains** what causes earthquakes. The lecture **describes** what happens in an earthquake.
Use *if* or *whether* for clauses that could be expressed as yes / no questions. (*Can earthquakes be predicted?*)	The professor **discusses** if / whether earthquakes can be predicted.

Practice Exercises

A Choose the correct phrase to complete each sentence.

1. The passage explains _____.
   a how hurricanes are they formed   b how hurricanes are formed
   c how are hurricanes formed

2. The examples illustrate _____ of hurricanes.
   a that the size and speed   b what the size and speed
   c the speed and size

3. The passage describes _____.
   a how forecasters predict hurricanes   b how hurricanes predict by forecasters
   c how forecasters hurricanes predict

4. The passage explains _____ in the United States during the fall months.
   a how most hurricanes form   b that most hurricanes form
   c how a most hurricanes form

5. Statistical data show _____.
   a how frequent are hurricanes   b how are frequent hurricanes
   c the high frequency of hurricanes

6. The lecture discusses _____.
   a if hurricanes are getting stronger   b if hurricanes getting stronger are
   c if are getting hurricanes stronger

B Complete each sentence so that it summarizes the content of the preceding sentence.

1. Dust storms frequently occur in the American southwest.
   The passage describes _____.

2. They are formed when the wind in a dry sandy region is strong enough to lift off the top layers of dirt from the ground.
   The passage explains _____.

3. There are two methods by which dust can be transported: suspension and saltation.
   The passage describes _____.

4. Small particles of soil are suspended in the air and carried by the wind. This is known as suspension.
   The passage explains _____.

5. The second method, known as saltation, is when large particles bounce along the ground.
   The passage explains _____.

6. In the 1930s, a series of dust storms devastated the Great Plains of North America. This period was known as the Dust Bowl.
   The example illustrates _____.

Test Practice

The following question is similar to question 3 in the speaking section (academic reading and lecture). In this question, you will read a paragraph and then listen to part of a lecture on the same topic. The lecture usually extends or gives examples of the information in the reading passage.

DICTIONARY SKILLS

POWERED BY COBUILD

The root *dict-* means *to say*. *Prediction* means *to say something before it happens*. Use your dictionary to find the meanings of these words: *jurisdiction, interdiction, indictment, contradict, dictatorial.*

Read the passage in 45 seconds and make notes below.

Earthquake Prediction

Early scientific efforts toward earthquake prediction were directed primarily toward the measurement of observable physical changes in areas where earthquakes occur. These warning signals or precursors included foreshocks, changes in animal behavior, and changes in the water table, stream flow, well levels, and patterns of electrical currents in the ground. It was hoped that by carefully recording these signals over a period of time, it would be possible to accumulate sufficient data to predict when and where future earthquakes would occur. A second approach to earthquake prediction studies the frequency of earthquakes along specific fault lines in order to establish a probability forecast based on the average time between earthquakes. This is based on the idea that a fault builds up pressure until it reaches a critical point, when it is released as an earthquake. Then the whole process starts again.

Notes

🎧 **Now listen to part of a lecture in a geology class and take notes.**

Track 24

> Notes

Complete the spoken response below. (Note that in the test, you will rely only on your notes.) Practice reading the response aloud. If possible record your response and listen to it. You have 60 seconds to give your spoken response.

The professor describes two examples of earthquake prediction. Use examples from the lecture to explain how successful they have been.

The lecture and the reading passage are about _____.

The reading passage describes two approaches _____.

The passage explains that one _____ is _____

_____.

The second _____ is _____

_____.

The lecture gives examples of _____.

The first example shows that _____

_____.

Unfortunately, _____.

The second example mentioned in the lecture _____

_____.

This example shows that _____

_____.

Both approaches illustrate that _____.

TEST TIP: Speaking section question 3 (academic reading and lecture)

First, analyze the prompt. Make sure you understand the specific information you should include in your response. Use your notes to create an outline for your response during the preparation time. Begin your response by briefly summarizing the main ideas of the reading passage and the lecture. Be sure to describe how the sources are related. Introduce both of the key points from the lecture. Include supporting details for each key point. Don't forget to describe how the key points relate to the reading.

Gerunds and infinitives

Study the explanations and examples in the chart. Make your own examples.

OVERVIEW

A **gerund** is the *-ing* form of a verb. It can be used like a noun.	
Gerunds can be subjects, objects, or complements.	**Reaching** oil deposits under the sea is a complex and dangerous process.
A gerund can be a compound noun.	**Offshore oil drilling** can have environmental hazards as well as economic benefits.
A gerund can have an object.	**Constructing offshore oil platforms** on the ocean bed requires expensive equipment.
Two gerunds can be combined to form one subject.	**Drilling and mining** for oil is a multi-million dollar industry.
A gerund can be negative.	**Not ensuring** the highest safety standards can have enormous environmental consequences.
A gerund can be used as the subject in a *that* clause.	The professor claims that **oil mining** is less destructive than coal mining.
Use a gerund after prepositions. Ex. *by / a reason for / in favor of / against / instead of / because of / without*	The lecture supports the argument **by giving two** examples of the environmental effects. The lecture presents several reasons **for developing** deep-sea oil fields. The lecture states three reasons **against using** fossil fuels.
Infinitives are formed with *to* + the base form of the verb.	
Infinitive clauses are used to show purpose (*in order to*).	The professor provides two examples **to illustrate** the dangers of nuclear energy.
The purpose clause can also start the sentence, followed by a comma.	**To illustrate** the dangers of nuclear energy, the professor provides two examples.
Infinitive clauses can modify abstract nouns. Ex. *evidence, opportunity, attempt, chance, need*	There is **evidence to show** that oil consumption is decreasing.
Infinitives can follow adjectives, especially those expressing an opinion. *It + be* + adjective + infinitive Ex. *important, easy, difficult, interesting, essential, possible, impossible* Note: It is important **for us** to remember that … .	It is important **to remember** that nuclear energy accidents can cause significant long-term damage to the environment.

Note: *way* can be followed by an infinitive, or *of* + gerund. For example: *Wind farms are a way **to generate / of generating** clean energy.*

Practice Exercises

A Rewrite the sentences using either a gerund or an infinitive construction.

1. An important goal is to increase energy from renewable sources.

    Increasing _____.

2. It is cleaner and safer to burn vegetable oil than gasoline.

    Burning _____.

3. Drilling for oil under the sea costs a lot of money. (expensive)

    It _____.

4. Finding alternative ways to produce energy is a priority. (important)

    It _____.

5. We can use new technology to harness solar energy.

    Harnessing _____.

6. We should develop new energy sources, and not look for new sources of fossil fuels.

    Instead of _____.

7. We can produce energy using water, sunlight, and wind. (possible)

    It _____.

8. Wind and solar energy have many benefits.

    There are many reasons for _____.

9. Increasing the number of wind farms can reduce dependence on oil and gas.

    To _____.

10. Biomass is another clean energy production method. (way)

    Biomass is _____.

B Choose the correct forms to complete the passage.

Alternative Energy Sources

Scientists have been working on ways [1]*capturing / to capture* energy directly from ocean waves. [2]*Blowing / To blow* wind and fluctuations in underwater pressure are the main reasons for waves. An innovative device has been designed [3]*taking / to take* advantage of variations in wave size and strength. [4]*By moving / To move* up and down on the ocean surface, it produces energy that can be transported to the shore. In the future, it may be possible [5]*establishing / to establish* wave power farms. [6]*Replacing / To replace* coal- or gas-powered energy plants would reduce global carbon emissions.

 Wind farms are another way [7]*to generate / generating* energy from renewable resources. [8]*To make / Making* use of strong winds from the ocean, wind farms are usually constructed on the coast or offshore. Wind turbines make it possible [9]*to convert / converting* mechanical energy into electricity. [10]*To design / Designing* wind turbines requires careful analysis of wind flow direction and speed.

STUDY TIP

The integrated writing task (Writing question 1) tests a wide range of both linguistic and academic skills. It tests your ability to organize your ideas and present them logically and clearly, using correct grammar and appropriate vocabulary.

Test Practice

The following question is similar to question 1 in the writing section (integrated task). In this question, you will read a passage and then listen to part of a lecture on the same topic. The lecture will support, extend, or contradict ideas in the passage.

DICTIONARY SKILLS

POWERED BY COBUILD

Hydraulic comes from the Greek root *hydro* (= *water*) and means *operated by pressure of water*. Use your dictionary to find the meaning of these words connected with water: *hydroelectric, hydrophobia, dehydrate, hydrogen*.

Read the passage and make notes on the left below.

Hydraulic fracturing (also known as fracking) is the process of drilling and injecting fluid into the ground at a high pressure in order to fracture shale rocks to release the natural gas inside. Although this method of extracting oil has been known since the 1940s, it is only recently that new technology has made it possible to extract this oil more cheaply and efficiently. Fracking offers an important new energy source at a time when traditional domestic supplies of coal and gas are diminishing. A new study concludes that the risk of contaminating water supplies is very low if fracking takes place at a depth of many hundreds of meters and the wells are properly constructed. Careful monitoring of chemicals in air and water would reduce any environmental hazards.

🎧 Track 25 Now listen to part of a lecture in an environmental science class and make notes on the right below. Then answer the question. Write your answer in 150 words.

Notes

Reading passage   *Lecture*

Summarize the points made in the lecture, being sure to explain how they cast doubt on the points in the reading passage.

_____

_____

_____

_____

_____

_____

_____

_____

_____

_____

_____

_____

_____

_____

_____

_____

_____

Extra Practice

Complete the following paragraph with the gerund or infinitive form of the verb in parentheses.

Both the reading passage and the lecture are about the process of hydraulic fracturing. In this process, water, chemicals, and sand are driven downward into rocks [1]_____ (access) oil. The reading passage argues in favor of [2]_____ (extract) oil in this way, as it offers an important way [3]_____ (increase) energy production. It suggests that careful [4]_____ (monitor) can reduce any environmental risks. The professor mentions that some researchers are concerned about [5]_____ (introduce) chemicals into the water supply. Others fear that intensive [6]_____ (drill) can trigger small earthquakes. The professor concludes that it is important [7]_____ (not start) large-scale drilling without first [8]_____ (study) the possible long-term impacts on the environment.

TEST TIP: Writing section question 1 (integrated writing task)

The integrated writing task tests a wide range of both linguistic and academic skills. It tests your ability to organize your ideas and present them logically and clearly, using correct grammar and appropriate vocabulary. In order to achieve a high score, identify the major points in the reading passage and the lecture. Then, determine whether the lecturer supports or challenges the points in the reading passage. You should analyze the writing prompt carefully and create an outline for your response. Remember to connect the information from both sources. Organize your response using clear transitions so that it is clear and easy to understand.

Reference words

Study the explanations and examples in the chart. Make your own examples.

OVERVIEW

Pronouns can be used to point back to previously mentioned nouns in the same or a previous sentence. A pronoun usually (but not always) refers to the last noun or nouns that agrees in number and gender, but it can also refer to another previous noun (or clause), depending on the meaning.

Personal pronouns	**he, she, it, they, I, we, you** (subject pronouns)	An Earth-sized planet was discovered in 2011. **It** is a rocky planet that does not have any liquid water.
	his, her, its, their, my, our, your (possessive pronouns)	Many planets orbit very close to **their** sun. **Their** surface temperature is too hot to support life.
	him, her, it, us, me, you, them (object pronouns)	There are eight planets and five dwarf planets in our solar system, although only one of **them** – Earth – is known to be habitable.
Demonstratives	**this, that, these, those** (demonstrative pronouns)	The universe is thought to have up to two billion galaxies containing a possible 200 million trillion planets. Is it possible that only one of **these** has had the capacity to develop life?
	this, that, these, those (demonstrative adjectives can refer back to a noun or a clause)	Stars emit light and for **this** reason they are much easier to detect than planets. Planets do not emit light and **this** makes them more difficult to detect.
Indefinite pronouns	**one, ones** (or **the one, the ones**)	Larger telescopes will enable scientists to photograph more planets. In addition, they will be able to detect smaller **ones**.

Note: Watch out for cases where the referent is separated from the noun it refers to by a long clause or phrase. For example: *Although humans have speculated about life on other planets for centuries, there has been no scientific evidence to suggest that **it** exists.*

Practice Exercises

A Circle the correct noun or clause that each highlighted word refers to.

1. As we discover more planets that are similar in size to Earth, the possibility of finding one that is habitable is becoming more likely.

    a planet   b size   c Earth

2. Some planets may have reservoirs of water or ice beneath their surface where life may exist.

    a planets   b reservoirs   c water or ice

3. Scientists have developed many large telescopes for hunting planets. There are three major ones that are used to locate exoplanets.

    a scientists   b telescopes   c planets

> **WORD BUILDING**
>
> The prefix *tele-* means far away. A *telescope* is an instrument that sees faraway objects. Use your dictionary to find out what these words mean: *teleport, telecommunications, teleworking.*

4. The Kepler telescope transmits data for 100,000 stars. This enables scientists to study multiple stars at once.

    a telescope   b data   c transmits data for 100,000 stars

5. Even if life forms existed on other planets, an asteroid collision or any number of other disasters may have destroyed them.

    a life forms   b planets   c disasters

B Complete the paragraphs with the correct words from the chart.

1. For a planet to support life, ᵃ_____ must lie within a certain zone from ᵇ_____ host star. Planets that are too close to ᶜ_____ star will be too hot. If ᵈ_____ are too far away, there will not be enough light or heat. An Earth-sized planet was discovered in 2011. ᵉ_____ discovery could indicate that our planet is not the only ᶠ_____ that has conditions to support life. ᵍ_____ surface has a temperature of about 767 degrees Celsius (1,410 degrees Fahrenheit). For ʰ_____ reason, it is not capable of sustaining life as we know it.

2. There are eight planets and five dwarf planets in our solar system. It is possible that some of ᵃ_____ may have supported life in the past. Mars and Jupiter's Moon Europa may once have had, or may still have, water under ᵇ_____ surface, but so far there is no concrete evidence to support ᶜ_____. If scientists find evidence of life on these planets, ᵈ_____ is most likely to consist of tiny microbial organisms. To find a planet with signs of life, it will be necessary for scientists to look for ᵉ_____ that is outside our solar system.

STUDY TIP

Find a study partner to help you practice for the test. Find academic articles and make questions for each other based on those you might find in the test. Be sure to include some reference questions. If you cannot find a study partner, practice making your own test questions for academic articles. They will help you understand how the questions are constructed and how the text is organized.

Test Practice

TEST TIP: Reading section (referent questions)

This question asks you to identify the relationship between different parts of the passage. These questions are often about a pronoun, a demonstrative, or a relative pronoun. When making your choice, try substituting your chosen answer for the highlighted word to see if it still makes sense.

Read the passage and answer the questions.

Searching for Exoplanets

[1] The possible discovery of life on other planets has been one of the most tantalizing and challenging questions for science and **one** that recent advances in scientific space technology have brought closer to reality. The search for exoplanets – planets outside our solar system – is one of the newest and most exciting developments in the field of astronomy.

[2] Previously, scientists were only able to find large hot planets that orbit their star within a very close range. These planets are so hot that there is very little likelihood of finding life on them. Larger and more powerful telescopes are now enabling scientists to track down smaller exoplanets. The aim is to find planets that are similar in size to Earth and are in a habitable zone. **This** means that their orbit does not take them so close to the sun that they are extremely hot and not so far away that they do not get enough heat or light for life to form.

[3] One problem in detecting planets is that they do not emit any light, so it is difficult to observe them directly. Telescopes, such as the Kepler telescope launched by NASA in 2009, observe thousands of stars constantly. One method of locating planets is the transit method. When a planet orbits a star, some of the starlight is blocked by the planet, so the star appears to dim slightly. When **this** occurs at regular intervals, it establishes the presence of a planet. This method can be used to measure the planet's size and mass.

[4] The first exoplanet that is similar to the size of Earth was found in 2011. Named Kepler 20-e, it has a radius of approximately 0.87 times that of Earth and has a rocky surface, just like Earth. Its orbit is very close to its star and takes just 6.1 days. **For this reason**, it is extremely hot and does not have the conditions to support water or life.

[5] In the coming years, scientists predict that it is very likely that telescopes will discover more planets that are **Earth-analogues**, and it is possible that some of them will be in the habitable zone.

---

1. What does **one** refer to in paragraph 1?
    - ○ discovery
    - ○ life
    - ○ planet
    - ○ question

2. What does **this** refer to in paragraph 2?
    - ○ to find planets
    - ○ a similar size to Earth
    - ○ in a habitable zone
    - ○ not too hot

3. What does this refer to in paragraph 3?

○ The planet is observed by telescope.　　○ The planet orbits the star.

○ The presence of a planet　　　　　　　○ The star becomes less bright.

4. What does this reason refer to in paragraph 4?

○ It is smaller than Earth.　　　　　　　○ It travels close to its star.

○ Its orbit is six days.　　　　　　　　　○ It has a rocky surface.

5. All of these are true of the Kepler telescope EXCEPT

○ it observes many stars and planets.　　○ it can estimate the size of a planet.

○ it records any decrease in light from stars.　　○ it observes planets directly.

6. Which is closest in meaning to the highlighted word in paragraph 5?

○ They can be reached from Earth.　　　○ They are near to Earth.

○ They are like Earth.　　　　　　　　　○ They are habitable.

7.　An introductory sentence for a summary of the passage is provided below. Complete the summary by selecting the THREE answer options that express the most important ideas in the passage. Some sentences do not belong in the summary because they express ideas that are not presented in the passage or are minor ideas in the passage.

This passage describes the search for exoplanets.

○ _____

○ _____

○ _____

Answer options

1.　New telescopes have made it possible to find planets outside our solar system.

2.　Habitable exoplanets are neither too close nor too far away from their star.

3.　It is easy to identify stars because they emit light.

4.　It may be possible to find life on an exoplanet one day.

5.　Planets without water are often very hot.

6.　Kepler 20-e is slightly smaller than Earth.

The passive

Study the explanations and examples in the chart. Make your own examples based on each rule.

OVERVIEW

The **passive** is used in formal and academic writing to focus attention on the event or the action when the agent of that action is already known, is not important, or is unknown. The subject of a passive sentence is the receiver of the action.

	Explanation	Example
Present	present simple	Oil **is derived** from fossilized organic material.
	is / are + past participle	Coal and oil **are found** under the ocean.
	present continuous	A new oilfield **is being explored** in the Arctic.
	is / are + *being* + past participle	New methods **are being developed**.
Past	past simple	Oil **was discovered** under the North Sea.
	was/were + past participle	Offshore oil platforms **were designed** to withstand ocean waves.
	present perfect	Oil **has been used** in many industries.
	has / have + *been* + past participle	Many products **have been derived** from oil.
	past perfect	Coal **had been extracted** from the mines for several decades before they were exhausted.
	had + *been* + past participle	
Future	*will* + *be* + past participle	New pipelines **will be constructed** in Alaska.
	be going to + *be* + past participle	
	future perfect	Oil reserves **will have been exhausted** by the end of the century.
	will + *have* + *been* + past participle	
Infinitives	passive infinitive (present and past forms)	The new pipeline is supposed **to be completed** by next year.
		It was supposed **to have been finished** last year.
Gerunds	passive infinitive (present and past forms)	The oil company denied **being told** about the leaks.
	passive gerund (present and past forms)	**Having been destroyed** by the storm, the oil well started to leak.
Modals	Passives can be formed with all modals (Ex. *could*, *can*, *may*, *might*, *should*) in present and past forms.	Oil **can be extracted** by drilling.
		Environmental factors **could have been considered** more carefully.
Passive with verbs of perception	Passives with verbs of perception are often used in academic English. They are followed by an infinitive. Ex. *think*, *believe*, *consider*, *predict*, *suppose*, *know*, *estimate*	Oil reserves **are predicted** to run out in a few years' time. Newly discovered oil reserves beneath the Arctic **are considered** to have huge potential.

Notes: 1. To mention the agent of the action, use *by*. For example, *The diamonds were discovered by a team of geologists.* 2. Some verbs cannot form the passive. These are: intransitive verbs (*happen*, *exist*), and verbs that describe states (*belong*, *seem*).

Practice Exercises

A Complete the paragraphs with the passive forms of the verbs provided.

1. Natural gas ª_____ (form) millions of years ago. As thousands of microscopic organisms ᵇ_____ (break down), gas ᶜ_____ (release) and it ᵈ_____ (trap) in the ground. The organic matter ᵉ_____ (turn) into coal or oil. That is why gas reservoirs ᶠ_____ (find) near reserves of fossil fuels.

2. Erosion is the process by which soil and rock ª_____ (remove) from the Earth's surface and then ᵇ_____ (transport) to other locations. Sometimes this ᶜ_____ (do) by natural processes such as wind, rainfall, or rivers. But in recent years, an increasing amount of erosion ᵈ_____ (cause) by human activities.

3. Volcanic lava ª_____ once _____ (think) to be liquid rock that ᵇ_____ (force) upward directly from the Earth's core. The Earth's core ᶜ_____ now _____ (know) ᵈ_____ (compose) of solid rock with a layer of liquid rock between the Earth's crust and the hot core.

B Rewrite each sentence using the passive form.

1. The presence of microfossils can identify oil and gas reserves.

    _____

2. Scientists need to study these fossils under a microscope.

    _____

3. Scientists can remove microfossils by dissolving the surrounding rock.

    _____

4. They will drill holes in the rock and transport rock particles to the surface.

    Holes _____.

5. They have to carry out this analysis under laboratory conditions.

    This analysis _____.

STUDY TIP

Passive constructions are helpful in the writing and speaking sections of the test. For the writing section, using the passive helps to vary your writing and to avoid repetition. It also helps to make your writing sound more objective and academic (but avoid using passives in every sentence!). In the speaking section, it can be helpful to use passives when paraphrasing content from the academic reading and lecture in question 3 and when summarizing the lecture in question 4.

Test Practice

Read the passage and answer the questions.

Paleolithic Cave Paintings

The Chauvet-Pont-d'Arc Cave is the location of some of the most famous prehistoric paintings in the world. Located in southern France, the cave was discovered in 1994 by a small team of cavers led by Jean-Marie Chauvet, after whom the cave was named. Not only are they some of the most beautiful prehistoric paintings ever discovered, they are also the earliest known. They are estimated to be between 30,000 and 33,000 years old. It is thought that the entrance to the cave was covered up by a landslide and as a result, the cave had been untouched until it was discovered in 1994. Due to the dry climate conditions inside the sealed cave, the paintings were more or less perfectly preserved.

Hundreds of animal paintings have been analyzed and recorded. At least 13 different species of animals are depicted, including some rarely or never found in other ice-age paintings. What is unusual about the choice of subject matter is that rather than depicting only familiar animals, such as horses, cattle, and mammoths, the Chauvet paintings also show many predatory animals, such as lions, panthers, bears, and hyenas. Typical of most paleolithic art, there are no complete human figures, although there is one partial female figure. There are also reddish-brown handprints and abstract marks – lines and dots – that are found throughout the cave.

The sophistication and beauty of these paintings have overturned long-held beliefs about the nature of paleolithic art. Although it is impossible to know the specific purpose of the paintings, it is believed that there may have been a religious, magical, or ritualistic use. Were they an attempt to communicate with spirits of the cave, or perhaps an expression of something seen in a trance? In addition to providing valuable scientific evidence, they raise tantalizing questions about why paeliolithic humans created these beautiful if still mysterious images.

---

1. Which is true of the Chauvet-Pont-d'Arc Cave paintings?

    ○ They were damaged by a landslide.

    ○ They did not portray horses.

    ○ They depict religious rituals.

    ○ They depict extinct animals.

2. Which word is closest in meaning the word predatory?

    ○ animals that eat plants

    ○ animals that hunt other animals

    ○ animals that are extinct

    ○ animals that can be eaten

3. What is implied in paragraph 3 about previously held opinions of paleolithic art?

   ○ They were thought to be simple and plain.

   ○ They did not include animals.

   ○ They were used for magic or religion.

   ○ They provide a record of prehistoric life.

4. Which of the following best expresses the essential information in the highlighted sentence?

   ○ Scientists are not sure if the paintings had a religious purpose.

   ○ Scientists are fairly certain that their purpose was religious.

   ○ The paintings do not provide any evidence of their purpose.

   ○ The paintings may have had many different purposes.

5. An introductory sentence for a brief summary of the passage is provided below. Complete the summary by selecting the THREE choices that express the most important ideas in the passage. Some sentences do not belong in the summary because they express ideas that are not presented in the passage or are minor ideas in the passage. This question is worth two points.

   The passage discusses the unique aspects of the Chauvet-Pont-d'Arc cave paintings.

   ○ _____

   ○ _____

   ○ _____

   Answer options

   1. The paintings are the oldest ever discovered.

   2. There aren't any human figures in the paintings.

   3. The paintings depict a wide variety of animals.

   4. The caves provide evidence of highly developed artistic skills.

   5. Scientists have carefully analyzed the paintings.

   6. The caves provide answers to many questions.

TEST TIP: Reading section (sentence summary questions)

The correct answer for a sentence summary question correctly rewords and simplifies the information from the original sentence. It will contain the essential information from the original sentence. Incorrect answers contradict or leave something out from the original sentence. Try paraphrasing the sentence in your own words before reading the answer options.

Conjunctions

Study the explanations and examples in the chart. Make your own examples.

OVERVIEW

Conjunctions are used to join clauses into one sentence and show the relationship between them. **Coordinating conjunctions** join two main (independent) clauses. **Subordinating conjunctions** join a main clause and a subordinate clause. The subordinate clause contains information that is less important than in the main clause.

Conjunction	Explanation	Example
Coordinating conjunctions		
and	adds information	Glaciers are rivers of ice, **and** (they) are known for their gradual pace.
but / yet	contrasts information	Most glaciers move about 30 centimeters a day, **but** some move at a much faster rate.
or	shows two alternatives	Increased glacial speeds can cause earthquakes, **or** (they can) send large amounts of ice into the ocean.
so	links a cause and a result	Glacial earthquakes are usually in uninhabited areas, **so** they do not cause much damage.
Subordinating conjunctions: Cause and result		
because / since / as	introduces a cause	Glacial earthquakes do not cause much damage **because** they are usually located in uninhabited areas.
so that	introduces a result	Glaciers move very slowly **so that** it is impossible to detect their movement with the naked eye.
Subordinating conjunctions: Contrast		
although / while	introduces a contradictory idea	**While** glacial earthquakes have limited effects, fast-moving glaciers can have a greater impact.
Subordinating conjunctions: Time sequence		
as / when / while	introduces something that happens at the same time as another event	**As** glaciers move forward, they carve deep holes in the valley floor.
when / as soon as / once / after	introduces the first in a sequence of two events	**After** the ice has melted, the holes fill with water to make lakes.
before / until	introduces the second in a sequence of two events	Glaciers transport rocks and ice downhill for many miles **before** they reach the ocean. Icebergs do not usually form **until** the glacier reaches the ocean.
Subordinating conjunctions: Condition		
when / whenever / if	introduces something that enables another event to happen (for more about *if*, see Grammar Unit 6)	**When** a glacier moves at a fast pace, it loses massive amounts of ice.

Notes: 1. With coordinating conjunctions, the subject can be omitted in the second clause if it is the same as in the first. 2. Notice the use of commas with subordinate clauses.

Practice Exercises

A Complete the sentences with a suitable conjunction. Sometimes more than one is possible.

after	although	and	as	because	but	since	so	when
whenever	while							

1. Rock erosion is caused by human activities, _____ it is also caused by wind, water, and ice.

2. Rainwater forms pools on the rock surface, _____ is trapped within tiny cracks.

3. _____ water turns to ice, it expands.

4. The water expands and contracts inside them, _____ the rocks start to break up.

5. In desert regions, rocks are rapidly heated up by the sun _____ they expand.

6. _____ the rocks cool down and contract, small pieces of rock break off.

7. Dry soil is eroded more easily _____ there is insufficient vegetation to hold it down.

8. _____ erosion is a natural process, it has been dramatically increased by the effects of human activities.

B Choose the sentence that best expresses the essential information in the sentence.

1. Since the cultivation of crops requires the clearing of existing vegetation, large areas of land are deprived of plant cover and become vulnerable to erosion.

   a Clearing land for crops is increasing erosion.

   b Erosion is occurring because there are too many crops.

   c There is too much erosion so plants cannot grow.

   d Planting crops will prevent erosion.

2. Although the erosion caused by storms is not as destructive as that produced during hurricanes and tornadoes, the amount of soil loss can be significant, especially when storms repeatedly affect a given region.

   a When storms occur, they cause soil erosion.

   b Storms are not very destructive because they are not strong.

   c Storms can cause soil erosion over a long time period.

   d Hurricanes cause more erosion than storms.

3. Because melting ice is causing sea levels to rise, habitats of humans as well as multitudes of other organisms will be in danger of being washed away.

   a Habitats are being destroyed by melting ice.

   b Ice is melting because sea levels are rising.

   c As sea levels rise, habitats are being destroyed.

   d Sea levels are rising so ice is melting.

WORD BUILDING

The root word *habit* means *to live in a place*. Use your dictionary to find the meaning of these words: *habitat, habitable, uninhabitable, inhabit, inhabitant.*

STUDY TIP

Using conjunctions correctly will help you in the writing and speaking sections of the test. Review your written work and notice if you have used a variety of conjunctions. Find places where you could add conjunctions to connect your ideas better. You should use a variety of conjunctions in the speaking section, too. For example, in question 1 (choice) you might start your response as follows: *Although some people prefer to travel alone, I prefer to travel with a friend because ...*; *Although I studied many different subjects at school, my favorite subject was always history.* Using *although* in this way shows that you have considered the opposing point of view.

Test Practice

Listen to part of a seminar in a geology class. Take notes as you listen. Then answer the questions.

Track 26

1. How does the professor explain plate tectonics?

   ○ By giving three examples

   ○ By describing three categories

   ○ By comparing three theories

   ○ By describing three steps in a process

2. Why does the professor mention Japan?

   ○ To give an example of convergent movement

   ○ To explain why volcanoes occur

   ○ To contrast convergent and divergent movements

   ○ To describe two kinds of material in the Earth's crust

Track 27

3. Listen. Why does the professor say this?

   ○ To check if students have understood the information so far

   ○ To find out how much students already know

   ○ To test students on information from the last lecture

   ○ To ask for students' opinions

4. Why does oceanic crust get compressed?

   ○ Because there is volcanic activity

   ○ Because it is under the ocean

   ○ Because it is weaker than continental crust

   ○ Because it is on a plate boundary

5. Match each type of tectonic movement with the correct description.

   Place a check mark (✓) in the correct boxes.

	Plates are pressed together	Gaps are formed between plates	There is volcanic activity
convergent			
divergent			
conservative			

When you take notes while listening, use symbols to express relationships between different ideas. For example:

→ (so, therefore)	b/c (because)	+ (and)	w. (when or while)
> (greater than)	< (less than)	b4 (before)	w/o (without)
ex. (example)	= (equal to)	esp. (especially)	

Extra Practice

🎧 Track 26

A In question 4 in the speaking section (academic summary), you will listen to a lecture and take notes. Then you will be asked to give a spoken summary of the information. Listen again and makes notes on the main ideas of the lecture. Remember to organize your notes clearly and use abbreviations.

> Notes

B Using points and examples from the lecture, explain the different types of tectonic plate movements. Write your spoken response here (or record your response and write the transcript here).

_____

_____

_____

_____

_____

_____

_____

_____

_____

_____

_____

_____

Relative clauses

Study the explanations and examples in the chart. Make your own examples.

OVERVIEW

Relative clauses provide additional information about a preceding noun.

Relative pronoun	Explanation	Example
A **restrictive relative clause** provides information that helps to define the noun. It can refer to the subject or the object of the preceding clause. Commas are not used.		
which, who, that, where, why	Use **which** or **that** for things or places, **who** or **that** for people, **where** for places, and **why** for reasons.	A child → **who / that** has not yet acquired language will point to objects. Language is a system of signs or symbols **that** represents things.
whose	Use **whose** when the clause describes something that belongs to the noun in the previous sentences (a person or a thing).	Children **whose** language skills have not yet developed will have difficulty explaining whether they understand a concept.
who or **whom**	Use **whom** when referring to a person who is the object. (*Whom* is more common in formal writing, especially after a preposition.)	Piaget is the behavioral scientist **to whom** many refer when discussing theories of cognitive development.
Omission of relative pronoun	The relative pronoun (except *whose*) can be omitted in clauses that refer to the object.	Intelligence is not something (**that**) you can easily measure.
Relative clauses with prepositions (who, whom, which)	In formal English, the preposition is placed before the relative pronoun.	The stage of development **at which** a child learns to remember objects usually occurs before two years old.
A **non-restrictive relative clause** provides additional information that is not essential to defining the noun. Commas are used to separate the clause from the rest of the sentence.		
which, who, whom, where (Note: These are not omitted in object clauses.)	Use **which** for things or places, **who** for people, **where** for places.	Language use, **which** shows evidence of symbolic thinking, does not develop until about two years of age.
which	**Which** can also refer back to a whole clause (see referent pronouns Grammar Unit 11).	Piaget designed tasks to measure children's intelligence, **which** led him to develop his theory of cognitive development.

Practice Exercises

WORD BUILDING

The root word *phobia* means *fear* or *extreme dislike*. Use your dictionary to find the meanings of these words: *claustrophobia, xenophobia, arachnophobia.*

A Combine the sentences into one sentence using relative clauses.

1.   A phobia is an irrational fear of a specific object, situation, or activity. It is accompanied by an intense wish to escape.

_____

_____

2.   Agoraphobia is a phobia. It is a fear of open spaces. People most often seek treatment for it.

_____

3.   Agoraphobia may be caused by stress. It is very difficult to treat. This may be connected to the cause of the phobia.

_____

4.   Agoraphobia is a complex condition. We don't fully understand the causes of it and there is so single explanation for it.

_____

B Complete the passage by writing the letter of each relative clause in the correct place.

> ### The Concept of Personal Space
>
> Personal space is the invisible area of space [1]_____. This personal space is important as it protects us from other people, [2]_____. The boundaries of this space vary depending on the people [3]_____. It also varies according to the culture [4]_____. In countries [5]_____, you can cause offence by standing too close to another person. Conversely, people [6]_____, could cause offence in countries [7]_____. Research also suggests that there is a difference between the personal space of men and women. Women tend to have a smaller personal space with friends than with people [8]_____. Men, [9]_____, especially when interacting with other men, have a more similar size of space for people [10]_____.

a   in which we live

b   that they dislike

c   they like and dislike

d   where personal space is larger

e   where personal space is smaller

f   which is why we feel uncomfortable if the space is invaded

g   that surrounds each individual person

h   who stand too far away

i   whose personal space is generally larger

j   with whom we interact

STUDY TIP

Using relative clauses correctly will help you in the writing and speaking sections of the test. Review your written work and find places where you could combine sentences using relative clauses. You can use relative clauses in the speaking section, too. For example, in question 1 of the speaking section (choice) you might include sentences such as: *People who travel alone don't have the chance to discuss their experiences, but people who travel with a friend can exchange opinions all the time. Traveling with a friend is something that I have always enjoyed because … .*

Test Practice

Read the passage and answer the questions.

Cognitive Development

The theory of cognitive development that was proposed by Jean Piaget and first published in the 1920s was based on observations and tests that were carried out with children of various ages and were designed to measure intelligence and development of conceptual understanding.

Piaget theorized that children's knowledge and understanding develops as a result of maturation of the brain and develops in the same way in all children, but that intelligence is something that depends on interaction between children and their environment. He concluded that knowledge develops through the construction of progressively more complex concepts.

He proposed four major stages of development that take place at different stages of childhood, and which progress from simple exploration of the environment through the baby's sense of sight, sound, taste, and touch, to symbolic thinking and the ability to understand manipulation of concrete forms and ideas.

One of the main difficulties in researching child cognition is to find ways of measuring how much the child knows, especially with children whose limited language makes it difficult to find out what they are thinking. It is clearly possible for children to develop concepts before they develop the ability to express them in language.

There has since been scientific criticism of the methods that Piaget used to carry out his research, which has cast doubt on the validity of his theories. Although Piaget's research tasks did not necessarily involve language, some of them were conceptually complex from the child's point of view, which may have affected the child's ability to do the task. Another factor he did not take into account was the social context, as it has been shown that children easily respond to the hints and cues provided by an adult and may try to give answers that the adult wants or expects.

Notwithstanding the criticisms of Piaget's research methods, his theories have provided the basis for research in the field of cognitive development. Subsequent research has largely supported the conceptual abilities he identified and the sequence and stages of their development, although they may not be as clearly defined as he suggested.

---

1. The word progressively in the passage is closest in meaning to

   ○ interestingly.

   ○ increasingly.

   ○ importantly.

   ○ rapidly.

2. According to paragraph 2, children

   ○ develop concepts at different ages depending on their environment.

   ○ continually develop conceptual knowledge as they get older.

   ○ need to interact with people to develop complex conceptual knowledge.

   ○ have similar conceptual process to those of an adult.

3. What is implied in paragraph 4?

   ○ Children can express complex concepts.

   ○ Children can understand concepts that they cannot express.

   ○ Children can talk about concepts before understanding them.

   ○ Children can talk about concepts they don't understand.

WORD BUILDING

The root word *cogn-* means *think*. Use your dictionary to find the meaning of these words: *cognate, cognition, recognize.*

4.   The word which in the passage refers to

○ research.

○ methods.

○ criticism.

○ theories.

5.   Which of the following best expresses the essential information in the highlighted sentence in the passage? *Incorrect* answer choices change the meaning in important ways or leave out essential information.

○ The children misunderstood the task.

○ The researcher misinterpreted the results.

○ The children were unable to explain their answers.

○ The researcher influenced the results.

6.   An introductory sentence for a brief summary of the passage is provided below. Complete the summary by selecting the THREE answer options that express the most important ideas in the passage. Some sentences do not belong in the summary because they express ideas that are not presented in the passage or are minor ideas in the passage.

Piaget's cognitive development theory is a way of understanding how intelligence develops in children.

○ _____

○ _____

○ _____

Choose 3 answers.

1.   Children's cognitive abilities develop in fixed stages according to age.

2.   Children's intelligence varies according to interaction with their environment.

3.   Children are easily influenced by adult expectations.

4.   A challenge is measuring the ability of children with learning difficulties.

5.   Overall, Piaget's research has been accepted in the area of cognitive development.

6.   It was difficult for children to do Piaget's research tasks because of the complex language.

TEST TIP: Reading section (sentence summary questions)

First, read the sentence and try to paraphrase it. Then read all the options. Eliminate options that are incorrect. In the remaining options, ask yourself these questions: Is there a contradictory detail? Is there a change in meaning? Has any extra information been added?

Office hours conversations

Read the examples. Think of your own examples based on situations that you have experienced.

OVERVIEW

Asking about a problem

How's everything going?	**How is** your research topic **coming along**?
How's … been going?	**Are you having any trouble** finding a topic?
How is your … coming along?	
How are you getting on with …?	
Are you having any trouble (with) …?	
Are you here to ask me about …?	

Asking for advice

Can you help me with …?	**I was wondering if I could talk to you about** the assignment.
I'd like to ask you about … .	
I have a couple of questions about … .	
I was wondering if I could talk to you about … .	
Would you be able to help me with …?	

Describing a problem

The thing is … .	**The thing is**, I'm having trouble keeping up with the assignment dates.
Well, one issue is … .	**I'm not sure** how to go about collecting data for my research project.
I have a concern about … .	
I'm worried about … .	
I'm not sure what to do about … .	
I was wondering if I should … .	

Offering advice

Have you thought of …?	**Have you tried** accessing information on the college website?
How about …?	**One option might be** to research news reports of that time period.
Maybe … could help.	
Have you already tried …?	
One option might be to … .	
It might be a good idea to try … .	

Responding to advice

Expressing a positive response	Sure! Definitely! You bet! Good idea!
	No problem. Sure thing.
	I hadn't thought of that. You're right. Why not?
Expressing doubt	I'm not sure that's a good idea. I don't know if that would work. I have one concern about that. That might not be the best idea.

Practice Exercises

A Complete the conversation with words from the box.

could I	have you thought of	how's it	I can see	I'm not sure about
I'm wondering	no problem	one concern	quick question	the thing is

Student: Excuse me, Professor Taylor. ¹_____ ask you a ²_____?

Professor: Sure. ³_____ been going with your research project?

Student: Well, ⁴_____, that's what I wanted to ask you about. I'm worried about the topic I chose. ⁵_____ if it's really broad enough. I'm researching the effects of recent fuel price increases on local businesses.

Professor: OK, so can you tell me why you think there's a problem?

Student: Well, ⁶_____ I have is that most people I interviewed gave similar answers, so there isn't much variety.

Professor: I see, well, ⁷_____ adapting your interview questions and interviewing them again?

Student: Well, ⁸_____ that because they're usually very busy, you see. They can't spare the time to help me.

Professor: Yes, I can see that. In that case, how about interviewing just one person in more depth? You could analyze their responses in more detail.

Student: Yes. ⁹_____ how that would work. Thanks so much for your help.

Professor: ¹⁰_____.

> **DICTIONARY SKILLS**
>
> ⟨Ɛ POWERED BY COBUILD
>
> Use your dictionary to find synonyms and antonyms. For example, two synonyms of the word *worried* are: *anxious* and *concerned*. Two antonyms of *worried* are: *relaxed* and *calm*.

B Match the sentences on the left with the most appropriate responses on the right.

1. Are you having trouble with the assignment? _____
2. Could I ask you about the research project? _____
3. How's everything been going this semester? _____
4. Have you tried accessing the website? _____
5. I was wondering if I should change my topic. _____
6. Would it be OK to change my topic? _____

   a What's the problem with it?
   b No, I'm worried about the presentation.
   c I'm sure it would be fine.
   d Yes, what do you want to know?
   e Just great! I'm really enjoying your class.
   f I tried that, but I couldn't find the information.

C Number the sentences in the conversation in the best order.

_____ Professor: Diana, I'm sorry I can't do that. It wouldn't be fair to the other students.

_____ Professor: Hi, Diana, of course! Let me guess … is it about last week's lecture?

_____ Professor: Oh yes. How's that going?

_____ Professor: Well, you still have a couple of weeks. I'm sure you'll be fine.

_____ Student: Do you think I could get an extension? I really need a few more days.

_____ Student: Hi, Professor Ezzaki. Could I ask you a quick question?

_____ Student: No … actually it's about the final paper.

_____ Student: OK. Thank you, anyway.

_____ Student: Well, I haven't started writing it yet. I've been overloaded with work recently.

D Read the following exchanges and identify the purpose of the visit.

1. A: I was wondering if I could talk to you about the final project.

   B: Of course. I'm guessing that you need help with research. I can recommend a couple of books if you like.

   A: I appreciate that but what I really want to talk about is the format of my project.

   The student

   ○ needs help with her project.

   ○ needs ideas for her topic.

   ○ doesn't understand the topic.

   ○ wants help with the design of her project.

2. A: Hi, Professor, is this a good time? Could I talk to you about my final paper?

   B: Yes! How far along are you? You know, it's due this Friday.

   A: Well, I've outlined it but I haven't started writing yet because I've been so overloaded.

   The student

   ○ needs help with his topic.

   ○ needs ideas for his topic.

   ○ wants more time to write his paper.

   ○ wants the professor to review his outline.

3. A: Hi, Sanjay, how's everything going? Do you have questions about the midterm?

   B: Well, I'm having a problem with the assignment. I haven't been able to find many references.

   A: Oh, I see. Well, have you tried accessing the library electronic database?

   The student

   ○ wants advice about the test.

   ○ needs advice on researching the topic.

   ○ wants help with choosing a topic.

   ○ asks for help with using the library.

STUDY TIP

Office hours conversations in the listening section are spoken at a natural speed. In conversational English, individual words are not always pronounced carefully and precisely. They tend to get shortened and run into each other. For example, _going to_ is often pronounced as _gonna_, and _what do you_ can sound like _whaddaya_. It is very important to get used to listening to American conversational English at natural speeds. Speak with native speakers of American English as much as possible, and listen to American TV and radio shows and movies. Please also note that the Listening section can include native-speaker English accents from the U.K., New Zealand and Australia as well as North America.

Test Practice

Track 28

Listen to part of a conversation between a student and a professor and take notes. Then answer the questions.

1. Why does the student visit the professor?
   - ○ To ask a question about the test
   - ○ To ask the professor about her research topic
   - ○ To ask the professor to recommend which books to read
   - ○ To get advice about revising her research project

2. What can be inferred about the student's visit?
   - ○ She usually sees this professor at this time every week.
   - ○ She confirmed the meeting earlier with the professor.
   - ○ She did not make an appointment to see the professor.
   - ○ It is not during the professor's office hours.

3. What can be inferred about the student?
   - ○ She has not written many research papers.
   - ○ She is not good at describing her research.
   - ○ She finds the research project difficult.
   - ○ She has not done much research about her topic.

4. What is implied about the student's project?
   - ○ The details are not clearly organized.
   - ○ The conclusions are too general.
   - ○ The arguments are not related to the topic.
   - ○ There are insufficient references.

5. What is the professor's attitude to the student's work?
   - ○ He is doubtful whether it will pass.
   - ○ It will need a lot of work to be acceptable.
   - ○ It has good points but needs some improvement.
   - ○ It needs to be completely rewritten.

TEST TIP: Listening section (office hours conversations)

Office hours are the hours when a professor is available in his or her office to see students individually. At the start of the audio, pay close attention to who the speakers are. This will be announced by the narrator and will help you predict what the conversation could be about. If the conversation is between a student and a professor, topics may include questions about grades, help with assignments, requests for extensions, or clarification of topics discussed in class. The first question is often a gist-purpose question asking about the purpose of the student's visit.

Causatives

Study the explanations and examples in the chart. Make your own examples based on each rule.

OVERVIEW

A **causative** is a verb that indicates that some person or thing helps to make something happen. It is followed by another verb.

Verbs	Examples
Verb + object + infinitive	
allow, *cause*, *enable*, *encourage*, *force*, *help*, *persuade*, *require* (infinitive with *to*)	Using the internet can **encourage** learners **to be** more independent. Communicating on social media can **cause** teenagers **to feel** a sense of connection. Learning online **enables** students **to learn** at their own pace.
have, *help*, *let*, *make* (infinitive without *to*)	Researchers studied whether watching TV **made children behave** differently. They **had groups of children watch** TV and then monitored their behavior afterward.
Verb + object + *from* + gerund	
discourage, *forbid*, *prevent*, *prohibit*, *stop*	Communicating on social media can **discourage children from spending** time in person with their friends. Some parents set time limits to **prevent their children from spending** too much time on their phones.
Passive forms	
These verbs can also be used in the passive (except for *have* and *let*, which have no passive form). Note that *make* is followed by an infinitive with *to* in the passive.	Teenagers **may be encouraged to** do better academically if they participate in sport. Children **could be discouraged from** face-to-face communication by using social media. Sometimes students **are made to** switch off their phones during lessons.

Note: There is another use of *have* as a causative: *to have something done*. Ex. *We had our TV repaired.* (= *We asked someone to repair our TV for us.*)

Practice Exercises

A Write two sentences using the words provided, one in the active and one in the passive form. The word in parentheses can be omitted in the passive sentence.

1. (schools) / should / allow / students / study any subject they like

_____

_____

2. (they) / students / prohibit / use cell phones / during the test

_____

_____

3. (some parents) / require / teenagers / limit their screen time

_____

_____

B Rewrite each sentence using the word in parentheses. You may need to add or change some words.

1. Teenagers who participate in sport at school are more confident. (make)

_____

_____

2. When children are watching TV, they have less opportunity to interact with other people. (discourage)

_____

_____

3. Teachers should tell their students to report online bullying. (encourage)

_____

_____

4. Schools should give students plenty of free time to socialize with their friends. (let)

_____

_____

STUDY TIP

Causatives are also useful in the speaking section and in the writing section of the test. Question 1 in the speaking section asks for your opinion on a topic. For example: _Do you think that technology enables students to study more or less effectively?_ When answering this question, you could say what the internet enables, allows, or helps students to do.

In the independent writing task, you may be asked for your opinion on whether something should be required or allowed, and why. In this case, you can support your argument by saying what kind of behavior would be encouraged or discouraged by this change.

Test Practice

A The following questions are similar to those in the writing section of the test (independent writing task). Write two sentences in answer to each question using verbs from the chart.

1. Some people think that students should be allowed to study any subjects they want at school. Do you agree or disagree?

   _____

   _____

   _____

   _____

2. Some people think that the internet has improved communication between people. Others think that it discourages people from speaking to each other in person. What is your opinion?

   _____

   _____

   _____

   _____

B The following is similar to question 1 in the writing section (integrated writing task). Read the passage and take notes.

> The influence of media on aggression was first investigated by Bandura in the 1960s and formed the basis of social learning theory, which states that we learn not only by reinforcement but also by observing others.
>
> In his famous Bobo Doll experiments, Bandura had children watch a video of an adult who displayed aggressive behavior toward a doll, while the control group watched a non-violent video. Afterward he let the children play with a range of toys, including the doll, and observed them to see how many incidents of aggressive behavior occurred.
>
> The results of this experiment showed that children who had watched the violent video displayed more aggressive behavior toward the doll afterward.
>
> Furthermore, he found that when the adult in the video was punished for being aggressive, this discouraged children from behaving aggressively. Conversely, when the adult was rewarded for being aggressive, this encouraged children to behave more aggressively.
>
> Finally, he found that when children were asked to reproduce the actions on the video, all the children were able to do so. This shows that even if children did not behave aggressively, they had still observed and learned the behavior.
>
> Bandura theorized from this that watching aggressive behavior in media such as movies or TV encouraged children to imitate the behavior and to become more violent.

Notes

Reading passage	Lecture
1.	1.
2.	2.
3.	3.

 Now listen to part of a lecture in a sociology class and take notes.

Track 29 Summarize the points made in the lecture, being sure to explain how they cast doubt on the points made in the reading passage. Write your response here (150–225 words).

_____

_____

_____

_____

_____

_____

_____

_____

_____

_____

_____

_____

_____

_____

_____

_____

TEST TIP: Writing section question 1 (integrated writing task)

In this question, you will be graded not only on grammar and vocabulary, but also on your ability to communicate clearly in writing and on how well your essay demonstrates the relationship between the points in the lecture and those in the reading passage. Remember to write a clear introduction and conclusion. The introduction should describe the main claim made in the reading passage and whether the professor supports or challenges the claim. For example, _The reading passage argues that … . However, the professor disagrees by stating that … ._

Introductory *there* and *it*

Study the rules and examples in the chart. Make your own examples.

OVERVIEW

There and **it** can be used as the subject of a sentence. They are sometimes known as "empty" subjects.	
There	
There + *be* + noun	**There has been** considerable progress in our understanding of animal intelligence.
	There are studies that show that some animals have excellent memories.
There + *be* + *no* / *many* / *some* / *several* / *a few* + noun	**There is no doubt** that some animals are more intelligent than others.
	There are several ways to measure intelligence in animals.
There + passive reporting verb + infinitive	**There is supposed to be** a relationship between brain size and intelligence.
	There are thought to be many different ways that whales communicate with each other.
There + adjective	**There is likely** to be more research in the future.
	There are certain to be many benefits from this study.
It	
It + *is* + adjective + clause	**It is true** that some animals can use tools and solve problems.
	It isn't clear whether all animals can learn to use tools.
It + *is* + adjective + infinitive	**It is possible** to measure perceptual processes.
	It is difficult to determine cognitive understanding.
It + passive reporting verb (impersonal passive)	**It has been argued** that animals can solve problems using abstract reasoning.
	It is sometimes thought that studying animals will help us understand the human brain.
It + *appear* / *seem* / *look as if*	**It looks as if** different species of animals have different cognitive processes.
	It **appears** likely that different species have different abilities.

Note: 1. After *there*, the verb agrees with the following noun. 2. Be careful not to overuse sentences that use *there* or *it* as a subject. Use them to add variety to your writing, but if you find there are too many, move the *real* subject to the front, as in practice exercise A opposite.

Practice Exercises

A Rewrite each sentence using the word provided so that it has the same meaning.

1. A great deal of research has been carried out in the study of animal intelligence.

    There _____.

2. Scientists use several criteria to determine an animal's cognitive skills.

    There _____

    _____.

3. Some studies provide evidence that animals can solve problems.

    There _____

    _____.

4. Scientists were able to teach a kind of sign language to a family of chimpanzees.

    It _____.

5. Animals that are able to recognize their own image are unusual.

    It _____.

DICTIONARY SKILLS

⊆ POWERED BY COBUILD

Use your dictionary to find the meaning of other expressions with *it* and *there*: Examples: *It's a good idea. It takes ages. It's not worth it. It's time to leave. There's nothing wrong. There's time to spare.*

B Complete the sentences with the words from the box.

considered	easy	important	likely	many examples	research
	some evidence		some expressions		

Nonverbal Language

There has been a great deal of ¹_____ into the universality of human facial expressions. There is ²_____ to suggest that there are ³_____ that are universal to all cultures. It seems ⁴_____ that people of all cultures interpret facial expressions such as smiling or frowning in the same way. However, it is ⁵_____ to realize that, unlike facial expressions, not all body language is universal. Although it is ⁶_____ to assume that gestures we have learned in our own culture have the same meaning in other cultures, there are ⁷_____ of gestures that can have an unintended meaning. For example, in some cultures, putting one's hands in one's pockets indicates a relaxed attitude whereas in others it is ⁸_____ very impolite.

C Complete the sentences with your own ideas to answer the question.

What do you think is the most interesting thing about researching animal behavior?

1. There is no doubt that _____.

2. It is possible that _____.

3. There are some basic differences between _____.

4. It is clear that _____.

5. There is some evidence to show that _____.

6. It is not certain whether _____.

STUDY TIP

When you read an academic article, practice taking notes using charts and diagrams. This will help you to answer the questions, as well as giving you practice with note-taking techniques.

Identify uses of *there* and *it* as a subject and try to paraphrase them. When you finish reading an article or listening to a lecture, try to paraphrase the whole article in your own words.

Test Practice

Read the passage and answer the questions.

The Purpose of Sleep

There has been much scientific research and discussion of the purpose of sleep. Although most scientists agree that sleep is essential to maintaining a healthy state, not all researchers agree on why.

The development of the electroencephalograph has allowed scientists to measure electrical patterns of activity produced by the brain while it is asleep. By recording brain waves during sleep, it has been possible to develop a description of five different stages of sleep. Stage one is shallow sleep and marks the transition between being awake and being asleep. Stage two features two forms of brain waves known as spindles and K-complexes. Stages three and four are the deepest sleep, often referred to as slow-wave sleep. The fifth stage is known as REM (rapid eye movement) because it is accompanied by rapid, jerky eye movements.

There are several theories for why sleep is important. One theory suggests that periods of activity and inactivity were a part of evolutionary development and are a means of conserving energy. According to this theory, all species adapt to sleep during periods of time when they need energy the least, so that they can have more energy at times when they need to hunt, or when there is a chance of danger. It appears, for example, that animals that have few natural predators, such as bears and lions, often sleep between 12 to 15 hours each day. Animals that have many natural predators, however, sleep for only short periods, usually no more than four or five hours each day.

A second theory is that sleep is essential for maintaining the physiological processes that keep the body and mind healthy. It has been suggested that shallow sleep is important for restoring physiological functions, while REM sleep is essential in restoring mental functions. In support of this theory, it is clear that when we are deprived of sleep, or after strenuous physical activity, we tend to sleep longer the next night or spend longer in deep sleep.

A third theory suggests that sleep is necessary in order to process information that has been acquired during the day. There is some research to suggest that memories are transferred from short-term memory to long-term memory during sleep. During sleep, the brain forgets unimportant information, and makes room for new information. There is no doubt that lack of sleep can affect our cognitive function. A study of college students found that students performed better in exams after a good night's sleep.

1. The word strenuous in paragraph 4 is closest in meaning to

   ○ lengthy.

   ○ tiring.

   ○ healthy.

   ○ important.

2. According to paragraph 3, some animals sleep very little because

   ○ they are afraid.

   ○ they are small.

   ○ they are not tired.

   ○ they need to hunt.

3. Why does the author mention college students in paragraph 5?

   ○ To differentiate between long- and short-term memory

   ○ To show how long-term memory affects exam performance

   ○ To provide an example of how lack of sleep affects the brain's function

   ○ To illustrate the purpose of sleep

4. An introductory sentence for a brief summary of the passage is provided below. Complete the summary by selecting the THREE answer options that express the most important ideas in the passage. Some sentences do not belong in the summary because they express ideas that are not presented in the passage or are minor ideas in the passage.

   New research methods now allow us to study sleep, which is essential in keeping us healthy.

   ○ _____

   ○ _____

   ○ _____

   Choose 3 answers.

   1. The animals that sleep least are natural predators that need to hunt often.

   2. There are different stages of sleep, each of which has a different function.

   3. College students have improved exam results after a good sleep.

   4. Sleep helps us to save energy so that we have energy when we need to be active.

   5. During sleep, humans process the information picked up while awake.

   6. REM sleep is characterized by jerky movements.

Paraphrasing

Study the examples in the chart. Think of other ways to paraphrase these sentences.

OVERVIEW

Paraphrasing means restating something in your own words. There are often multiple ways of paraphrasing a sentence or a paragraph, but it is important that the meaning of the paraphrase be the same as the original.	
Comparative structures (see Grammar Unit 4)	
Navigation was far more difficult in ancient times than it is today.	Navigation is easier today than it was in ancient times.
Maps were less accurate in those days than they are today.	Maps were not as accurate then as they are today.
Active / passive structures (see Grammar Unit 12)	
Many voyages of exploration in the 16th century were funded by the kings of Spain and Portugal.	The kings of Spain and Portugal funded many voyages of exploration in the 16th century.
New trade routes were discovered from Europe to India and China.	Explorers discovered new trade routes from Europe to India and China.
Prepositions (see Vocabulary Unit 18)	
Owing to the 16th-century voyages of exploration, navigators learned new methods of navigation.	Methods of navigation improved because of the explorations of 16th-century voyages of exploration.
In addition to observing the stars, they navigated by measuring speed and direction.	They navigated by observing the stars, as well as by measuring speed and direction.
Conjunctions (see Grammar Unit 13)	
When Columbus returned from his voyage, he established contacts between Old and New Worlds.	Before Columbus's voyage, there had been no contact between Old and New Worlds.
They knew that the earth was round but they did not know the extent of the oceans.	They did not know the extent of the oceans, although they knew that the Earth was round.
Modals (see Grammar Unit 5)	
The effects of his arrival couldn't have been more significant.	It is not possible to overestimate the effects of his arrival.
Some historians consider that this event may have been the beginning of the process of globalization.	This event may be considered the beginning of the process of globalization.

Note: To paraphrase successfully, it is a good idea to change the order of the information in the sentence as well as some of the vocabulary. For further practice with paraphrasing, see Vocabulary Unit 19.

Practice Exercises

A Rewrite each sentence so that it has the same meaning. Try to vary the sentence as much as possible.

1. The European expansion westward across the Atlantic was dominated in the 15th and 16th centuries by the Spanish.

    The Spanish _____

    _____.

2. India and China had been known by Europeans for centuries, but the existence of the Americas was totally unsuspected.

    Whereas _____

    _____.

3. The compass was in wide use, but most captains did not really understand why its needle pointed north.

    Although _____

    _____.

4. Voyages could take several years and sailors sometimes died from lack of food and water.

    Owing to _____

    _____.

5. Once the benefits of expansion had been proven, the Spanish and Portuguese monarchies decided to send soldiers to conquer these new lands.

    Because _____

    _____.

6. The Spanish established an empire in the Americas, and Portugal created a trade monopoly in Asia.

    While _____

    _____.

7. Portugal and Spain discovered new lands, and also pioneered the European discovery of sea routes that would connect the world.

    In addition _____

    _____.

B Read the paragraph and paraphrase it in your own words.

European Colonization of North America

The European colonization of North America had an enormous impact on the lives of Native Americans. At first, Native American tribes traded with the Europeans. They trapped animals for fur and traded furs for metal objects and guns. It is possible that this resulted in a decline of the animal population and endangered the food supply. Native Americans used the guns to fight with other tribes. Europeans also brought diseases that were fatal to Native Americans. Then the Europeans started to occupy Native American land. They killed many Native Americans and forced tribes to leave their homelands. The result was the complete devastation of the Native American people and their way of life.

STUDY TIP

What is the difference between paraphrasing and summarizing? Paraphrasing means restating something in your own words. Summarizing means restating only the main ideas. Practice paraphrasing and summarizing regularly. You can paraphrase anything you read or listen to, especially academic articles, news articles, news programs, and lectures. Try recording your response and asking someone to evaluate it for you. Paraphrasing is useful in all sections of the test, especially in the speaking section questions 2–4 and the writing section (integrated task). Summarizing is especially useful in the speaking section question 4.

Test Practice

The following question is similar to question 3 in the speaking section (academic reading and lecture). In this question, you will read a paragraph and then listen to part of a lecture on the same topic.

Read the passage and make notes.

TEST TIP: Speaking section question 3 (academic reading and lecture)

Record your response to this question and analyse your recording. Ask yourself the following questions: Did I answer the questions correctly? Did I speak clearly and pause often? Did I paraphrase the information in my own words? Did I organize my ideas clearly using signposting words? Did I make many grammatical errors?

In the 15th century, voyages were undertaken in order to gain knowledge about the world. There were three main developments that enabled sailors to make these long voyages. First, there was the development of more detailed maps. Second, there were improved methods of navigation. Finally, there was a better understanding and knowledge of the wind patterns and systems in the Atlantic Ocean.

Notes

Track 30

Now listen to part of a lecture in a history class and take notes. Then write your spoken response below. (Note that in the test, you will rely only on your notes.) Practice reading the response aloud. If possible record your response and listen to it. You have 60 seconds.

The professor describes three developments in 15th-century marine navigation. Use examples from the lecture to explain why they were important.

Notes

Nominalization

Study the examples in the chart. Make your own examples.

OVERVIEW

Nominalization is the process by which a verb, adjective, or other part of speech is changed into a noun. Noun phrases are frequently used in academic writing and make your writing sound more abstract and more formal. It changes the focus from the agent to the action.

Changing adjectives and verbs into nouns

More people are becoming addicted to video gaming.	*Video gaming addiction* is becoming more common.
Children couldn't stop playing video games, and parents were concerned.	Children's *inability* to stop playing caused *concern* among parents.
When people participate in video gaming, they develop a variety of skills.	*Participation* in video gaming facilitates the *development* of a variety of skills.

Using the passive

Scientists conducted a study into how video gaming affected children's behavior.	*A study* was conducted into *the effects* of video gaming on children's behavior.
Children who did not play games were compared with children who played games every day.	*A comparison* was made between children who did not play games and children who played games every day.
They concluded that video gaming had no negative effects.	*A conclusion* was reached that video gaming had no negative effects.

Using *there* as a subject

Many people perceive video games as a waste of time.	*There is a (general) perception* that video games are a waste of time.
The number of video games on the market has risen dramatically.	*There has been a dramatic rise* in the number of video games on the market.
Some evidence suggests that they interacted less frequently with other people.	*There appears to be* some evidence of a decrease in social interaction.

Using a noun to summarize information from a previous sentence

Some children spent a lot of time thinking about games, became restless if they could not play. These *symptoms* seem to indicate that … .

Children can learn social skills, planning skills, as well as spatial coordination skills. These *benefits* confirm that video games can have an educational purpose.

Practice Exercises

A Write the noun forms of the verbs and adjectives.

Verbs	Nouns	Adjectives	Nouns
1. accumulate		7. able	
2. analyse		8. accurate	
3. choose		9. aware	
4. grow		10. diverse	
5. involve		11. dominant	
6. modify		12. flexible	

B Rewrite each sentence to include more nouns.

1. They analyzed the data and it revealed that boys spent more time on video gaming than girls.

   _____

2. They investigated whether children were more tired after playing video games.

   _____

3. Children used video games to construct alternative worlds and scientists studied this.

   _____

4. Studies have linked video games with poorer relationships with family and friends.

   _____

5. If children play video games excessively, it can lead to addiction.

   _____

6. Video games can help adults to learn how to process information and solve problems.

   _____

7. People increasingly use video games to educate and instruct.

   _____

8. Many games emphasize cooperation and working in a team.

   _____

9. Children who played video games were more self-confident than those who did not.

   _____

10. Some studies suggest that video game players are able to respond more quickly.

   _____

STUDY TIP

When you record new words in your vocabulary notebook, always make a note of the noun forms and verbs that collocate with them, For example: *draw a conclusion, reach a decision, conduct / carry out an experiment, find / discover a link, discover / reveal a connection.*

Test Practice

TEST TIP: Writing section question 1 (integrated writing task)

When listening to the lecture, make sure to organize your notes clearly so that you can understand them later. Your essay should have an introduction, three body paragraphs, and a conclusion. The introduction should summarize the main idea of the lecture and the reading passage. Each body paragraph should address one point from the reading and the professor's supporting or contradictory point from the lecture. Write a concluding sentence that restates the main point of the reading passage and the main point of the lecture. Use the time given to plan, write, and proofread your essay.

The following question is similar to question 1 in the writing section (integrated task). In this question, you will read a passage and then listen to part of a lecture on the same topic. The lecture may support or challenge the ideas in the passage.

Read the passage.

> Video games are a part of everyday life for most children growing up today. Several recent studies suggest that excessive video gaming may have negative effects on children's development. There are several reasons for this.
>
> First, researchers found that children who played video games regularly reported that they spend less time on social life, sports, and school studies. In particular, if they spend all their time looking at a screen, they will not develop the social skills they need for personal interaction.
>
> Furthermore, researchers also found that children who played video games are less likely to get enough physical exercise and are at risk of becoming overweight. Some studies also suggested that they have more difficulty sleeping and experience persistent tiredness as a result.
>
> Finally, there is a danger of addiction. These games are designed so that children want to keep playing. Researchers found that children who played video games regularly reported that they spend most of their time thinking about video games, even when they were not playing.

Main idea of passage

point 1

detail

point 2

detail

point 3

detail

🎧 **Now listen to part of a lecture in a sociology class and complete the notes below.**
Track 31

Main idea of lecture

point 1   point 3

detail   detail

point 2

detail

Now summarize the main points in the lecture, being sure to explain how they support or cast doubt on the ideas in the reading passage.

Write your written response below. You may use your notes.

_____

_____

_____

_____

_____

_____

_____

_____

_____

_____

_____

_____

_____

_____

_____

_____

_____

_____

_____

_____

_____

_____

_____

_____

_____

Common errors

Study the examples in the chart. Editing your own written work is an important part of improving your writing.

OVERVIEW

Error	Problem	Revised version
Sentence fragments		
People who work hard are usually more successful. For example, earning more money.	Every sentence must be grammatically complete with a subject and a verb.	*People who work hard are usually more successful. For example, they earn more money.*
Some people don't earn much money. Even though they work hard.	Make sure every sentence is complete and join subordinate clauses to a main clause.	*Some people don't earn much money, even though they work hard.*
Run-on sentences		
In my experience, it is important to be flexible so that you can always adapt to any context and take advantage of new opportunities because they could help you to succeed.	Too many clauses in one sentence make it difficult to follow.	*It is important to be flexible so that you can always adapt to any context. Taking advantage of new opportunities can help you to succeed.*
I prefer to take risks because I am an adventurous person and I like challenges and they help me to develop and learn.	Use adjective clauses, or break up sentences. Use a variety of linking words and conjunctions.	*I prefer to take risks because I am an adventurous person. I like challenges that help me to develop and learn.*
Structures are not parallel		
My goals include starting a business, a family, and a house.	Two or more matching ideas in a sentence should follow the same grammatical structure.	*My goals include starting a business, having a family, and buying a house.*
Some people are not so much successful as just having luck.		*Some people are not so much successful as just lucky.*
Incorrect pronoun agreement		
When someone learns a new language, they learn about a new culture as well.	It is better to use a plural subject in order to avoid having to use *he or she*.	*When people learn a new language, they learn about a new culture as well.*
Everyone needs to have some experience of making mistakes, otherwise they will not learn anything.	Because *everyone* is singular, it is not usually possible to use *they* as a subject. You can change the subject to *people* or break up the sentence.	*Everyone needs to have some experience of making mistakes. People who don't make mistakes will not learn anything.*
Incorrect subject-verb agreement		
There is many reasons why some people are successful.	The verb agrees with the noun following *there*.	*There are many reasons why some people are successful.*
Neither success nor money are sufficient for happiness.	The verb agrees with the last noun in a pair joined by *neither/nor*.	*Neither success nor money is sufficient for happiness.*

Practice Exercises

A Correct these sentences.

Question: Is it more important to be able to work with a team or to work independently?

1. Working with a team or working independently. It's difficult to decide which is better.

   _____

2. If someone works with a group, they learn many skills. For example, co-operation and how to be tolerant.

   _____

3. Everyone who work in a team should have a chance to say your opinion.

   _____

4. It is not always easy to work with a team because there can be a personality problem and it can cause conflicts and this can be very destructive.

   _____

5. Everyone who work in a team have to co-operate with the others.

   _____

6. People who work alone only has to think about themself.

   _____

7. You need to have initiative, creative, and having a lot of confidence.

   _____

8. I learned that it is important to be on time and having a positive attitude.

   _____

B In the Paper Edition of the TOEFL iBT, you will write your opinion on a topic. Read the question below, and the essay. Correct the errors.

In your opinion, what is the most important characteristic that a person can have to be successful in life?

Most people want to be successful in life. They may measure their success in different ways. Some people think it is earning money, others think it is being famous or being respected in the community. Others think it is owning their own house, having a car or be able to travel to other countries. Whatever kind of success you choose. I believe that there are one personal characteristic that is essential if they want to be successful and that is honesty. Honesty is important for several reasons.

First, honesty is important if you want to earn the trust of your friends and colleagues. No matter what job you do, whether in business, law, education, or medicine, it is important for other people to know that you will always tell him the truth. I believe that someone who are honest will usually be more successful in the end because more people come to them for advice and ask for their help.

Second, honesty is very important for your own self-esteem. How can you enjoy your success if it has been built on dishonest actions in the past? Or by deceiving other people? If you want to feel calm and relaxed in your heart, it is important to feel that you have always tried your best to be honest with others and if you feel confident, you can make better decisions and you will be more successful in your relationships with others. Everyone who are honest will be rewarded for their honesty.

Finally, honesty is important to society as a whole. If we try to be honest. We can be a role model for our children and also for other people. If there were more honest people in the world, we would live in a better society.

STUDY TIP

Analyze your written work carefully to identify the errors that you make most frequently. What kind of errors are they? Are they errors in articles, prepositions, or tenses? Keep a list of frequent errors and their revised versions in your notebook. Revise your written work carefully, looking out for these types of errors.

Test Practice

The following question is similar to question 2 in the writing section (independent task: personal experience) of the Paper Edition of the TOEFL iBT test.

Many students choose to attend schools or universities in another country. Why do some students study abroad? Use specific reasons and details to explain your answer.

Write a plan for your essay. Use this plan.

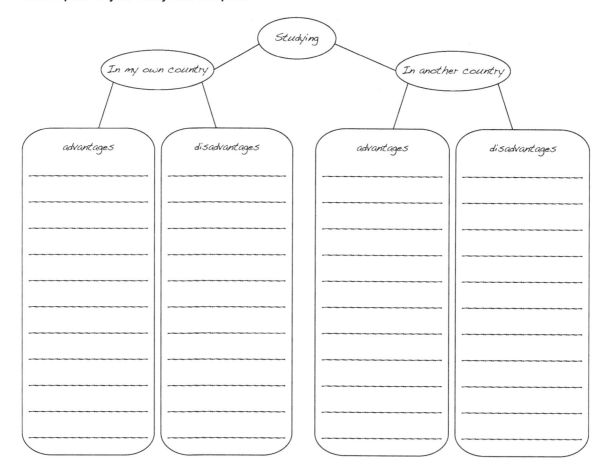

Now write your essay. You have 30 minutes. You should write about 300 words. When you have finished, edit your work carefully.

_____

_____

_____

_____

_____

_____

_____

_____

_____

_____

_____

_____

_____

_____

_____

_____

_____

_____

_____

_____

_____

_____

_____

_____

_____

TEST TIP: Writing section

When answering questions in the writing section make sure to allow enough time for planning, and also for editing. Time yourself when you do test questions. Allow at least five minutes for editing your written work.

Evaluate your work: Does it address the question effectively? Is it well organized? Did you give supporting details for each point? Have you used a range of grammatical structures, signposting words, and vocabulary?

Writing question 2 academic discussion task

This is Writing question 2 for the computer-based test and Home Edition of the TOEFL iBT test (academic discussion task). For information on the units that contain Writing question 2 for the Paper Edition of the TOEFL iBT test (Personal Experience Essay), see page 5.

For this task, you will read an online discussion. A professor posted a question about a topic, and some classmates responded with their ideas.

In your notebook, write a response that contributes to the discussion. In the actual test, you will have 10 minutes to write your response. It is important to use your own words in the response. Including memorized reasons or examples will result in a lower score.

Here are eleven practice questions for you, each linked to a different unit in this book. Sample answers can be found on page 195.

Academic discussion practice task 1 (linked to Vocabulary Unit 3, Music and dance)

Your professor is teaching a class on popular culture. Write a post responding to the professor's question.

In your response, you should do the following.

- Express and support your opinion.
- Make a contribution to the discussion in your own words.

An effective response will contain at least 100 words.

Professor Eniko

With the development of popular music, some musicians and groups wrote and played their own songs while others performed songs written by other people. For the purposes of this assignment, I'm going to refer to music, written by people (sometimes with the help of computers), but not performed by them as a 'commercial' genre. This type of music is developed for a wide audience and with the aim of making money. It is globally popular, but tends to have a similar style and sound. From one perspective, a lot of people enjoy commercial music, but other people think that music is becoming less individual. Is this true in your opinion? Let me know what you think.

Celine

It is true that a lot of popular music nowadays sounds very similar. But that's because people enjoy listening to certain types of music. In my view, music is for enjoyment and listening to in the background, if people like watching people singing and dancing to music, then this isn't a bad thing. It doesn't matter who writes and performs it as long as people enjoy it.

Tamako

I tend to disagree with Celine, I think that music, like art, shows something about our culture and helps us to express our feelings or say something about ourselves. Furthermore, I worry that we are in danger of losing something special to companies who simply want to make money by getting computer programs to write the music we listen to.

_____

_____

_____

_____

_____

_____

_____

_____

TEST TIP: Writing section question 2 (academic discussion)

When you read the opening statement from the academic (the professor or doctor), look for the theme of the subject and quickly note any words associated with it so that you can use them in your response. General words (hypernyms) connected to the theme of the question, like *performance*, *genre* and *instrument* (words that cover a wide range of sub-categories) are likely to be useful in your answer. Look at the vocabulary in this book and identify these general words to use in a possible response.

Academic discussion practice task 2 (linked to Vocabulary Unit 6, Medicine and healthcare)

Your professor is teaching a class on pharmacy. Write a post responding to the professor's question.

In your response, you should do the following.

- Express and support your opinion.
- Make a contribution to the discussion in your own words.

An effective response will contain at least 100 words.

Doctor Edwards

This week, we discussed the growing interest in the effectiveness of traditional plant-based medicine. For centuries herbs and plant-based medicines were prescribed to treat people and prevent illness in all parts of the world. They are available and easy to use, and because they are based on natural products, they are frequently seen as safe and healthier to use than manufactured drugs – by this I mean man-made drugs that are produced by pharmaceutical companies. What are the arguments for and against using traditional herbal medicines?

Kaveetha

I worry about traditional medicines for many reasons. First of all, the perception that all natural remedies are beneficial just isn't true. Some plants can have harmful side effects and they can't treat serious disorders. We need pharmaceutical medicines for bacterial infections and lots of other serious illnesses.

Emily

I see your point, Kaveetha, but plant-based remedies have a long history, and we know that they can be effective. In my opinion, humans are part of nature and natural medicines can be used to prevent illnesses. We shouldn't ignore the learning from the past.

_____

_____

_____

_____

_____

_____

_____

_____

_____

_____

_____

TEST TIP: Writing section question 2 (academic discussion)

In your response to the academic discussion question, you will not need specialized knowledge of the subject. Your score will be marked on giving a relevant contribution to the discussion that is supported by good examples with accurate grammar and appropriate vocabulary. A response that adds to the discussion rather than just repeating points in the posts will get higher marks.

Academic discussion practice task 3 (linked to Vocabulary Unit 8, Opinions)

Your professor is teaching a class on life science. Write a post responding to the professor's question.

In your response, you should do the following.

- Express and support your opinion.
- Make a contribution to the discussion in your own words.

An effective response will contain at least 100 words.

Doctor Rogers

There are billions of people on the Earth and a limited amount of land for agriculture to feed people. Natural food crops can develop diseases and cannot tolerate certain conditions. By growing crops that were genetically changed to resist disease or are able to tolerate harsh climate conditions, or produce more food per plant, we can feed the world on limited resources. These are called genetically modified or GM crops. Some people, however, think that GM crops are bad for the environment, and potentially bad for humans. What do you think?

Ceci

In my opinion, GM food is the only way to go. With our climate changing so rapidly, we need a quick solution to feeding the billions of people on the planet. We cannot keep cutting down forests for new land, so we have to be more efficient with what we have – GM crops are the way forward.

Frankie

While I agree that food security is important, so is food diversity. Plants evolved over millions of years to adapt to their environment. They are perfect for the environment they grow in. If the genes from GM crops get into other plant species, we will pollute their genetic pool, and this will affect the diversity of the plants on our planet.

_____

_____

_____

_____

_____

_____

_____

_____

_____

_____

_____

_____

_____

_____

_____

<u>Academic discussion practice task 4 (linked to Vocabulary Unit 12, Cause and effect)</u>

Your professor is teaching a class on economics. Write a post responding to the professor's question.

In your response, you should do the following.

- Express and support your opinion.
- Make a contribution to the discussion in your own words.

An effective response will contain at least 100 words.

Doctor Laszlo

As we saw last week, there are many different models of company ownership. Some companies are owned privately by individuals or families while some are owned by shareholders – the investors in the company. Other businesses are owned by the people who work there; these are often called non-profit-making companies. Finally, some companies are owned by the state – these are often utility companies. Of course, there are many other versions, and each model has its own advantages and disadvantages. I would like to hear from you which type of company you think is the best and why.

Vinnie

I think that from the list above, companies which are owned by individuals are the best because one person has control. This means that the person who had the idea for the business originally still runs the company and that they have the experience and ideas to keep running it successfully.

Rie Lee

I'm afraid that don't agree with Vinnie. People can become too fixed in their ideas – even successful businesspeople – but business has to change. That's why companies which have investors are better. Investors will give their money to companies that are leading in the market and making money for them. Alternatively, if the company does not perform well, investors will leave.

_____

_____

_____

_____

_____

_____

_____

_____

_____

_____

_____

_____

_____

_____

_____

_____

Academic discussion practice task 5 (linked to Grammar Unit 1, Review of verb forms)

Your professor is teaching a class on education. Write a post responding to the professor's question.

In your response, you should do the following.

- Express and support your opinion.
- Make a contribution to the discussion in your own words.

An effective response will contain at least 100 words.

Doctor Amit

Not very long ago, students went to class in a school or college for their education. Students who were studying distance-learning courses, received course materials by email or video. Today this has changed, and students are learning on the internet – but not alone – in classes over video and with a variety of interactive materials. Some students never meet their classmates in person. But is this a good thing? Can you let me know your thoughts? Is education better in person or online?

Debbie

In my opinion, being able to access education wherever you are is the important thing. I don't think it really matters if everyone is in the same place at the same time. In some ways it is better if they are not in class because you can meet a wider variety of people in different counties and different time zones. Online is definitely an improvement.

Hari

I really miss the personal interaction you got when you met people on campus. My view is that online education doesn't have the excitement of learning in person, where people are talking and discussing in one place and even laughing and joking together. I am great with tech but in my opinion, we need personal interaction.

_____

_____

_____

_____

_____

_____

_____

_____

_____

_____

TEST TIP: Writing section question 2 (academic discussion)

A good range of verb tenses used with correct subject-verb agreement is important in gaining a good score. Your introductory statement will probably contain a present tense to describe something that you believe to be true. Make sure that you include modals because these are an important way of contributing to a discussion in which two or more points are being put forward. Using modals, you can write about things that you believe in a less direct and more polite way.

Academic discussion practice task 6 (linked to Grammar Unit 2, Review of articles)

Your professor is teaching a class on education. Write a post responding to the professor's question.

In your response, you should do the following.

- Express and support your opinion.
- Make a contribution to the discussion in your own words.

An effective response will contain at least 100 words.

Professor Kaitlin

This week we will be looking at education patterns. Many students take time out before going to university. Some students prefer to take a year out to work because it gives you experience of work and, of course, money to fund your education. Other students spend a year studying their subject, in order to give themselves the best chance at being successful at university. Again, because university is expensive, they want to give themselves the best chance of succeeding. What are your thoughts? Which is the best way to spend the year before going to university?

Noah

I definitely think that a year between high school and university is a great idea, but the question is how to use it wisely. For me, money is always an issue. Education is expensive, and if you don't have money, you can spend a lot of your time worrying, or working, instead of concentrating on your studies. I would choose to work and save money, not volunteer or travel.

Kalidou

I don't agree with Noah. In my opinion, you are going to university for a reason: to study. So, if you are going to take a year out, then you should spend it preparing for your degree – read around the subject, go to lectures, really understand the subject you are going to learn. I would stay at home and get ready.

_____

_____

_____

_____

_____

_____

_____

_____

_____

_____

_____

_____

_____

_____

_____

_____

Academic discussion practice task 7 (linked to Grammar Unit 3, Subject-verb agreement)

Your professor is teaching a class on education. Write a post responding to the professor's question.

In your response, you should do the following.

- Express and support your opinion.
- Make a contribution to the discussion in your own words.

An effective response will contain at least 100 words.

Professor Burhan

In the next class, we'll look at work-based learning. Generally speaking, this is learning academic and technical skills by working in a real-world environment, and this term covers a wide range of options including apprenticeships and jobs that you do after graduating. There are a number of positive outcomes for students in work-based learning programmes. They can help students apply their classroom learning to real-world situations and help them explore career choices, as well as increasing job-related skills. While many regard work-based learning as a plus, others see it as distraction from the real aim of education – the acquisition of knowledge from a professional educator. So, what are the benefits of work-based learning? Tell me what you think.

Alice

For me the main benefits are experiencing a work environment. In class, we are taught a lot of things about our subject, and if you can get work-based learning in your subject area, for example, as a laboratory technician assistant, then that is great. Furthermore, when you are working with people then you can learn from them, and if you are lucky to work in your area, it gives you a new perspective on what you are studying.

Steve

I like what Alice said, this sounds like an ideal situation, but I know that this situation doesn't always happen. Sometimes work-based learning can sound better than it actually is, and students change their minds and find that the area they are working in is not what they want to do. I think you need to be careful about saying that there are always benefits.

_____

_____

_____

_____

_____

_____

_____

_____

_____

_____

_____

Academic discussion practice task 8 (linked to Grammar Unit 4, Comparative structures)

Your professor is teaching a class on housing. Write a post responding to the professor's question.

In your response, you should do the following.

- Express and support your opinion.
- Make a contribution to the discussion in your own words.

An effective response will contain at least 100 words.

Doctor Scarlett

As geographers, we study where and how people live. An interesting feature is the number of people who rent versus the number of people who prefer to own a home. There are benefits to both, based on an individual's circumstances and location. Generally speaking, renting is more common in large cities where it is more expensive to buy a home. Also, people may need to move more frequently as their jobs change, in addition to the fact that some people do not want to have the trouble of dealing with repairs. But is it better to rent or own your home? Do you have an opinion about this? What is it and why?

Nick

The main reason renting is better than owning a home is the costs. In my view, renting is far more common because it is not as expensive and more convenient. When you are young, you do not need a big house, nor can you probably afford a big down payment and all the bills and repairs that come together with ownership.

Drake

I understand what Nick is saying. Home ownership can be significantly more costly than renting. But on the other hand, renting has difficulties too; you don't have much control over the property and you cannot do what you want with it. Finally, if the landlord wants to increase the rent, then you have much less say in what happens.

_____

_____

_____

_____

_____

_____

_____

_____

_____

_____

TEST TIP: Writing section question 2 (academic discussion)

The academic discussion question often asks you to write a response to questions such as *Which is better? What is the best way? Which approach do you agree with? What is the most significant advantage of ...?, etc.* For these questions, you will need to use comparative structures that say how two things or people are similar or different. Try to use a range of comparative structures from this book, including negative comparative and equal comparative structures.

<u>Academic discussion practice task 9 (linked to Grammar Unit 5, Modals)</u>

Your professor is teaching a class on space exploration. Write a post responding to the professor's question.

In your response, you should do the following.

- Express and support your opinion.
- Make a contribution to the discussion in your own words.

An effective response will contain at least 100 words.

Professor Rinvolucri

In the last lecture, we saw that the global space industry is worth around 500 billion dollars per year. Now, that is a lot of rockets! Some space programmes are designed to explore space and deepen our knowledge of other planets. Other space programmes are set up to launch satellites for communication or to learn about our world. However, it raises serious questions about how important it is to spend so much money on going to space, and whether we could spend the money better on protecting our planet. In your view, is it right to spend so much money on space? Or should our priority be to spend money protecting our planet? Tell me what you think in your post.

Augustus

There are so many important discoveries from space exploration that I think it is vital to continue. Furthermore, satellite photos from space showing the ice melting from the poles or greenhouse gas emissions or deforestation help us to understand how to protect the earth and how urgent it is. You can't have one without the other.

Pablo

I agree with Augustus on that point, but the cost of the space programmes is enormous. Think of what we could do with 500 billion dollars per year. We could invest it into developing green energy or stopping people cutting down the rainforest or providing clean water for everyone. The answer is clear to me.

<u>Academic discussion practice task 10 (linked to Grammar Unit 16, Causatives)</u>

Your professor is teaching a class on psychology. Write a post responding to the professor's question.

In your response, you should do the following.

- Express and support your opinion.

- Make a contribution to the discussion in your own words.

An effective response will contain at least 100 words.

Professor Fender

If you look at the trending topics online today, you will immediately see that the mental health of young adults is up there. Most people use social media to keep in touch or share information with friends. However, people are concerned that social media can cause problems with concentration or even result in dependence. Let me know what your thoughts are. Is social media harming young peoples' lives and impacting their behavior or is it just another form of communication and entertainment?

Lynn

I agree with the last point. Young people are sharing social media posts to communicate or share something entertaining with friends. However, they are not really concentrating on the content or focussing on what they are doing. These posts are instant and distracting – it's all about what is important in the moment. Unfortunately, some people can become dependent on social media, and it stops them doing other things.

James

Social media is a great development in my opinion. Anyone can get involved and post or share information. You can form groups, find old friends, follow topics that you are interested in and even buy and sell stuff. It's true that some people use social media too much, but they are in the minority. Most of us use social media responsibly, and it does not prevent us doing other things.

_____

_____

_____

_____

_____

_____

_____

_____

_____

_____

TEST TIP: Writing section question 2 (academic discussion)

A good academic discussion response will provide reasons why you agree, disagree or partially agree with a point. You should link your opinion to your reasons with causative verbs. Causative verbs show why something happens and are important to use when you are supporting your opinion with examples and reasons. Use the causative structures in this book to make your argument, explanation and reasons clear.

Academic discussion practice task 11 (linked to Grammar Unit 20, Common errors)

Your professor is teaching a class on business. Write a post responding to the professor's question.

In your response, you should do the following.

- Express and support your opinion.
- Make a contribution to the discussion in your own words.

An effective response will contain at least 100 words.

Doctor Zhi

This week we are looking at risk-taking in business. Risk is a normal part of life and doing business, and what often makes someone successful in business is how well they can balance being brave with being careful. Knowing when to take a brave or risky decision is one of the most important business skills. But how do you get to the correct balance? Which is more important in business decisions – being a risk-taker or being careful? Let me know what you think.

Henri

One of the first things we think of when we consider business is taking risks. Some very successful businesspeople were risk-takers. Think about the entrepreneurs of the online business world or the people who set up the big tech companies – they all took risks and they and their companies became hugely successful.

Mei

I agree in part with you, Henri, but even though we only hear about the risk-takers who were successful, we need to think about the risk-takers who didn't succeed. I think there are many more people who took a risk and lost, so I believe that being cautious in business and doing detailed research, careful planning and preparing for success is the best way.

_____

_____

_____

_____

_____

_____

_____

_____

_____

_____

_____

_____

_____

_____

_____

_____

Overview of the TOEFL iBT® Test

The TOEFL iBT® Test (Test of English as a Foreign Language) measures your proficiency in English. The TOEFL iBT test does not evaluate your knowledge of the English language. Rather, it measures your ability to use English in a variety of academic settings. The test is divided into four timed parts: Reading, Listening, Speaking, and Writing. Each section tests key skills that you will need in order to succeed as a student at an English-speaking university.

Reading section

The reading section is the first section on the test. It measures your reading comprehension abilities by presenting you with a series of academic passages. Then, you will answer a set of questions based on each reading. The questions in this section test your ability to:

- identify the main idea.
- understand the main details.
- make inferences.
- understand the organizational structure.
- use context clues to determine the definitions of key words.

There are two, three or four academic reading passages per reading section, depending on which version of the test you are taking. Each passage is between 600 and 750 words long. After each reading passage, you will answer a set of questions. There are ten questions per passage. In the reading section, you are allowed to go back to previously answered questions to review or change your answers. For more information on the reading section, see *Skills for the TOEFL iBT® Test: Reading and Writing*.

Listening section

The listening section is the second section on the test. In order to evaluate your listening comprehension abilities, you will first listen to a lecture or conversation through your headphones. Then, you will answer a set of questions based on each listening passage. The questions in this section test your ability to:

- identify the main idea or purpose.
- understand the main details.
- make inferences.
- identify the speaker's purpose.

There are five listening passages per listening section in the computer-based version of the TOEFL iBT test, and seven listening passages in the Paper Edition. Each listening is between three and five minutes long. After each listening passage, you will answer a set of questions. There are five or six questions per passage. In the listening section, you are not allowed to review questions you have answered previously. For more information on the listening section, see *Skills for the TOEFL iBT® Test: Listening and Speaking*.

Speaking section

The speaking section is the third section on the test, unless you are taking the Paper Edition. In this section, you will speak into the microphone your responses to a variety of tasks. The tasks test a number of speaking abilities, including:

- giving opinions.
- understanding and responding to questions in the classroom.
- synthesizing (combining) information from two sources.
- summarizing a lecture.

There are four speaking tasks in the speaking section: one independent task and three integrated tasks. Each item requires different skills, including reading, listening and speaking, and listening and speaking only. For more information on the speaking section, see *Skills for the TOEFL iBT® Test: Listening and Speaking*.

Writing section

The writing section is the fourth section on the test (or third section if you are taking the Paper Edition). In this section, you will type or write your responses for each item. The tasks measure your ability to:

- plan and organize an essay.
- develop a written response by using examples or specific details.
- use a variety of grammatical structures and vocabulary.
- use correct spelling and punctuation.

There are two writing tasks in the writing section: the first task is the integrated writing task.

TOEFL iBT test on the computer

The second writing task on the computer-based TOEFL iBT test is the academic discussion task. In this task, you will write a response to the professor's question using the information in the posts and your own ideas.

TOEFL iBT Paper Edition

The second writing task on the Paper Edition of the TOEFL iBT test is the independent writing task. In this task, you will answer a question using your own background knowledge.

For more information on the writing section, see *Skills for the TOEFL iBT® Test: Reading and Writing.*

QUICK GUIDE: TOEFL iBT® Test Computer Based / Home Edition

Section	Tasks	Timing
Reading Section	Reading Passages: 2 Number of Questions: 20	**Total Section Time: 35 minutes**
Listening Section	Listening Passages: 5 3 Lectures 2 Conversations Number of Questions: 28	**Total Section Time: 36 minutes**
Speaking Section	Number of Questions: 4 1 Independent 3 Integrated	**Total Section Time: 16 minutes**
Writing Section	Number of Tasks: 2 1 Integrated 1 Academic Discussion	Integrated Task: 19 minutes Academic Discussion Task: 10 minutes **Total Section Time: 29 minutes**

QUICK GUIDE: TOEFL iBT® Test Paper Edition

Section	Tasks	Timing
Reading Section	Reading Passages: 3 or 4 Number of Questions: 30 questions if the test comprises 3 reading passages, or 40 questions if the test comprises 4 reading passages	54 minutes if the test comprises 3 reading passages, or 72 minutes if the text comprises 4 reading passages. **Total Section Time: 54–72 minutes**
Listening Section	Listening Passages: 5 or 7 3 or 4 Lectures 2 or 3 Conversations Number of Questions: 28 questions if the test comprises 5 listening passages, or 39 questions if the test comprises 7 listening passages	41 minutes if the test comprises 5 listening passages, or 57 minutes if the test comprises 7 listening passages. **Total Section Time: 41–57 minutes**
10-Minute Break		
Writing Section	Number of Tasks: 2 1 Integrated 1 Independent	Integrated Task: 20 minutes Independent Task: 30 minutes **Total Section Time: 50 minutes**
Speaking Section	Number of Questions: 4 1 Independent 3 Integrated	**Total Section Time: 17 minutes**

Scoring

You will receive a score for each section of the test. The score ranges per section are as follows:

Reading	0–30
Listening	0–30
Speaking	0–30
Writing	0–30

In order to calculate your total score, the individual scores for the four sections are added together. Thus, the highest score you can possibly achieve on the TOEFL iBT test is 120.

The reading and listening sections are both scored by computer. However, in order to determine your scores for the speaking and writing sections, your responses are saved and sent to ETS, where they are scored by certified raters. Each of the four responses in the speaking section is assigned a score of 0–4. The scores for each task are added together and converted into a score on the 30-point scale described above. Similarly, the two tasks on the writing section are each given a score of 0–5. Again, the scores for both tasks are added together and then converted to a score between 0 and 30.

Accommodations

Testing accommodations are available for test takers with disabilities or health-related needs. See www.ets.org/toefl for a list of accommodations test takers can request during the registration process. For needs that are not on the list, test takers can contact ETS Disability Services via a web link. Note that accommodation requests are subject to approval by ETS.

Score reports

There are several ways to review your scores. First, you may view your scores online 4–8 days after the test. All you have to do is visit www.ets.org/toefl and sign in to your ETS account with the username and password that you created when you registered for the test.

Your online score report will show the following information:

- The date that you took the test
- Your scores for each section
- Your total score
- Performance evaluations for each section that describe whether your performance was low, medium, or high.

You may access your scores online for tests that you have taken within the past two years. (Note that the universities and institutions you have selected to receive your scores will also be able to view your scores online.) You will also receive a paper score report via mail two weeks after the test date. Note that a paper copy of your score report must be requested before you take the test.

Overview of the Reading Section

The reading section is the first part of the TOEFL iBT test. It tests your comprehension of written English by presenting you with a series of reading passages and then asking you a set of questions based on each one.

QUICK GUIDE: TOEFL iBT® Computer Test

Definition	The reading section tests your ability to understand written academic English. The section includes different types of reading passages that are based on a variety of academic subjects.
Targeted Skills	In order to do well on the reading section, you must be able to: • understand basic academic vocabulary in context. • quickly scan a written passage and understand its main ideas and supporting details. • understand how information is organized. • understand inferences, relationships, paraphrases, and the purpose of a passage. • answer questions within the given time.
The Reading Passages	The reading section includes two reading passages. Each passage is usually 650–700 words long. Each passage will appear on your screen and remain there while you answer the questions based on that passage. There are three different types of passages in the reading section: expository, argumentative, and historical. In addition, each passage is arranged according to a particular organizational style, which include compare and contrast, cause and effect, problem and solution, theory and support, and classification.
Questions	There are ten questions per reading passage. The questions are multiple choice and can usually be classified as one of the following question types: • Detail • Vocabulary • Referent • Sentence Summary/Simplification • Negative Fact • Passage/Prose Summary • Function • Insert A Sentence/Text • Inference
Timing	You will have **35 minutes** to read and answer the questions for a set of two reading passages.

PAPER EDITION: Please note that, in the Paper Edition of the TOEFL iBT test, the testing company ETS may include extra sample material. This sample material is not scored. However, since you will not know which passages are sample materials, you should try your best on all of the passages.

This means that the Paper Edition of the Reading section could be 30–40 questions, and you will be given 54–72 minutes to complete the Reading section of the Paper Edition.

Overview of the Listening Section

The listening section is the second part of the TOEFL iBT test. It tests your ability to understand spoken English by presenting you with a series of listening passages and then asking you a set of questions based on each listening passage.

QUICK GUIDE: TOEFL iBT® Computer Test

Definition	The listening section tests your comprehension of English lectures and conversations. The section includes different types of listening passages spoken by native speakers. Some passages are about academic topics, while others are about experiences that a student may encounter on campus.
Targeted Skills	In order to do well on the listening section, you must be able to: • understand basic academic vocabulary. • identify a speaker's meaning based on intonation and tone. • take good notes. • answer questions within the given time.
The Listening Passages	The listening section consists of five listening passages, which you hear through your headset. There are three different types of passages in the listening section: academic lectures, office hours conversations, and service encounter conversations. Each passage is between three and five minutes long, and you will hear each passage only once.
Questions	There are five or six questions per listening passage. After an academic lecture, you will answer six questions. After office hours and service conversations, you will answer five questions. The questions usually fall into the following categories: • Main Idea • Function • Detail • Attitude • Purpose • Organization • Inference • Connecting content
Timing	The clock will <u>not</u> run while you are listening to the passages. In other words, no time will be deducted while you are listening to the lectures / conversations. The entire section, including listening time, takes **36 minutes** to complete.

PAPER EDITION: Please note that, in the Paper Edition of the TOEFL iBT test, the testing company ETS may include extra sample material. This sample material is not scored. However, since you will not know which passages are sample materials, you should try your best on all of the passages.

This means that the Paper Edition of the Listening section could be 28–39 questions, and you will be given 41–57 minutes to complete the Listening section of the Paper Edition.

Overview of the Speaking Section

The speaking section tests your ability to speak English by presenting you with a variety of tasks. During this section, you will wear a headset. The headphones of the headset are noise-canceling, which means that you will not be able to hear noise around you, including the other test takers giving their responses while you are working on the section. The headset is also equipped with a microphone that you can adjust so that your spoken responses can be digitally recorded.

QUICK GUIDE: TOEFL iBT® Test

Definition	The speaking section tests your ability to understand written and spoken English and respond to questions appropriately. For each question, you will be presented with a specific task that may test the following skills: reading, listening and speaking, listening and speaking, and speaking only.
Targeted Skills	In order to do well on the speaking section, you must be able to: • understand and respond to questions. • express your opinion about a subject. • report the ideas and / or opinions of other people. • summarize the main idea of a listening passage. • combine information from different sources. • answer questions within the given time.
The Questions	The speaking section includes four distinct questions. The first question is an independent question, and the remaining three are integrated tasks.
Timing	The time that you have to prepare and respond to each question varies by question type. See the list below for the order in which the questions appear on the test and the preparation and response times for each question type.

Question Type	Preparation	Response
1. Paired Choice	15 seconds	45 seconds
2. Campus Matters	30 seconds	60 seconds
3. Academic Reading and Lecture	30 seconds	60 seconds
4. Academic Summary	20 seconds	60 seconds

The entire section takes approximately **16 minutes** to complete.

Please note that the computer version and Paper Edition of the TOEFL iBT test are the same. The speaking section is the third part of the TOEFL iBT computer-based test and the Home Edition of the TOEFL iBT test.

If you are taking the Paper Edition of the TOEFL iBT test, the Speaking test is taken at home in a separate session monitored online by a human proctor, within three days of the test center appointment.

Overview of the Writing Section

The writing section tests your ability to create written responses based on two different types of prompts. For the first prompt, you will read a short passage, listen to an academic lecture on the same topic, then write an essay which combines information from both sources. For the second prompt, the question differs depending on whether you are taking the computer-based version of the TOEFL iBT test or the Paper Edition.

The second question in the computer-based version of the Writing section requires you to state and support an opinion in an online classroom discussion (Writing for an Academic Discussion).

In the second question in the Paper Edition of the Writing section, you will read a short question about a familiar topic and write an essay in response to that question (Personal Experience Essay).

QUICK GUIDE: TOEFL iBT® Test Computer Test

Definition	The writing section tests your ability to understand written and spoken English and respond to prompts in writing. For each question, you will be required to understand the task, know how to write a well-organized response, and incorporate main ideas and details to answer the question.
Targeted Skills	In order to do well on the writing section you must be able to: • understand prompts that appear in writing. • take notes on material you hear and/or read, then combine them to create a well-organized response. • summarize and paraphrase ideas from a listening and/or reading passage. • express your ideas or the ideas of other people about a subject. • create a well-organized response in a limited time.
The Questions	The writing section comprises two questions. The first is an integrated writing task and the second is an academic discussion writing task.
Timing	The time that you have to prepare and respond to each question varies by question type.

Question 1: Integrated Task		Question 2: Academic Discussion Task	
Reading*	3 minutes		n / a
Listening	3–5 minutes		n / a
Writing Time	20 minutes	Writing Time	10 minutes

You will have **29 minutes** to complete the entire section.

*Remember, in Question 1 you will be able to see the reading on the screen while you write your essay but you will not be able to replay the listening passage. The reading passage will disappear from the screen while you listen to the lecture that follows but it will reappear when you begin writing so that you can refer to it as you work.

PAPER EDITION: Please note that, in the Paper Edition of the TOEFL iBT test, Question 2 is an Independent task, where test-takers have 30 minutes to answer. The total test time is 50 minutes.

Answer key

Vocabulary

UNIT 1
Practice Exercises
A 1. **a** considerable **b** impact
   c contemporary
   2. **a** seeks **b** convey **c** an image
   3. **a** create **b** designs
   4. **a** A unique **b** aspect **c** depict
B 1. a 2. b 3. b 4. c
C 1. depiction 2. illustrator
   3. creativity 4. innovations
   5. analysis

Test Practice
A 1. Cubist art portrayed real people.
   2. Modern art is abstract.
   3. Modern architecture is not
      influenced by old architecture.
B 1. To explain aspects of Kahlo's
      inner life.
   2. The influence of her life on her art
   3. It challenges the viewer.
   4. It expressed the unconscious.
   5. He thinks this view is doubtful.

UNIT 2
Practice Exercises
A 1. b 2. c 3. a 4. b 5. c
B 1. pseudonym 2. novels
   3. portrayal 4. style 5. original
   6. narrated 7. perspective
   8. inspiration

Test Practice
A 1. unplanned 2. thought-provoking
   3. technique
B *Answers will vary.*
C *Answers will vary.*

UNIT 3
Practice Exercises
A 1. transformed 2. instrumental
   3. evolves 4. combine
   5. concept 6. reject 7. genre
   8. release 9. rhythm
   10. choreographic
B 1. develop 2. consisted
   3. performed 4. rejected
   5. incorporated 6. transformation
   7. emergence 8. based on
   9. choreographer 10. combined

Test Practice
A 1. use musical instruments
   2. send
   3. a set of lines
   4. popular
   5. 2. Blues music often expresses
      sadness and suffering.
   4. Blues developed from songs
      that were sung by enslaved
      people on plantations.
   5. The music developed a unique
      pattern and rhythm.
B *Answers will vary.*

UNIT 4
Practice Exercises
A 1. b 2. b 3. a 4. b 5. c
B 1. both 2. like 3. however
   4. differ 5. difference 6. Whereas /
   While 7. resemble 8. on the other
   hand / however 9. in common
   10. unlike / in contrast to

Test Practice
1. How to compare art and graphic design.
2. They start with a fixed purpose in mind.
3. It is more commercial.

Extra Practice
A *Answers will vary. Suggested
   answers.*
Similarities
1. Create *visual works*
2. Have a range of *materials and tools*
3. Use *their imagination*
Differences: Art
1. Expresses *a feeling or point of view*
2. Can have *several meanings*
3. Artist's presence is *visible*
Differences: Graphic design
1. Has a *fixed purpose*
2. Persuades *people to take action*
3. Sells *a product or service*

UNIT 5
Practice Exercises
A 1. a 2. c 3. a 4. b 5. c
   6. a 7. c 8. b
B 1. cellular 2. microscope
   3. identification 4. survival
   5. characterized

Test Practice
A 1. Use of technology to alter DNA
   2. To distinguish it from genetic
      modification
   3. Altering the genetic structure of
      organisms
   4. To find out what students already
      know
   5. It has a huge number of potential
      uses.
   6. To increase the food supply

Extra Practice
A
Topic: *genetic modification*
Definition: *altering genetic makeup of
living organisms*
Reasons for: *grow faster, resistant to
disease, survive drought, add nutrients,
medicines*
Why needed? *increase food supply*
New technology: *genome sequencing*

UNIT 6
Practice Exercises
A 1. d 2. c 3. g 4. e 5. a
   6. b 7. f
B 1. b 2. a 3. b 4. c 5. a
   6. c 7. b
C 1. persistent, bacteria, antibiotics
   2. interpret, diagnose, prescribe
   3. advances, procedures, infection
   4. monitor, side-effects, modify

Test Practice
A 1. highlight the difference between
      traditional and modern surgery.
   2. They each present a different
      type of medical procedure.
   3. To identify illnesses
   4. They minimize recovery time.
   5. cuts
B *Answers will vary.*
C *Answers will vary.*

UNIT 7
Practice Exercises
A 1. **a** populations **b** triggered
   2. **a** species **b** migratory
   3. **a** trait **b** defense **c** predators
   4. **a** colonies **b** function

5. a endangered **b** extinct
6. a theory **b** habitat
7. a an average **b** herbivores
8. a mechanisms **b** contribute
B 1. patterns **2.** migrate
3. endanger **4.** climate
5. research **6.** average
7. migration **8.** contribute
9. decline **10.** extinction

Test Practice
1. functions of ants.
2. Males do not reproduce.
3. search.
4. infertile.
5. Forager ants hunt for food despite facing constant danger outside the colony.

Extra Practice
Answers will vary.

UNIT 8
Practice Exercises
A 1. On **2.** In **3.** As **4.** For
5. for **6.** In **7.** In
8. Additionally **9.** In
10. Furthermore
B 1. In general / On the whole **2.** In my opinion **3.** For instance **4.** In fact **5.** such as **6.** In addition **7.** especially **8.** on the whole / in general
C *Answers will vary.*

Test Practice
Answers will vary.

UNIT 9
Practice Exercises
A 1. a **2.** a **3.** b **4.** b **5.** c
6. c **7.** b **8.** b
B 1. settled **2.** founded
3. documents **4.** society
5. hierarchy **6.** rulers
7. constructed **8.** overthrown
9. declared **10.** period

Test Practice
1. important. **2.** eliminated. **3.** [1]
Extra Practice
Answers will vary.

UNIT 10
Practice Exercises
A 1. a compete **b** consumer
2. a budget **b** economy
3. a investors **b** capital
4. a measured **b** output
5. a inflation **b** a crisis
6. a sector **b** generates
7. a firms **b** promote

8. a demand **b** supply
B 1. promoting **2.** firm
3. consumers **4.** market
5. competitive **6.** demand
7. profit **8.** budget **9.** allocated
10. supply

Test Practice
1. Different ways of managing the economy
2. Only profitable goods are produced.
3. Goods are of poor quality.
4. It can have a range of economic effects.
5. To review what students know

Extra Practice
A
Main topic *economic systems*
Type 1 *free market economy*
Benefits *firms compete --> best products + price*
Problems *only profitable products made, some services too exp.*
Type 2 *planned economy*
Benefits *govn't decide prices and supply*
Problems *no reason to make best products*
Conclusion *most countries have a balance of both types*

UNIT 11
Practice Exercises
A 1. a investigating **b** structure
2. a issue **b** institutions
3. a conduct **b** involves
4. a excavated **b** artifacts
c evidence
5. a survey **b** conducted
B 1. nature **2.** structure
3. involve **4.** observing
5. participant **6.** data
7. identity **8.** conducted
9. investigation **10.** institution

Test Practice
A 1. environment **2.** direct
3. They did not base their theories on observation.
B 1. dry
2. equal
3. daily lives
4. [2]
5. We can guess details of their lives even without written records.

UNIT 12
Practice Exercises
A 1. A decline in the number of bookstores. People are buying books online.
2. More people are working from

home. Communication by computer is faster and more efficient.
3. People watch movies at home on the internet. Fewer people are going to movie theaters.
4. Too many people try to text and drive at the same time. There are many car accidents.

Answers may vary. Suggested answers.
1. One reason for the decline in the number of bookstores is that many people are buying books online. / Many people are buying books online. Consequently, there has been a decline in the number of bookstores.
2. More people are working from home owing to the fact that communication by computer is faster and more efficient. / Communication by computer is faster and more efficient. As a result, more people are working from home.
3. People watch movies at home on the internet. One of the effects has been that fewer people are going to the movie theater. / There are several reasons why fewer people are going to the movie theater. One reason is that people watch movies at home on the internet.
4. Owing to the number of people who text while they are driving, there are many accidents. / One of the main reasons for many car accidents is because too many people text and drive at the same time.

B 1. resulted **2.** cause **3.** Because of / Due to **4.** meant that
5. Consequently / As a result
6. effect / result **7.** As a result / Consequently **8.** reason
9. Consequently / As a result
10. therefore **11.** effect
12. Due to / Because of **13.** result / effect **14.** result in

Test Practice
Answers will vary.

UNIT 13
Practice Exercises
A 1. c **2.** b **3.** b **4.** c
5. b **6.** c **7.** b **8.** c
B 1. a **2.** f **3.** j **4.** g **5.** h
6. c **7.** i **8.** d **9.** e **10.** b

Test Practice
A 1. To find out how to access the internet

2. He has not accessed the library network before.

3. Listen to a lecture online.

B

Notes

Main change *fines for overdue laptops $20 per day*

Student's opinion *good idea*

Reason 1 *people will return them on time*

Detail *usually none available when he wants to borrow one*

Reason 2 *more laptops available*

Detail *often need repairs*

UNIT 14
Practice Exercises
A **1.** e **2.** f **3.** a **4.** b
    5. c **6.** d
B **1.** c **2.** a **3.** b **4.** c
    5. c **6.** a
C **1.** role **2.** temperature
    3. atmosphere **4.** ecosystems
    5. Ecologists **6.** reflected
    7. depleted **8.** absorb
    9. sustainable **10.** fossil fuels

Test Practice
1. explain why trees are being cut down.
2. the destruction of large areas of forest.
3. vulnerable.
4. Fewer trees mean less rain.
5. [3]
6. 2, 3, 5

UNIT 15
Practice Exercises
A **1. a** hydrogen **b** element
    2. a satellite **b** orbits
    3. a density
    4. a mass **b** gravitational
    5. a altitudes **b** oxygen
    6. a acceleration **b** velocity
    7. a nucleus **b** atom
    8. a protons **b** electrons
B **1. a** electron **b** atom
    c nucleus **d** orbit
    e satellites
    2. a protons **b** neutrons
    c mass **d** hydrogen **e** oxygen
    f phenomenon
    3. a velocity **b** gravity
    c generate **d** acceleration
    e altitude

Test Practice
1. Differences between planets and stars
2. To correct

3. To avoid confusion with nuclear fusion
4. It cannot exist in stars
5.

	Planets	Stars
Generate light		✓
Have a hot center		✓
Have hydrogen and helium	✓	✓
Reflect light	✓	
Generate energy		✓
Have low density	✓	

UNIT 16
Practice Exercises
A **1.** suggest **2.** proposed
    3. took **4.** disagreed with
    5. argued **6.** had
    7. claimed **8.** demonstrate
    9. challenged **10.** argued
B **1.** proposed **2.** demonstrated
    3. identify **4.** believed
    5. expanded **6.** supported
C **1.** defined **2.** illustrates
    3. mentions **4.** identifies
    5. challenges / queries, argues / makes the point / emphasizes
    6. believes / holds the view that
D **1.** The professor defines *the meaning of the term nanotechnology.*
    2. He claims that *nanotechnology will improve our daily lives.*
    3. He identifies *two examples of everyday uses of nanotechnology.*
    4. The two examples illustrate *how nanotechnology can help us in our daily lives.*
    5. He expands on *the topic of advances in nanotechnology.*
    6. He makes the point that *microchips have been getting smaller and smaller.*
    7. Some people query *whether this technology will always be used wisely.*
    8. He asserts that *this technology has a great deal of potential.*

Test Practice
A

Notes

Topic *negative environmental effects of CFC gases*

Point 1 *release chlorine, deplete ozone*

Reason *UV rays from sun harm plants, animals, + humans*

Point 2 *greenhouse gas*

Reason *trap heat + make earth warmer*

UNIT 17
Practice Exercises
A **1.** absent, make-up test
    2. grad school, academic adviser
    3. financial aid, tuition
    4. credits **5.** dorm, freshman
    6. Assignments, due date
    7. transcript
    8. major, sophomore
B **1.** dorm **2.** scholarship **3.** tuition
    4. financial aid **5.** freshman
    6. sophomore **7.** due dates
    8. assignments **9.** academic adviser **10.** grad school
C **1.** declare **2.** GPA **3.** semester
    4. faculty **5.** associate's degree
    6. commencement **7.** community college **8.** mandatory
    9. prerequisite **10.** transfer

Test Practice
A

Notes

Student's opinion *disagrees*

Reason 1 *difficult to find accommodation*

Detail *save time and money by living on campus*

Reason 2 *safer when studying late*

Detail *doesn't like to go home alone at night*

B

Answers will vary.

UNIT 18
Practice Exercises
A **1.** Thanks to **2.** as a result of
    3. Rather than **4.** Given
    5. Instead of **6.** compared to
    7. In the case of **8.** In terms of
B **1.** During the dot com bubble, many new internet companies did not make any profits, despite the fact that they received capital investment.
    2. Internet companies aimed to develop new technologies, in addition to increasing their market share.
    3. Instead of continuing to rise, shares in internet companies fell sharply.
    4. Thanks to the crash, many people lost their investments.
    5. Most internet companies collapsed, except for two companies that eventually exceeded market expectations.
    6. Compared with share values in technology stocks, other share prices did not fall as much.

7. In terms of social benefits, the dot com bubble enabled many developments in technology that are used today.

Test Practice
Answers will vary.

Extra Practice
The reading passage asserts that economic bubbles are a natural correction to unrealistic prices. It suggests that instead of focusing on their negative impact, we should look at the positive effects. The passage explains that thanks to the dot com bubble, society benefited from many new technologies that were developed, in spite of the financial losses that were incurred by investors. The professor disputes this view. He argues that, with the possible exception of the dot com bubble, economic bubbles rarely have any positive impact. In the case of the housing bubble, for example, risky lending practices by banks caused many people to lose their homes.

UNIT 19
Practice Exercises
A   1. wealth, rich, poor
   2. rapidity, fast, slow / gradual
   3. similarity, like, different
   4. strength, powerful, weak
   5. certainty, sure, doubtful / uncertain
   6. rise, increase, fall
   7. creation, make / design, destroy / abolish
   8. removal, eliminate, replace
   9. departure, leave, arrive
   10. transmission, send, receive

B   1. Many people are *leaving* *country* areas and *moving* to *urban* areas.
   2. Young people are *uncertain* about *jobs*.
   3. People in the cities are *usually wealthier.*
   4. Life in the city has many *benefits*.
   5. They have better access to *social facilities*.
   6. Some people *believe* that life in the country is more *peaceful*.

C   1. in the last hundred years
   2. available resources
   3. decrease, used up
   4. are dying, are living longer
   5. poor people, increasing rapidly
   6. rising, richer

Test Practice
1. huge.

2. absence of infrastructure.
3. More people are moving to the city because demand for resources is destroying rural areas.
4. facilitate better facilities in cities.
5.   1. Large cities have many wealthy as well as many poor people.
   4. The high demand for resources is damaging to the environment.
   5. The increasing world population presents many problems.

6   [2]

UNIT 20
Practice Exercises
A   1. e   2. f   3. d   4. c
   5. b   6. a
B   1. triangle   2. centenarian
   3. multitude   4. miniature
   5. compel   6. duplicate
C   1. bigger   2. large   3. changed
   4. four   5. tiny   6. carry
   7. three, same   8. five
   9. two   10. one
D   1. a system based on units of multiples of 10
   2. in the 1700s
   3. a system that was the same everywhere
   4. varied greatly
   5. advances in science
   6. sending and receiving goods to and from other countries
   7. unchanging
   8. instead of
   9. put forward
   10. the same as
   11. obligatory
   12. changed

Grammar

UNIT 1
Practice Exercises
A   1. are getting   2. is starting
   3. provides   4. communicated
   5. didn't use to take   6. have enabled
   7. have been communicating   8. had
   9. will   10. will have stopped
B   *Answers will vary*
C   1. In 20 years' time, artificial intelligence **will have changed** the way we live.
   2. When I started work 25 years ago, nobody **had** a computer on his or her desk.
   3. I've noticed that people who commute by train to work often **work** on the train.

4. Classrooms now **have** interactive whiteboards, so teachers can access the internet while they **are** teaching.
5. The government **has** implemented a new policy for the use of technology in education.
6. Due to the budget cuts, the university **will have** 10% less to spend on technology next year.
7. At the beginning of the last century, most people **didn't have** the opportunity to go to university.
8. Many people **consider** the internet as the most significant invention of all time.

Test Practice
A   1. has affected   2. has transformed   3. say / are saying
   4. agree   5. have changed
   6. used to take / took   7. send
   8. hold   9. have started
   10. will develop
   11. will stop / will have stopped
B   *Answers will vary.*
C
Notes
Main topic *Media Studies course will be online*
Reason *to facilitate larger student numbers*
Woman's opinion *she isn't happy with this change*
Reason 1 *learns better in person*
Reason 2 *worried she won't get a good grade*

Extra Practice
In the reading passage, the author states that ebooks **have become** more popular in the United States. The professor **supports** this view and says that ebooks have had an effect on reading habits. It was **predicted** that by 2015, the number of ebooks **would outnumber** print books. However, this has still not happened. The use of ebooks **continues** to lag behind the use of print books.

UNIT 2
Practice Exercises
A   1. –   2. the   3. the   4. a
   5. –   6. The   7. the   8. The
   9. the   10. –
B   a. 10   b. 1   c. 7   d. 5   e. 4
   f. 6   g. 2   h. 3   i. 9   j. 8
C   1. Many people visit ~~the~~ Nepal to climb *the* Himalayas.
   2. *The* most important subjects to study at school are ~~the~~ history and geography.

3. I kept *a* journal about my trip while I was traveling in *the* United States.

4. Some of *the* people in ~~the~~ my family went on a trip down *the* Amazon River in Brazil.

5. We traveled by train around ~~the~~ India and visited *the* capital city of New Delhi.

6. *The* hotel where we stayed in New York was across from *a* large art gallery.

7. I have a picture of Thailand on my wall. *The* picture reminds me of *the* best holiday I have ever had.

8. ~~The~~ Travel is an important way to learn about *the* culture and people of other countries.

9. My trip across ~~the~~ Asia was *the* most exciting adventure I've ever had.

10. Paris and London are ~~the~~ popular destinations for ~~the~~ tourists.

Test Practice

A *Answers will vary.*

B

In my opinion, it is far more interesting to travel with [a] companion than it is to travel alone. Although [ ] some people prefer to travel alone, and don't like to take [a] companion with them, I think that if you travel with [a] friend it is better for two main reasons: it is safer and you are never lonely.

First of all, traveling alone in [a] strange country can be quite dangerous. If you don't know [the] customs or [the] language, you can easily find yourself in [a] difficult situation. It is better not to be alone. In addition, it sometimes helps to have [a] friend who can watch [ ] your bags while you go to buy [ ] tickets, or if you want to get [ ] some food. A friend can help you out if you feel tired or sick. Once when I traveled to [ ] Malaysia, I got a bad case of the flu, and my friend was able to go to [a/the] pharmacy for me and get [ ] some medicine. If I had been alone, I don't think [a] stranger would have done that for me.

Another good reason to travel with a friend is that you always have someone to talk to. You can discuss [the] sights that you saw that day. You can exchange [ ] opinions and experiences and compare [ ] your impressions. Furthermore, it is fun to make [ ] plans for [the] next day. You can discuss

problems such as how to get from one place to another, and find [a] solution by working on it together. It is a good way to learn about [ ] cooperation. When I traveled with a friend on [a] trip to [ ] Europe, we became good friends and are still friends today.

In conclusion, it is my opinion that traveling with a friend is a much more enjoyable way to travel. I would advise anyone to go with a friend when they go on [a] trip.

UNIT 3
Practice Exercises

A 1. are 2. are 3. is 4. is 5. are 6. is 7. is 8. are 9. is 10. are 11. is 12. is

B 1. have 2. are 3. helps 4. is 5. is 6. are 7. is 8. doesn't 9. is 10. likes 11. isn't 12. are

Test Practice
Answers will vary.

UNIT 4
Practice Exercises

A 1. smaller 2 fewer 3. as 4. friendlier 5. considerably 6. more 7. much 8. content

B
If a factory is built in my hometown, there will be many advantages. First, there will be **(1)** *much* more employment. Second, roads will be **(2)** *better* and transportation will be **(3)** *faster*. There will also be **(4)** *many* more educational and recreational facilities. Unfortunately, there will also be some disadvantages. The town will not be **(5)** *as* peaceful as before and it will be **(6)** *much / far* more polluted. **(7)** *Many* more people will come to work here. The town will probably become more crowded and there will be **(8)** *fewer* parks and trees. On the whole, however, I feel that there are more advantages than disadvantages and I would support this plan.

C *Answers will vary.*

Test Practice
Answers will vary.

UNIT 5
Practice Exercises

A 1. may 2. will 3. don't have to / don't need to 4. have to / need to 5. should 6. should not 7. might 8. might 9. can 10. could

B 1. More should be done to protect the environment.

2. The effects on the environment should have been detected much sooner.

3. Gas and coal shouldn't be used to produce energy.

4. Stricter laws have to be passed to protect the environment.

5. The harmful effects of global warming could have been prevented.

6. Nuclear power plants shouldn't have been built in an earthquake zone.

C 1. should 2. would 3. would 4. may 5. needn't 6. might 7. could 8. may 9. might 10. wouldn't 11. might 12. might

D *Answers will vary.*

Test Practice
Answers will vary.

UNIT 6
Practice Exercises

A 1. won't / won't be able to 2. will have to 3. won't get 4. wouldn't have failed 5. would get 6. hadn't gone

B 1. you will / can get a discount on books

2. I won't have enough money

3. you would spend more time travelling

4. she won't get a grade

5. if he doesn't study harder

6. if she joins an academic study group

7. if I didn't have so many classes

8. if you had saved your work onto a flash drive

C *Answers will vary.*

Test Practice
A
Notes
Main change *have to do a required writing class*
Reason 1 *make students familiar with writing standards*
Reason 2 *help students learn about academic rules for writing*
Woman's opinion *agrees*
Reason 1 *need to improve grammar and writing*
Detail *took study skills class, v. helpful*
Reason 2 *will get better grades in other classes*
Detail *can bring essays to class*

B

Notes

Main topic *students need to buy a campus parking permit*

Reason *to reduce traffic on campus*

Man's opinion *he isn't happy with this change*

Reason 1 *thinks it should be free*

Detail *already pays a facility fee*

Reason 2 *it isn't worth buying a permit*

Detail *he doesn't drive to campus much*

UNIT 7

Practice Exercises

A 1. Both 2. however 3. Compared with 4. Therefore 5. Unlike

B 1. Both moths and butterflies belong to the category *Lepidoptera*. / Moths and butterflies both belong to the category *Lepidoptera*.

2. Cheetahs live in groups. Leopards, on the other hand, are solitary.

3. Food is scarce in the winter. Consequently, bears go into hibernation in order to conserve energy.

4. Like alligators, crocodiles have large, pointed teeth.

5. Pandas are good swimmers. Moreover, they are good at climbing trees.

6. Elephants have very thick wrinkly skin. As a result, it can retain water to help them stay cool.

7. Iguanas eat leaves and plants. However, chameleons are carnivores. / Iguanas eat leaves and plants. Chameleons, however, are carnivores.

8. Bats not only help to pollinate plants, they also eat insects and disperse seeds. / Not only do bats help to pollinate plants, but they also eat insects and disperse seeds.

C 1. First 2. Then 3. Not only 4. also 5. On the other hand 6. In addition 7. Consequently

Test Practice

Answers will vary.

UNIT 8

Practice Exercises

A 1. b 2. a 3. a 4. c 5. c 6. b

B 1. argues 2. with 3. gives 4. shows 5. that 6. refutes 7. to 8. concludes

C

The passage agrees **(1)** *with* the idea that TV has educational benefits for children. The author refers **(2)** *to* a study that found improved language development in pre-school children. The professor contradicts **(3)** ~~to~~ this idea. She claims that several studies **(4)** ~~to~~ show the opposite. She refers to evidence **(5)** *that* language skills were delayed in some children. She identifies **(6)** ~~that~~ three ways in which educational TV can be improved.

D

1. The reading passage states that language controls our thoughts and perceptions of the world. The lecture contradicts this view and maintains that language can cause differences in thought, but it does not determine how we think.

2. The reading passage claims that it is easier for children to learn a second language than for adults and refers to the critical period when children can easily learn languages. The passage does not contradict this view but suggests that adults have other advantages such as study strategies that can help them learn faster.

3. The passage asserts that children learn to understand words before the age of ten months and provides evidence that language helps to stimulate a child's brain. The lecture supports this argument and furthermore suggests that there is a danger that negative criticism can inhibit language development.

Test Practice

Notes

Main idea of passage *benefits of learning languages*

Benefit 1 *learn other languages more easily*

Reason *transfer skills*

Benefit 2 *increases critical thinking and creativity*

Reason *involves problem-solving*

Main idea of lecture *benefits of being bilingual*

Benefit 1 *achieve higher scores*

Reason *process data and multi-tasking*

Benefit 2 *protects against aging*

Reason *keeps the brain active*

UNIT 9

Practice Exercises

A 1. b 2. c 3. a 4. a 5. c 6. a

B 1. The passage describes *where dust storms most frequently occur.*

2. The passage explains *how dust storms are formed.*

3. The passage describes *two methods by which dust can be transported.*

4. The passage explains *the process of suspension / what suspension is.*

5. The passage explains *the process of saltation / what saltation is.*

6. The example illustrates *the devastation that can be caused by dust storms / the damage caused by dust storms.*

Test Practice

Answers will vary.

UNIT 10

Practice Exercises

A 1. Increasing energy from renewable sources is an important goal.

2. Burning vegetable oil is cleaner and safer than gasoline.

3. It is expensive to drill for oil under the sea.

4. It is important to find alternative ways to produce energy.

5. Harnessing solar energy is possible by using new technology.

6. Instead of looking for new sources of fossil fuels, we should develop new energy sources.

7. It is possible to produce energy using water, sunlight, and wind.

8. There are many reasons for using wind and solar energy.

9. To reduce dependence on oil and gas, we should increase the number of wind farms.

10. Biomass is another way to produce / of producing clean energy.

B 1. to capture 2. Blowing 3. to take 4. By moving 5. to establish 6. Replacing 7. to generate 8. Making 9. to convert 10. Designing

Test Practice

Answers will vary.

Extra Practice

1. to access 2. extracting 3. to increase 4. monitoring 5. introducing 6. drilling 7. not to start 8. studying

UNIT 11
Practice Exercises
A **1.** a **2.** a **3.** b **4.** c **5.** a

B **1. a** it **b** its **c** their **d** they
e This **f** one **g** Its **h** this

2. a them **b** their **c** this **d** it
e one

Test Practice
1. question
2. in a habitable zone
3. The star becomes less bright.
4. It travels close to its star.
5. It observes planets directly.
6. They are like Earth.
7. 1. New telescopes have made it possible to find planets outside our solar system.

2. Habitable exoplanets are neither too close nor too far away from their star.

4. It may be possible to find life on an exoplanet one day.

UNIT 12
Practice Exercises
A **1. a** was formed **b** were broken down **c** was released **d** was trapped **e** was turned **f** are found

2. a are removed **b** transported **c** is done **d** has been caused

3. a was once thought **b** was forced **c** is now known **d** to be composed

B **1.** Oil and gas reserves can be identified by the presence of microfossils.

2. These fossils need to be studied under a microscope.

3. Microfossils can be removed by dissolving the surrounding rock.

4. Holes will be drilled in the rock and rock particles transported to the surface.

5. This analysis has to be carried out under laboratory conditions.

Test Practice
1. They depict extinct animals.
2. animals that hunt other animals
3. They were thought to be simple and plain.
4. The paintings may have had many different purposes.
5. 1. The paintings are the oldest ever discovered.

3. The paintings depict a wide variety of animals.

4. The caves provide evidence of highly developed artistic skills.

UNIT 13
Practice Exercises
A **1.** and / but / although **2.** and
3. When / As / Whenever **4.** so
5. so **6.** When / As **7.** because / since / as **8.** While / Although

B **1.** a **2.** c **3.** c

Test Practice
1. By describing three categories
2. To give an example of convergent movement
3. To find out how much students already know
4. Because it is weaker than continental crust
5.

	Plates are pressed together.	Gaps are formed between plates.	There is volcanic activity.
convergent	✓		✓
divergent		✓	✓
conservative			

UNIT 14
Practice Exercises
A **1.** A phobia is an intense fear of a specific object, situation, or activity which is accompanied by a wish to escape.

2. Agoraphobia, which is a fear of open spaces, is the phobia for which people most often seek treatment.

3. Agoraphobia may be caused by stress, which is very difficult to treat and may be connected to the cause of the phobia.

4. Agoraphobia is a complex condition whose causes we don't fully understand and for which there is no single explanation.

B **1.** g **2.** f **3.** j **4.** a **5.** d
6. h **7.** e **8.** b **9.** i **10.** c

Test Practice
1. increasingly
2. continually develop conceptual knowledge as they get older.
3. Children can understand concepts that they cannot express.
4. criticism
5. The researcher influenced the results.
6. 1, 2, 5

UNIT 15
Practice Exercises
A **1.** could I **2.** quick question
3. How's it **4.** the thing is
5. I'm wondering **6.** one concern
7. have you thought of **8.** I'm not sure about **9.** I can see **10.** No problem

B **1.** b **2.** d **3.** e **4.** f
5. a **6.** c

C
1. Student: Hi, Professor Ezzaki. Could I ask you a quick question?
2. Professor: Hi, Diana, of course! Let me guess ... is it about last week's lecture?
3. Student: No ... actually it's about the final paper.
4. Professor: Oh yes. How's that going?
5. Student: Well, I haven't started writing it yet. I've been overloaded with work recently.
6. Professor: Well, you still have a couple of weeks. I'm sure you'll be fine.
7. Student: Do you think I could get an extension? I really need a few more days.
8. Professor: Diana, I'm sorry I can't do that. It wouldn't be fair to the other students.
9. Student: OK. Thank you, anyway.

D **1.** The student wants help with the design of her project.

2. The student wants more time to write his paper.

3. The student needs advice on researching the topic.

Test Practice
1. To get advice about revising her research project
2. She confirmed the meeting earlier with the professor.
3. She has not written many research papers.
4. There are insufficient references.
5. It has good points but needs some improvement.

UNIT 16
Practice Exercises
A **1.** Schools should allow students to study any subject they like. Students should be allowed to study any subject they like at school.

2. Students are prohibited from using cell phones during the test. Using cell phones is prohibited during the test.

3. Some parents require teenagers to limit their screen time.

Some teenagers are required to limit their screen time.

B **1.** Participating in sport at school can make teenagers more confident.

2. Watching TV discourages children from interacting with other people.

3. Teachers should encourage children to report online bullying.

4. Schools should let students have plenty of free time to socialize with their friends.

Test Practice

B

Notes: Reading passage

Topic: *Influence of the media on aggression*

1. *expt. to find out if we learn violence by watching others*

2. *result: children who watched violent videos were more aggressive*

3. *all children had learned the aggressive behavior*

Notes: Lecture

1. *children tend to imitate adults, different from watching TV*

2. *social approval is an important factor*

3. *other social factors influence aggression*

UNIT 17
Practice Exercises

A **1.** There has been a great deal of research in the study of animal intelligence.

2. There are several criteria (used) to determine an animal's cognitive skills.

3. There is some evidence that animals can solve problems.

4. It was possible to teach a kind of sign language to a family of chimpanzees.

5. It is unusual for animals to be able recognize their own image.

B **1.** research   **2.** some evidence
3. some expressions   **4.** likely
5. important   **6.** easy   **7.** many examples   **8.** considered

C *Answers will vary.*

Test Practice

1. tiring.

2. they are afraid.

3. To provide an example of how lack of sleep affects the brain's function.

4. 2, 4, 5

UNIT 18
Practice Exercises

A **1.** The Spanish *dominated the European expansion westward across the Atlantic in the 15th and 16th centuries.*

2. Whereas *India and China had been known for centuries, the existence of the Americas was totally unsuspected.*

3. Although *the compass was in wide use, most captains did not really understand why its needle pointed north.*

4. Owing to *the fact that voyages could take several years, sailors sometimes died from lack of food and water.*

5. Because *they realized the benefits of expansion, the Spanish and Portuguese monarchies decided to send soldiers to conquer these new lands.*

6. While *the Spanish established an empire in the Americas, Portugal created a trade monopoly in Asia.*

7. In addition *to discovering new lands, Portugal and Spain also pioneered the European discovery of sea routes that would connect the world.*

B

Native Americans were greatly impacted by the European colonization of North America. Native Americans sold furs to the Europeans, which may have caused a decrease in the food supply. The Europeans sold guns to the Native Americans, which they used to fight other tribes. Native Americans were also affected by diseases that were brought over by the Europeans. Many Native Americans died, or were killed, or were forced to leave their homelands. Their population and way of life were completely devastated.

Test Practice

Answers will vary.

UNIT 19
Practice Exercises

A

1. accumulation

2. analysis

3. choice

4. growth

5. involvement

6. modification

7. ability

8. accuracy

9. awareness

10. diversity

11. dominance

12. flexibility

B **1.** Analysis of the data revealed that boys spent more time on video gaming than girls.

2. An investigation studied whether children were more tired after playing video games.

3. Children's use of video games to construct alternative worlds was studied.

4. There have been several studies that link video games with poorer relationships with family and friends.

5. Playing video games excessively can lead to addiction.

6. Some evidence suggests that video games can help adults to learn how to process information and solve problems.

7. Video games are increasingly used for education and instruction.

8. There is an emphasis on cooperation and working in a team in many games.

9. There was an increase in self-confidence in children who played video games.

10. Some evidence suggests that video game players are able to respond more quickly.

Test Practice

Main idea of passage *effects of video gaming on children*

point 1 *inhibits social skills*

detail *spend less time with friends and family*

point 2 *not enough exercise/weight gain*

detail *possible link to being permanently overtired*

point 3 *danger of addiction*

detail *children won't stop playing*

Main idea of lecture *positive impact of video gaming*

point 1 *learn a variety of skills*

detail *planning, organisational, social skills*

point 2 *many games are educational*

detail *violence caused by other factors*

point 3 *creative and imaginative*

detail *children love playing, it's not addiction*

UNIT 20
Practice Exercises

A 1. Working with a team or working independently both have advantages, so it is difficult to decide which is better.

2. If someone works with a group, they learn many skills. For example, they can learn how to co-operate and how to be tolerant.

3. Everyone who works in a team should have a chance to say his or her opinion.

4. It is not always easy to work with a team because there can be a personality problem. This can cause conflicts and can also be very destructive.

5. Everyone who works in a team has to co-operate with the others.

6. People who work alone only have to think about themselves.

7. You need to have initiative, creativity, and a great deal of confidence.

8. I learned that it is important to be on time and have a positive attitude.

B

Most people want to be successful in life **(1) although** they may measure their success in different ways. Some people think it is earning money, others think it is being famous, and others think it is owning houses, cars, and **(2) going** on expensive holidays. Whatever kind of success you choose, I believe that there is one personal characteristic that is essential if **(3) you** want to be successful and that is honesty. Honesty is important for several reasons.

First, honesty is important if you want to earn the trust of your friends and colleagues. No matter what profession you are in, whether in business, law, education, or medicine, it is important for other people to know that you will always tell them the truth. I believe that **(4) people** who are honest will usually be more successful in the end because more people come to them for advice and ask for their help.

Second, honesty is very important for your own self-esteem. How can you enjoy your success if it has been built on dishonest actions in the past, **(5) or** by deceiving other people? If you want to feel calm and relaxed in your heart, it is important to feel that you have always tried your best to be honest with others. **(6) If** you feel confident, you can make better decisions and you will be more successful in your relationships with others. **(7) People** who are honest will be rewarded for their honesty.

Finally, honesty is important to society as a whole. If we try to be honest, **(8) we** can be a role model for our children and also for other people. If there were more honest people in the world, we would live in a better society.

Test Practice
Answers will vary.

UNIT 21
Writing Question 2 For The Computer-Based Test And Home Edition Sample Answers

Academic discussion practice task 1 (linked to Vocabulary Unit 3)
Sample Answer

I can see both sides of the argument. If people didn't enjoy this 'global' music, they simply wouldn't listen to it. Moreover, we like to listen to background music where we don't pay attention to the music because we are doing something more important. At the same time, I would add that some of the greatest popular music came from individual musicians and bands – people who want to express something about themselves, their situation or something happening in society. These songs are often about love! The thing that worries me is that one genre of music becomes too dominant and doesn't leave enough room for the other. On the other hand, I guess that people always have and always will make their own music.

Academic discussion practice task 2 (linked to Vocabulary Unit 6)
Sample Answer

In my view, plant-based medicines have a role in treating mild symptoms of illnesses; after all, some modern medicines are based on plants. However, we need to be careful because some plants and herbs can be poisonous and have bad side effects, especially if they are eaten in large amounts. Furthermore, when it comes to serious illnesses like viral infections, herbal medicines will not work, and we need antibiotics and stronger modern treatments. Of course, when invasive surgery is needed, plant-based medicines can't help. However, to go back to my first point, traditional herbal medicines were used for thousands of years and people get benefits from them, so we need to understand their properties better and see them as another aid against disease.

Academic discussion practice task 3 (linked to Vocabulary Unit 8)
Sample Answer

In my view, GM crops are the solution to a growing world population and a more unpredictable climate causing poor growing conditions, crop diseases and pests. Because our world is changing, humans need to adapt and also to adapt the way we grow food. For example, GM foods are much better at resisting diseases and pests so that farmers get better crops. As another example, GM rice is able to grow during floods so that farmers do not lose their produce because of extreme weather. Frankie raises the point that the genetic pool of non-GM plants could be polluted. In some ways this is true, but governments put regulations about where GM crops can be planted in order to avoid this happening. Overall, I think GM foods could help to solve an urgent problem.

Academic discussion practice task 4 (linked to Vocabulary Unit 12)
Sample Answer

There is no easy answer to this question, but I think employee-owned companies, or non-profit-making companies, are interesting alternatives. One reason for saying this is motivation – when all the workers are sharing the profit rather than giving it away to shareholders, then employees' motivation increases. This is due to people seeing a direct connection between their work and salary. One of the other effects could be better productivity. However, I take Rie Lee's point about investment. Companies need a lot of investment, and if it is non-profit-making, then it may result in a lack of investment and consequently poor growth.

Academic discussion practice task 5 (linked to Grammar Unit 1)
Sample Answer

I believe that online learning and classroom learning aren't two different things, but that they can work well together. As an example, at my college we will often have tutorials and small group work online for specific topics. We used to have lots of classes, but these are less frequent now, and we do more preparation outside class. The advantages are that students with jobs can work and learn, people don't have to travel every day, and they can save money and time. But I would like to add that the best thing is that when we are all in class, we're well prepared and have some really good discussions because we want to be there and make the best use of our time with the tutor.

Academic discussion practice task 6 (linked to Grammar Unit 2)

Sample Answer

My thought is that it is really good to work and save some money for your studies. At the same time, it is true that staying at home to study and making sure that your do not fail the first year is also very valuable. However, my opinion is that you can get some work experience without committing to a full-time job by doing volunteer work. That way, you can learn about being employed, and if you are lucky you can do volunteer work in the area that you are going to study. For example, if you want to study veterinary science, you could volunteer to work with animals and study about them at the same time. In this way, you can get the best of both worlds.

Academic discussion practice task 7 (linked to Grammar Unit 3)

Sample answer

I appreciate that there are some people who don't think there are many benefits to work-based learning, but overall, I think that there are many advantages. I agree with Alice that working can be a great experience, particularly if you can get work in an area that you are interested in or want to study later. If you can balance your time working and continue studying, then that is the best option. In addition, I think that there are extra benefits – work-based learning looks great on your resume and makes you more employable. Companies are always looking for people with relevant skills and experience. Moreover, you are meeting new people who you would not normally meet, and you can get to understand the work environment much better. All in all, I agree with Alice.

Academic discussion practice task 8 (linked to Grammar Unit 4)

Sample Answer

In my view, it depends on your individual circumstances. Nowadays, for people starting out in the job market, who are moving from one job to another more frequently and may need to relocate more often, renting a home is the best option. Unfortunately, renting is less stable than buying a property, but if you find a good landlord, then you may stay for a longer period. This also means that you don't need to pay for expensive house maintenance. The downside is that good landlords are becoming harder and harder to find, and so are good rentals.

People are spending large amounts of time finding a home they want to rent. Finally, saving money is harder than ever, and seeing a large amount of your income go to another person instead of towards buying your own home can be the worst feeling.

Academic discussion practice task 9 (linked to Grammar Unit 5)

Sample Answer

There are already a lot of benefits from the space exploration programme. For me the most significant ones are the satellites that we use to monitor the Earth and how human activity is affecting it. These images and information are key indicators of how urgent the problem is. In contrast, we have to think about the effect of space exploration on the environment. For example, each time a rocket is launched, it releases a huge amount of carbon dioxide. Moreover, some space missions are planned to establish bases on the Moon or Mars, so that humans can live on other planets. I think these missions are really unnecessary. The money spent on these projects should be spent making sure that humans can live in our own world, especially now that satellite images show how much damage we are doing.

Academic discussion practice task 10 (linked to Grammar Unit 16)

Sample Answer

Personally, I think that social media brought a new dimension to how we live, but at the same time, I recognise that it can have negative effects, like impacting people's attention spans or even causing dependence or addiction. The best thing is that it enables people to keep up to date with developments in each other's lives. On the other hand, because posts are so short, viewers don't need to focus and it encourages us to switch from one post to the next without really engaging with the subject matter. In some cases, this can make our behavior dependent on using social media and prevent us concentrating. In addition, it can affect your studies if you cannot pay attention to what you are doing for a long period. Overall, I think it is an individual's judgement as to whether social media is affecting their concentration or not and if they need to stop.

Academic discussion practice task 11 (linked to Grammar Unit 20)

Sample Answer

I believe that there is a balance between taking risks and being cautious that is very difficult to achieve. If you are too cautious and you take too long, your business idea could be taken up by someone else. You have to remember that it is a competition and to win you need to take risks. Furthermore, without risking something, you won't fail, and failure is a really important way of learning. Another point is that it can be risky to do nothing and be too cautious. In my view, there is a decision to make about what type of risk you are taking and what are the chances of succeeding – you need to plan and prepare well to be able to make that judgement.

Audio script

Vocabulary

Unit 1 🎧 Track 2

Professor: Undoubtedly, one of the most influential artists in 20th century Mexican art was Frida Kahlo. And perhaps the most innovative aspect of her work was the use of the self-portrait to convey the emotions of her inner life. Let me show you an example. Here's a picture of one of her most famous paintings. It's entitled *The Two Fridas* and was painted in 1939. On the right is the Mexican Frida in traditional Mexican dress. On the left is the European Frida in a colonial white dress, possibly a wedding gown. The two women are seated on a green bench, holding hands, looking very composed and calm. But the shocking aspect of the picture is their two hearts that are depicted as if in a medical anatomy illustration and are joined together by veins and arteries. One vein is connected to a miniature portrait of Frida's husband which she holds in her hand. The peaceful expressions on their faces and their body language contradict the graphic medical imagery and illustrate Kahlo's internal psychological conflict and is influenced by principles of surrealism that seek to externalize the inner processes of the mind. This painting was created at a time in her life when she was experiencing conflict in her relationship with her husband, the artist Diego Rivera, but there was also conflict for her in terms of her identity as a person with both European and Mexican roots. Some have also suggested that the painting offers us an insight into the contradictions in women's identity in society, although I'm not sure whether that was really her intention.

Although Kahlo's work is intensely autobiographical on the surface, her vision also transcends the personal in expressing dualities in the identity of the individual as well as that of a nation or a society. The image forces us to analyze how identity is constructed, deconstructed, and reminds us of its fragility. Now let's move on to another example of her work … .

Unit 4 🎧 Track 3

Professor: Today I'm going to discuss the hotly debated issue of the difference between art and graphic design. The difference between art and graphic design is not always easy to define. There is a great deal of overlap between the two. However, I think that attempting to compare them will help give us a greater understanding of each field.

OK, so what do artists and graphic designers have in common? To begin with, it's clear that artists and designers are both concerned with creating visual compositions. They have at their disposal a range of materials and tools, whether paint and canvas, or digital tools, with which to create a visual image. And it's up to them to use their imagination and originality to create something that is memorable, that expresses something new, that makes an impact on the viewer.

What is the difference, then, between art and graphic design? Perhaps the most fundamental difference is the purpose for which the work is created. A work of art is intended to express a feeling, or a point of view that the artist wishes to share with his or her audience. The artist sets out to create something that effectively expresses his or her personal view of life, society, art. A work of art can have different meanings for different people – there isn't one single message that is being conveyed. Just think of famous works like the painting of the *Mona Lisa*. Part of her beauty – and her mystery! – lies in the fact that we can interpret her smile in many different ways. In fact, a successful piece of art is one that can be interpreted and reinterpreted on many levels. Whereas the graphic designer's viewpoint is largely absent from the final product, with art, the artist's presence is extremely visible in the work and when we look at the work, we experience a kind of bond with the person who created it.

By contrast, a graphic designer usually has a fixed starting point. That starting point is the purpose of the design – which may be to advertise a product, or a service, or an event, or to give information. Artists start with a blank canvas. Graphic designers, on the other hand, usually have a specific set of instructions to follow. They don't convey their own feelings – they communicate a message and persuade people to take some action. For example, an exciting design for a can of soup will persuade you to buy it. Unlike artists, graphic designers create their work to sell a product or promote a service.

Unit 5 Recording 1 🎧 Track 4

Professor: Now today I'd like to talk about the concept of genetic modification. By the way, we shouldn't confuse genetic modification with biotechnology, which is a far more general term. In fact, biotechnology refers to any use of organisms to make products and includes for example, something as simple as using enzymes to make cheese or yogurt. But to get back to the main topic of today's lecture. Let's try to establish a definition of the term genetic modification. Anyone?

Student 1: Altering the genetic structure of plants?

Professor: That's partly right, but not just plants. It can also refer to altering the genetic makeup of animals, or bacteria, or any living organism. Combining genes from different organisms is known as recombinant DNA technology, and the resulting organism is said to be "genetically modified," "genetically engineered," or "transgenic."

Now, why would we want to alter the genetic makeup of a plant or an animal?

Student 2: To make it grow faster?

Student 3: To make it resistant to disease?

Professor: Yes, both of you are correct. Those are two important reasons. There are a number of other reasons, too, for example, improving a crop's ability to survive in drought conditions, or adding important nutrients that will improve people's diet, or adding a medicinal vaccine that will protect humans against infectious diseases such as hepatitis. It's impossible at this stage to predict where this technology will take us. As the world's population continues to increase, I don't think there's any doubt that GM products will be a major factor in helping us to meet the challenges of the 21st century.

All organisms have adapted their genetic structure in order to survive, but now for the first time we have the opportunity to control this process. Now, the first and most important step in this process is identifying genes with important characteristics. And here's where genome sequencing is helping us with detailed information about the genetic sequencing of organisms, and of course we are also developing new technologies to analyze and use this data. Now, let's consider the steps in the process of creating a genetically modified product... .

Unit 5 Recording 2 🎧 Track 5
Professor: Let's try to establish a definition of the term genetic modification. Anyone?

Unit 7 🎧 Track 6
Professor: So ... we've been discussing how animals have adapted to the extreme conditions of living in the desert. Desert animals have developed a wide range of *physical and behavioral* mechanisms to survive the extremes of heat and dryness in the desert. Some animals have developed special *physiological* structures to help them regulate body heat. Jackrabbits, for example, have large ears that allow air to cool their blood as it circulates.

Other animals have developed *behavioral* adaptations. An example of a behavioral adaptation is estivation. You probably know that bears go to sleep during the coldest part of the winter? That's known as hibernation. Well in the desert there are a few types of animals, such as the round-tailed ground squirrel, that go to sleep during the hottest part of the summer, and wake up when the temperature has gone down. This is known as estivation.

Unit 9 🎧 Track 7
Professor: The steam engine was one of the most significant inventions of the 19th century, especially when we consider how it impacted Western society, which was particularly evident in two areas: transportation and manufacturing.

First, let's look at transportation. The steam engine enabled the development of steam trains and steam ships. Until then, communication had been slow-paced, and fairly leisurely. People depended on horses or ships. With the

increased speed of travel, goods and raw materials such as wool or metal could be transported around the country more quickly, increasing output as a result.

Second, the steam engine had an enormous impact on manufacturing. In England and in the U.S., steam engines led to the construction of factories which increased the rate of production. Previously, textiles and clothing, for example, were made by individual workers in their homes. With the construction of factories, workers started to leave the rural areas and came to the towns to work, creating the beginning of the highly urbanized society we have today. It was the beginning of the industrial revolution that would have a profound effect on social, economic, and cultural conditions all around the world.

Unit 10 Recording 1 🎧 Track 8
Professor: As we discussed in the previous lecture, there are two main types of economic systems: a free market economy and a planned economy. Before moving on to today's topic, I'll recap the main points from last week.

In a free market economy, as I'm sure you recall, there is a limited public sector. The majority of all goods and services are produced by private companies with the goal of making a profit. One advantage of this type of economy is that firms will compete with each other to make the best possible products for the cheapest price. A disadvantage is that only products that will make a profit will be produced. Additionally, some services that everyone needs such as health or education may be too expensive for everyone to afford.

In a planned economy, on the other hand, there is a limited private sector. Most economic decisions are made by the government. The government decides what will be produced and how much it will cost, based on what they think are in the best interests of the people. One problem with this type of economy is that there is little incentive for firms to produce the best products as they do not have to compete for the market.

Most countries in the world today have elements of both types of economy. The balance between the two varies widely. In the United States, for example, almost all economic activity is run by private companies, with a very small proportion of activity, in areas such as Medicare and Social Security, being funded by the government.

Now to move on to the main topic of today's lecture, what happens when an economy switches over from a planned to a market economy? What are the implications of this transition and how does it impact on labor, production, and the supply and demand of goods and services?

Unit 10 Recording 2 🎧 Track 9
Professor: Before moving on to today's topic, I'll recap the main points from last week.

Unit 13 Recording 1 🎧 Track 10
Student: Hi. Could you please help me with something?

Librarian: Yes, of course. Do you need help finding materials?

Student: I'm just having a problem accessing the Wi-Fi network on my laptop. Could you help me with that?

Librarian: Oh yes, it's a little tricky doing this the first time. Let's take a look. Mmm. Yes, it seems to be configured correctly ... Oh yeah, you need to click this icon here to enable access to Wi-Fi networks.

Student: Oh, I see! And then which network do I choose?

Librarian: Then click on this one here that says college internet network ... Now try opening up your browser.

Student: It works! That's great! Is it OK to listen to audio here in the library?

Librarian: Yes, as long as you use your headphones.

Student: Awesome! Thanks so much for your help.

Librarian: No problem.

Unit 13 Recording 2 🎧 Track 11
Student 1: Wow! According to the announcement, the library is going to charge $20 for every day your laptop is overdue.

Student 2: Really! Does it say why?

Student 1: Yes, they give a couple of reasons. One is to reduce the number of overdue laptops, which makes sense I guess. Whenever I ask to borrow a laptop, there's none available. So this way people won't keep them so long. You don't pay anything if you return them on time.

Student 2: Still I think that's a lot of money.

Student 1: That's true, but it says the second reason is to help pay for laptop repairs. So I guess that's a good thing too because there will be more laptops in circulation. Last time I borrowed a laptop, someone had downloaded some computer software program onto it and it kept crashing.

Student 2: Yes, that's why I prefer to use my own laptop.

Unit 15 Recording 1 🎧 Track 12
Professor: Now let's continue our discussion from last week where as you'll remember we started to come up with a definition of what a planet is. As you know, scientists believe that the sun and all the planets were originally formed from clouds of gas and dust left over from old stars when they exploded. So what are the differences between a star and a planet?

Student 1: A planet doesn't generate light, it only reflects light from its star.

Professor: That's correct. Stars shine because they have atomic energy at their core, which makes them extremely hot. And they shine all the time, although we only see them at night. What else?

Student 2: Stars are mostly made of hydrogen and helium.

Professor: Yes. A star is a mass of gas held together and given its shape by its own gravity. Gravity is constantly exerting pressure on the star, trying to make it collapse. The matter inside a star is extremely hot – millions of degrees in fact! – and unlike matter on earth which is mostly made of atoms, ordinary atomic matter cannot exist inside a star. The matter inside a star is a mixture of ions and electrons known as plasma. We can observe small explosions of plasma on the sun's surface, for example. As a result of the pressure and intense heat, some of the hydrogen nuclei start to fuse together and create a new element, helium, thus releasing energy that keeps the furnace going. Note that this is nuclear fusion, *not* nuclear fission, which is something quite different!

But let's get back to understanding the differences between a planet and a star. After all, hydrogen and helium are also found on planets. And carbon-based material, which is found on Earth, is also found on stars. So what is another characteristic of a planet – that is not found in a star?

Student 1: Planets orbit their star, while stars stay in the same place?

Professor: Well ... in a way. They don't actually stay still, but they stay in the same position relative to each other, that is true. Any other ideas?

So think about mass. Planets have less mass and are therefore less dense than stars. Planets can generally be divided into two main types: large, low-density gas giants, and smaller planets with a rocky surface. Mercury, Venus, Earth, and Mars are rocky planets. The outer planets are made up mostly of gases, although they may have rocky cores. But all nine planets have sufficient gravity to maintain a spherical shape and have cleared the area of space around their orbit.

OK, so let's move on to talk about asteroids, which are sometimes mistaken for planets.

Unit 15 Recording 2 🎧 Track 13
Professor: Well ... in a way. They don't actually stay still, but they stay in the same position relative to each other, that is true.

Unit 16 🎧 Track 14
Professor: So let's talk a little more about chlorofluorocarbons, or CFCs, which as you know are an organic compound that contain carbon, chlorine, and fluorine. CFCs are widely used in refrigerators, air conditioners, packaging, and in aerosol sprays. By the way, they were first developed in the 1920s as a safer method of refrigeration. However, it was not until the 1980s that scientists realized how much damage they were causing to the Earth's atmosphere.

When CFCs are released into the outer layers of the Earth's atmosphere, they start to break down under ultraviolet radiation. This process of decomposition means that they release chlorine into the stratosphere and this depletes ozone. Ozone is extremely important because it absorbs ultraviolet radiation from the sun. If the layer of ozone is too thin, then UV rays will pass through into the Earth's lower atmosphere, harming plants and animals. It can also cause medical problems in humans, such as increased cases of skin cancer.

Ozone depletion is not the only way that CFCs affect the Earth's atmosphere. They are also a greenhouse gas, that is, a type of gas that, like carbon dioxide, both captures and stores solar radiation. In other words, solar heat is absorbed by the gas and it can't get out. By trapping heat in the Earth's atmosphere, CFCs contribute to the general increase in the Earth's temperature, which is known as the greenhouse effect.

Now we're going to take a look at recent developments of alternatives to CFCs and see how their molecular structure makes them less harmful to the atmosphere ... .

Unit 17 🎧 Track 15
Student 1: Did you hear about the decision to throw sophomores out of the dorms next year?

Student 2: Yes ... It's because there isn't enough space.

Student 1: I know, but it's so difficult to find a rental apartment that's close enough to campus, and has a reasonable rent. That's why so many sophomores prefer to stay in the dorms because they save time and money. After all, tuition is so high here, at least they could give us reasonably priced accommodation.

Student 2: That's true.

Student 1: Plus, it's safer to be on campus if you're studying late at night for example. I wouldn't like to go home alone at night. I really hope they reconsider their decision.

Unit 18 🎧 Track 16
Professor: We've been discussing some of the causes of economic cycles, but let's think about some of the effects.

Many economists consider economic cycles to be generally efficient as a way for a market-driven economy to regulate itself. But what if we take the opposing view for a moment and look at some of the disadvantages.

First, it's clear that the boom part of the cycle—the period of expansion—is good for the economy. There's plenty of investment, lots of jobs, it's easy to get credit. Great, right? But what if there is over-investment in a particular sector, which results in an oversupply, as in the case of the recent housing boom in the U.S.? Capital is wasted on goods and products that aren't really needed. This is an inefficient use of resources.

Second, when we look at the contraction phase of the cycle, what happens when people lose their jobs and their incomes decline? They lose their homes, they have to move to find work, communities are broken up. There are many long-term effects that impact workers, their families, and their communities causing economic hardship as well as social instability and given these disadvantages ... .

Unit 20 🎧 Track 17
Professor: So we've been discussing the significance of the Magna Carta in U.S. history, specifically the ways in which it has influenced the Bill of Rights and the Constitution.

As you know, at the time the Magna Carta was first proposed in England back in 1215, it was intended as a way for the barons to restrict the powers of the king. Although the document preceded the establishment of the American colonies by several centuries, it included several clauses that were to prove inspirational to later generations of lawmakers and especially to the authors of the Bill of Rights and the Constitution.

The Magna Carta declared that no free man could be punished except through the law of the land. Now this is a clear precedent for the Fifth Amendment to the Constitution, which declares that "no person shall … be deprived of life, liberty, or property, without due process of law."

This was an important step, because it asserts that *everyone* has the right to a fair trial. Even though, at the time of the Magna Carta, the barons were referring only to themselves. Nevertheless, its meaning has since been extended to include everyone and is generally considered to have laid the foundation for the concept of universal human rights that we are all familiar with today.

Grammar

Unit 1 🎧 Track 18
Woman: Hey Zain! How's it going?

Zain: Good! How about you?

Woman: I'm really annoyed because they just announced that my media studies course will be online instead of in person.

Zain: Is that a bad thing? I mean it could be really interesting.

Woman: I just think it's better to meet other students and teachers in person. I think I learn better that way. You know, it's easier to generate ideas and ask questions, that sort of thing.

Zain: I know what you mean but I've done several online courses and they were a lot of fun.

Woman: I'm sure there are some advantages, but I'm worried that I won't be able to participate enough to get a good grade. Maybe I won't be able to pass the course!

Zain: You'll be fine—don't worry! Just give it a try and see how it goes.

Unit 2 🎧 Track 19
Professor: Now, last week we discussed the formation of volcanoes. Today let's move on to the classification of volcanoes.

Volcanoes can be active, dormant, or extinct. Active volcanoes are volcanoes that have recently erupting or are expected to erupt in the near future. The Hawaiian Islands are a string of islands formed by volcanic activity and there are several active volcanoes including Mauna Loa, the largest volcano in the world, which erupted in 2022. Another example is in Italy where Mount Stromboli has been erupting almost constantly for the last 2000 years.

Dormant volcanoes are no longer erupting, but might become active again in the future. One example of a dormant volcano is Mount Fuji in Japan. Some volcanoes can be dormant for hundreds of years and suddenly become active as happened in 2008, when a volcano in southern Chile erupted following a dormancy of nine thousand years.

Extinct volcanoes are unlikely to erupt again. An example of an extinct volcano is Mount Capulin in New Mexico, which last erupted about 60,000 years ago and isn't expected to erupt again.

Unit 6 Recording 1 🎧 Track 20

Student 1: Did you hear about the new rule about academic writing for freshmen?

Student 2: Yes, I heard about that. I think it's a good idea, because I really need to improve my grammar and written expression.

Student 1: But if I have to take that class, I won't be able to take all the other courses that I planned.

Student 2: Yeah, but if you improve your writing, you can get better grades in your other classes! If I hadn't taken that study skills class, last semester, I would have been completely lost!

Student 1: OK, I can see that it's useful. But do we have to do a whole class? Why not just one or two sessions?

Student 2: I think it's a great way to get feedback on the writing that we're doing in our other classes. If we bring our assignments into the class, the teacher will help us.

Student 1: Oh yes, mmmm I hadn't thought of that.

Unit 6 Recording 2 🎧 Track 21

Woman: Have you signed up for your parking permit yet?

Man: No, I haven't. I don't understand this new rule. Parking used to be free for students! We already pay a student facility fee.

Woman: I guess too many people were parking their cars here, even though they aren't students. Anyway, if there are fewer cars, the campus will be quieter and safer for pedestrians.

Man: I know what you mean. If I used my car every day it would be worth it, but I don't drive to campus that much.

Woman: Maybe you could use campus transportation instead?

Man: That's true. I'll certainly think twice about driving from now on.

Unit 7 🎧 Track 22

Professor: Whales travel in groups and use a variety of methods to communicate. Researchers have recorded their vocalizations and have found three main types of sounds: clicks, whistles, and pulsed calls. Clicks are mainly used for navigation, helping them to identify surrounding objects. Whistles and pulsed calls on the other hand are used to communicate with each other. It has been discovered that different groups of whales have different whistles and that the whistles of individual whales within one group may also vary. This helps them to identify one another.

A very different form of communication can be found in ants. Scientists have discovered that ants use a variety of small chemicals called pheromones to communicate. They can sense the pheromones using their antennae. These pheromones hold a great deal of information for other ants. They can indicate a path to food sources, warn other ants of dangers, and they can also identify which nest an ant is from, as well as their status within the ant colony

Unit 8 🎧 Track 23

Professor: Now let's take a look at some of the possible effects of being bilingual. Let's keep in mind that there are varying levels of bilingualism, but I'm using this term generally to refer to individuals who are fluent in two languages and probably learned both languages as children. That means they were brought up speaking two languages at home, or one language at school and a different language at home.

What do you think are the effects of being bilingual? You know, sometimes parents worry that having to cope with two languages will slow down children's general cognitive development and they won't do as well in their academic skills, but recent studies indicate the opposite.

Bilingual children tend to achieve higher scores than monolingual children on both verbal and nonverbal tests of intelligence. Why do you think that is?

Well, when children learn to select which language to communicate in, they are in fact learning to process many different types of data at one time. As a result, they become much more skilled at prioritizing tasks and working on multiple projects or multi-tasking.

But you know, that's not the only benefit. Another study of older bilingual speakers found that being bilingual may also help to protect against problems associated with aging, such as Alzheimer's disease and dementia. In fact, several studies have shown that language learning keeps the brain more active for longer … .

Unit 9 🎧 Track 24

Professor: Let's look at a couple of different approaches to earthquake prediction.

The first approach looks at precursors or warning signals such as changes in water level or animal behavior. This approach was used most successfully in 1975, when the Chinese government made a successful prediction based on reports of a wide range of unusual observations and ordered the evacuation of the city of Haicheng, which has a population of about 1 million. An earthquake struck the region just days later on February 4, 1975. However, such predictions are not always possible as was shown just a year later in 1976, when there was another major earthquake in northern China. One reason may have been the difficulty of identifying precursor signs.

A second approach utilizes frequency data to create a prediction based on probability. In 1983, scientists predicted that a moderate earthquake was due to strike near Parkfield,

California. The prediction was based on the observation that earthquakes with magnitudes of about 6.0 had occurred there on average every 22 years, so the prediction was made for 1988 plus or minus five years. When the quake did not hit by 1993, the prediction was canceled. So this approach also has proved to be ineffective.

Unit 10 🎧 Track 25

Professor: Hydraulic fracturing is a type of oil mining that has recently become a hot topic for the energy industry and for environmental science.

The process involves driving water, chemicals, and sand at high pressure down into rocks to break them apart in order to access oil and gas deposits that are located in small fissures or cracks in the earth.

Previously, it was considered too expensive to be worthwhile, but recent technological innovations have made it possible to open up previously unreachable gas resources on a large scale.

One argument in favor of extracting oil in this way is that it may offer an important new energy source and a way to boost domestic energy production.

But Hydraulic fracturing, or fracking as it is more commonly known, has also become a highly controversial environmental issue.

Two recent studies suggest that there may be major environmental hazards. One study found that pressurized fluids can find their way into water supplies and contaminate the drinking water.

Another study found that intensive fracking can trigger small earthquakes, something that has already happened in Ohio in the U.S., and also in Australia, and in the UK.

Although fracking has many supporters, notably amongst those concerned with creating jobs and domestic energy supplies, it also has critics who say it is important to first study the environmental impact before rushing ahead with this potentially dangerous form of energy extraction.

Unit 13 Recording 1 🎧 Track 26

Professor: OK let's get started. The topic we'll be focusing on today is mountain formation and the theory of plate tectonics. What is the definition of plate tectonics?

Student 1: Is it the way in which the earth's crust moves?

Professor: Right. Plate tectonics is the term used to describe the way in which pieces of the earth's crust, or *lithosphere*, move around.

Each plate is in contact with the surrounding plates on all sides of it but they're all moving relative to each other. Yes?

Student 2: Are there any gaps between the plates?

Professor: That's an interesting question. While there are places where we *can* see magma being forced upward … where do you think that is?

Student 1: Active volcanoes?

Professor: Correct. But there are no real gaps between the plates because if there were, we would be able to see deep chasms where we could look down into the magma or molten rock that lies below the earth's surface.

Now the plates actually all move around horizontally, but they move in different ways. One type of plate movement is known as convergent, which means that plates are moving toward each other.

Now let's consider what happens in Japan. Japan is located on the edge of a major plate. The floor of the Pacific Ocean is a different plate and it is moving gradually toward Japan. When two plates meet, there is intense pressure on the lithosphere. Now, since continental crust is much denser than the oceanic crust, what happens?

Student 3: The oceanic crust gets squeezed?

Professor: That's right. The oceanic crust goes underneath the continental crust. As one plate slides over the other, the front of the plate is compressed, and the rock tends to crumple and fold to form mountains.

Of course it isn't possible for *all* plates to move toward each other because otherwise the earth's surface would be constantly shrinking. So the other main kind of plate movement is divergent, that is to say, the plates move away from each other. On this type of boundary, magma gets forced up between the plates and become part of the earth's crust.

Many of earth's mountain ranges are located along plate boundaries, or former plate boundaries. In fact, returning to the previous point, volcanoes are a type of mountain that is built up when liquid and solid rock erupt from the earth's interior, so this is why we often see volcanic activity located along plate boundaries.

However, that isn't the whole picture, because not all boundaries are convergent or divergent. Sometimes plates simply slide along past each other. These are known as conservative plate boundaries. There is rarely any volcanic activity found along these types of boundary.

Unit 13 Recording 2 🎧 Track 27

Professor: Now, since continental crust is much denser than the oceanic crust, what happens?

Unit 15 🎧 Track 28

Professor: Hey, Susan, how are you doing?

Susan: Hi, Professor, thanks for making time to see me.

Professor: No problem. I'm always available at this time. How's it going with your research topic?

Susan: Um, well … the thing is … that's just what I wanted to ask you about

Professor: Are you having trouble revising your work?

Susan: Yes, that's just it. Could I ask you about some of the comments you made on my first draft?

Professor: Sure. Go ahead.

Susan: Well um this point here. You said that I have to clarify my sources here. What did you mean exactly?

Professor: Ah yes, I see. Well you've made a lot of claims here based on your reading around this topic, which is great, but in academic writing you have to cite clearly where this information is from. For example, you could mention here what type of study was involved, when it was done, and what kind of context was analyzed. For example, here you could say that "a Swedish study of banking trends in 2010 showed that Internet banking had increased by 25 percent over the previous year."

Susan: Oh, right, so I should tell the reader exactly where the information came from?

Professor: That's it. It's definitely a good idea to refer to research-based studies, in fact you should include more of them if you can, but you need to make it clear what kind of studies they are so the reader can see how well they relate to the topic.

Susan: Oh yeah, I can see that. That's really helped. Thanks!

Unit 16 🎧 Track 29

Professor: It seems that there are increasing levels of violence in many of the media sources that surround us, from TV and movies to cartoons and computer games. So how does this level of violence affect young children and does it in fact make them behave more aggressively?

Several studies have focused on this issue. In one particular study, children who had been shown a video of an adult acting aggressively toward a doll showed higher levels of aggression afterward.

There are, however, several reasons to question whether this proves that violence in the media causes people to act aggressively.

First, we should consider the validity of the research method. When children are shown behavior by an adult, they are more likely to think that this behavior is appropriate and should be imitated. They may feel that they are expected to imitate it in some way. This is quite different from watching aggressive behavior in a cartoon performed by an animated character, for example.

Second, most video games have interesting and often informational content that is very educational.

Finally, when children were asked to describe what they had seen on the film, all were able to do so, even though they had not imitated the behavior. This means they had observed and learned the behavior, but had not imitated it. This suggests that there may be other factors, such as social or cultural factors, influencing the tendency toward aggression that were not included in this study.

Unit 18 🎧 Track 30

Professor: Right, so we've discussed in some detail the economic motives for the European expansion of the 15th century. And these were of course the primary motives, but we should also ask ourselves what made the voyages possible? What kinds of developments enabled them to make these long and often treacherous voyages?

Well, let's think about the method of travel and also about the types of navigation that were used in those days. By the end of the 15th century, European ships were making regular trips to India and China. Until then, maps had not been very accurate, but when Europeans started to make longer journeys, their maps became more detailed and they gained a better understanding of the shape of the earth.

In addition, Europeans were developing better systems of marine navigation. Sailors mainly used celestial navigation. That means they located their position relative to the position of the sun or another star using a device called an astrolabe. Unfortunately, this method was difficult to use at sea, especially in windy conditions. And it was not until the 18th century, with the development of clocks that could keep time at sea, that sailors were able to determine both latitude and longitude with any accuracy.

Finally, a significant development that helped to extend the range of their voyages was their improved knowledge of the wind patterns in the Atlantic Ocean. Sailors had figured out that they needed to sail out into the Atlantic Ocean in order to catch westerly winds that would bring them back home. This was the technique that was used by Christopher Columbus in his voyages to the Americas.

Unit 19 🎧 Track 31

Professor: Video gaming is becoming more and more popular with young children nowadays. There are a lot of contradictory views about the impact of video games on children. Overall, though, evidence indicates that video gaming can have a very positive impact. There are several reasons for this.

First, children learn a variety of different skills by playing video games. They learn planning and strategy and organizational skills. Furthermore, many video games are very social. They involve interacting with other players, and working in a team.

Second, most video games have interesting and often informational content that is very educational.

Finally, video games can be very creative. Children enjoy using their imagination to create their own worlds, and their own characters. Although some studies suggest that children can become addicted to video gaming, in general this is not the case. Video gaming is just like any other fun activity—if children love doing something, it is difficult to get them to stop! Spending a lot of time on video games does not necessarily mean they are addicted.

Word list

Note:
Words in *italics* are from the Coxhead Academic Word List.
http://language.massey.ac.nz/staff/awl/index.shtml
The number given after each word denotes the Vocabulary Unit number.

absent (adj) 17
absorb (v) 14
abstract (adj) 1
academic adviser (n) 17
acceleration (n) 15
access (n or v) 13
accompany (v) 3
adapt (v) 5
additionally (adv) 8
advances (n) 6
allocate (v) 10
altitude (n) 15
anaesthesia (n) 6
analyze (v) 1
ancient (adj) 9
anonymous (adj) 2
antibacterial (adj) 6
app (application) (n) 13
argue (v) 16
artifact (n) 11
aspect (n) 1
assert (v) 16
assignment (n) 17
associate's degree (n) 17
atmosphere (n) 14
atom (n) 15
author (n or v) 2
autobiographical (adj) 2
average (n or v) 7
bachelor's degree (n) 17
bacterial (adj) 6
believe (v) 16
beneficial (adj) 6
besides (adv) 8
browser (n) 13
budget (n or v) 10
capital (n) 10
cause (n or v) 12
cell (n) 5
challenge (n or v) 16
character (n) 2
characteristic (n or adj) 5
choreographic (adj) 3
civilization (n) 9
claim (n or v) 16
classic (n) 2
classify (v) 5
climate (n) 7
collapse (n or v) 10
colony (n) 7
combine (v) 3

commencement (n) 17
community college (n) 17
compare (v) 4
compete (v) 10
concept (n) 3
conduct (v) 11
configure (v) 13
consequently (adv) 12
consider (v) 16
considerable (adj) 1
consist of (v) 3
construct (v) 9
consumer (v) 10
contemporary (adj) 1
contraction (n) 3
contradictory (adj) 2, 16
contrast (n or v) 4
contribute (v) 7
convey (v) 1
creative (adj) 1
credit (n) 17
crisis (n) 10
data (n) 11
declare (v) 9, 17
decline (n or v) 7
defence (n) 7
define (v) 16
deforestation (n) 14
delete (v) 13
demand (n or v) 10
demonstrate (v) 16
dense (adj) 15
depict (v) 1
deplete (v) 14
design (n or v) 1
develop (v) 3
diagnosis (n) 6
differ (v) 4
difference (n) 4
disorder (n) 6
distinguish (v) 5
diversity (n) 11
DNA (n) 5
document (n) 9
dorm (dormitory) (n) 17
download (v) 13
drought (n) 14
due date (n) 17
ecologist (n) 14
economy (n) 10
ecosystem (n) 14

elective (n) 17
electron (n) 15
element (n) 15
emerge (v) 3
emission (n) 14
emphasize (v) 16
endangered (adj) 7
establish (v) 9
estimate (v) 5
evidence (n) 11
evolve (v) 3, 5
examine (v) 11
excavate (v) 11
expand on (v) 16
experience (n) 2
extension (n) 17
extinct (adj) 7
factor (n) 5
faculty (n) 17
fiction (n) 2
financial aid (n) 17
firm (n) 10
fossil fuel (n) 14
found (v) 9
freshman (n) 17
function (n or v) 7
fundamental (adj) 14
furthermore (adv) 8
fuse (v or n) 15
generate (v) 10, 15
genetic (adj) 5
genre (n) 3
goods (n) 10
GPA (grade-point average) (n) 17
grad (graduate) school (n) 17
gravity (n) 15
habitat (n) 7
hard drive (n) 13
herbivore (n) 7
hierarchy (n) 9
hydrogen (n) 15
hygiene (n) 6
identify (v) 5, 16
identity (n) 11
illustrate (v) 1, 16
image (n) 1
impact (n or v) 1, 9
imply (v) 16
incorporate (v) 3
indicate (v) 16
infection (n) 6

inflation (n) 10
innovative (adj) 1
insight (n) 1
inspired (adj) 2
install (v) 13
instead of (adv) 18
institution (n) 11
instrument (n) 3
interpret (v) 6
invention (n) 9
investigate (v) 11
investment (n) 10
involve (v) 11
issue (n) 11
junior (n) 17
kingdom (n) 14
laptop (n) 13
layer (n) 5
lead to (v) 14
like (prep) 4
likewise (adv) 4
link (n or v) 5
log on (v) 13
major (n) 17
make the point (v) 16
mandatory (adj) 17
market share (n) 10
mass (n) 15
measure (v) 10
mechanism (n) 7
mention (v) 16
microscopic (adj) 5
migration (n) 7
modification (n) 6
monarchy (n) 9
monitor (n or v) 6
moreover (adv) 8
narrate (v) 2
nature (n) 11
neither (conj) 4
network (n or v) 13
neurology (n) 6
neutron (n) 15
novel (n) 2
nucleus (n) 15
nutrient (n) 5
observe (v) 11
orbit (n or v) 15
organism (n) 5
originality (n) 2
output (n) 10

overall (adj) 8, 10
overthrow (v) 9
oxygen (n) 15
participant (n) 11
password (n) 13
pattern (n) 7
perception (n) 6
performance (n) 3
period (n) 9
persist (v) 6
perspective (n) 2
phenomenon (n) 15
population (n) 7
portray (v) 2
precipitation (n) 14
predatory (adj) 7
prerequisite (n) 17
prescribe (v) 6
prevent (v) 6
procedure (n) 6
process (n) 5
profit (v or n) 10
promote (v) 10
prose (n) 2
proton (n) 15
pseudonym (n) 2
query (n or v) 16
range (v) 11
rather than (adv) 18
realistic (adj) 2
reason (n or v) 12
reflect (v) 14
refute (v) 16
reject (v) 3
release (n or v) 3, 14
removable media (n) 13
research (n or v) 7
resources (n) 10
restrict (v) 9
revolutionary (adj) 9
rhythm (n) 3
role (n) 14
rule (v) 9
satellite (n) 15
scholarship (n) 17
sector (n) 10
seek (v) 1
semester (n) 17
senior (adj) 17
services (n) 10
set (n or v) 2

settler (n) 9
shares (n) 10
shift (n or v) 1
shortcut (v) 13
side-effect (n) 6
signal (n or v) 1
similarity (n) 4
similarly (adv) 4, 8
site (n) 11
society (n) 9
sophomore (n) 17
species (n) 7
spreadsheet (n) 13
sterilize (v) 6
structure (n) 11
style (n) 2
subjective (adj) 1
suggest (v) 16
supply (n or v) 10
support (v) 16
surgery (n) 6
survey (n or v) 11
survive (v) 5
sustainable (adj) 14
symptom (n) 6
system (n) 5
technique (n) 2
temperature (n) 14
theory (n) 7
therefore (adv) 12
trait (n) 7
transcript (n) 17
transform (v) 3
treatment (n) 6
trigger (n or v) 7
tropical (adj) 14
tuition (n) 17
unique (adj) 1
unlike (prep) 4
utilize (v) 1
vary (v) 5
velocity (n) 15
version (n) 2
virus (n) 6
vision (n) 1
whereas (conj) 4
while (conj) 4
wireless (Wi-Fi) (adj) 13

Please note there is no direct correlation between the words found on the TOEFL iBT® test and those found on the Coxhead Academic Word List. This list has been included only as a reference for vocabulary commonly found in academic texts.